JIM BUTCHER'S

The DRESDEN FILES®

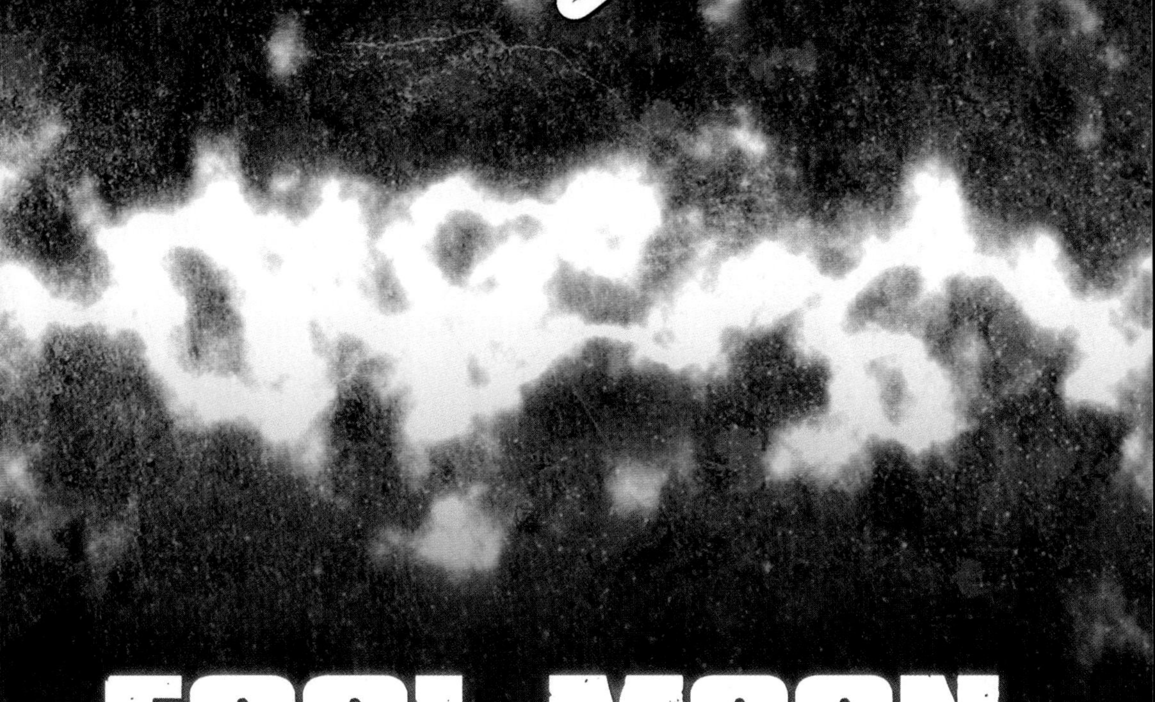

FOOL MOON

volume one

FOOL MOON

volume one

WRITTEN BY:
JIM BUTCHER
& MARK POWERS

ARTWORK & COLLECTION COVER BY:
CHASE CONLEY

COLORS BY:
MOHAN

LETTERING & TRADE DESIGN BY:
BILL TORTOLINI

CONSULTING EDITOR:
RICH YOUNG

THEMATIC CONSULTANTS:
PRISCILLA SPENCER,
MICHAEL ASHLEIGH FINN
& FRED HICKS

CONSULTANTS:
LES DABEL & ERNST DABEL

DYNAMITE
ENTERTAINMENT

NICK BARRUCCI • PRESIDENT
JUAN COLLADO • CHIEF OPERATING OFFICER
JOSEPH RYBANDT • EDITOR
JOSH JOHNSON • CREATIVE DIRECTOR
RICH YOUNG • DIR. BUSINESS DEVELOPMENT
JASON ULLMEYER • SENIOR DESIGNER
JOSH GREEN • TRAFFIC COORDINATOR
CHRIS CANIANO • PRODUCTION ASSISTANT

ISBN13: 978-1-60690-210-3   ISBN10: : 1-60690-210-5

10 9 8 7 6 5 4 3 2

JIM BUTCHER'S THE DRESDEN FILES: FOOL MOON, VOLUME ONE. Contains materials originally published in Jim Butcher's The Dresden Files: Fool M
#1-4. Published by Dynamite Entertainment. 155 Ninth Ave. Suite B, Runnemede, NJ 08078. Copyright © Jim Butcher. THE DRESDEN FILES: FOOL MOON
all characters featured in this issue and the distinctive names and likenesses thereof, and all related indicia are trademarks of Jim Butcher. All rights reser
DYNAMITE, DYNAMITE ENTERTAINMENT and the Dynamite Entertainment colophon are ™ and © 2011 DFI. All names, characters, events, and locales in
publication are entirely fictional. Any resemblance to actual persons (living or dead), events or places, without satiric intent, is coincidental. No portion of
book may be reproduced by any means (digital or print) without the written permission of Dynamite Entertainment except for review purposes. The scann
uploading and distribution of this book via the Internet or via any other means without the permission of the publisher is illegal and punishable by law. Pl
purchase only authorized electronic editions, and do not participate in or encourage electronic piracy of copyrighted materials. **Printed in Canada.**

For media rights, foreign rights, promotions, licensing, and advertising: **marketing@dynamiteentertainment.com**

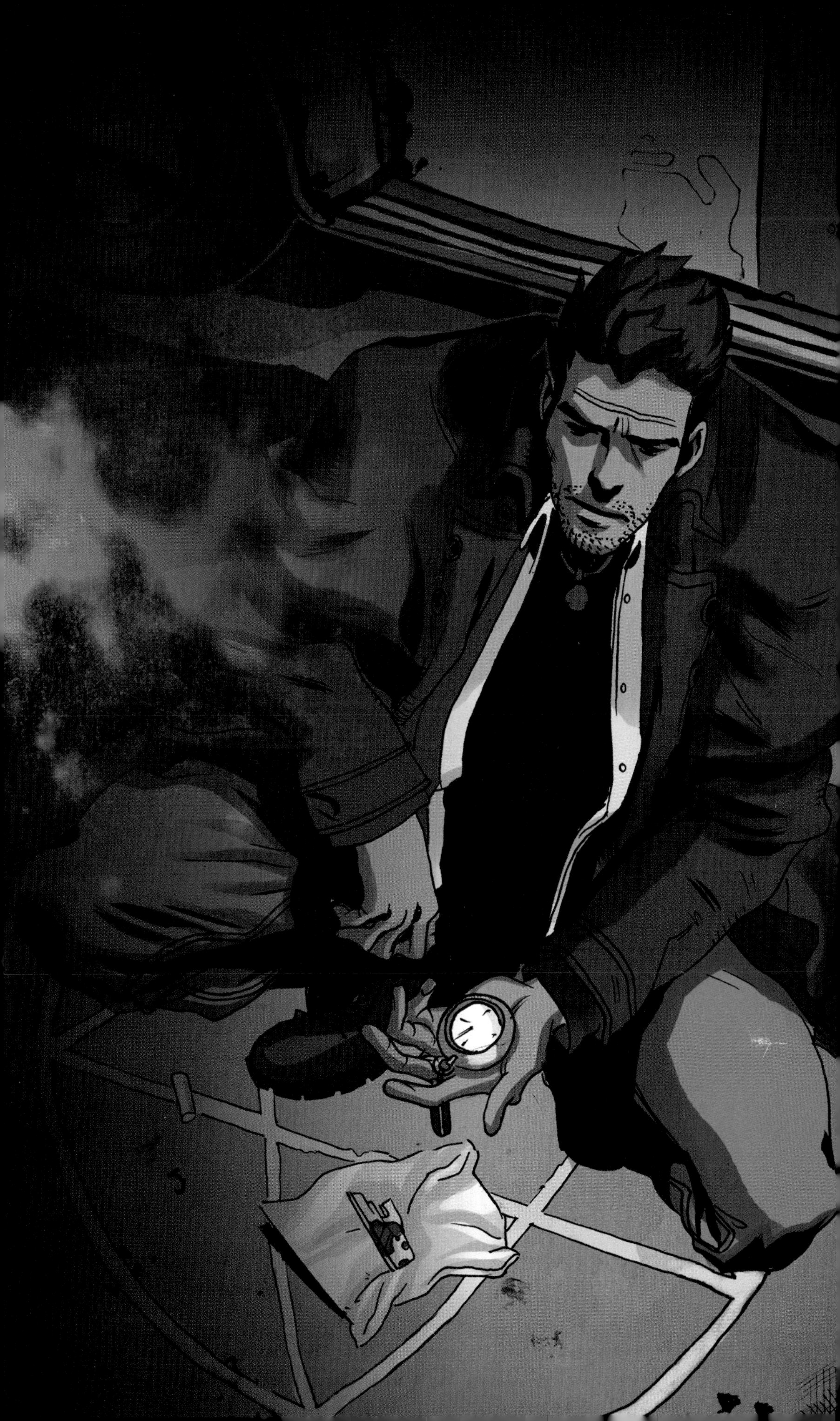

Know the old saying, "when it rains, it pours"? Well, if you're Harry Dresden--Chicago's only wizard for hire--"when it rains, it monsoons" would be far more appropriate. Take this case, for example: a string of brutal, bloody murders that seem to have been committed by wild animals.

In a city like Chicago, brutal murders are nothing new. But when one of the victims turns out to be one of mobster "Gentleman" Johnny Marcone's associates, it's only a sign that things are about to get a whole lot worse--and a whole lot more personal for Harry. See, Harry's old school in his approach to life and justice: protect your friends, no matter what. Stand tall against your enemies, no matter how much stronger they are. But what happens when you need to protect your enemies from your friends? What happens when your sacrifices drive a wedge between you and those you care about most?

The moon is full. A predator's howl echoes through the windy city's dark alleys.

Harry Dresden's life is about to change forever...

Harry Dresden
WIZARD

1273 Grand Avenue
Chicago IL 60612   312-555-0199

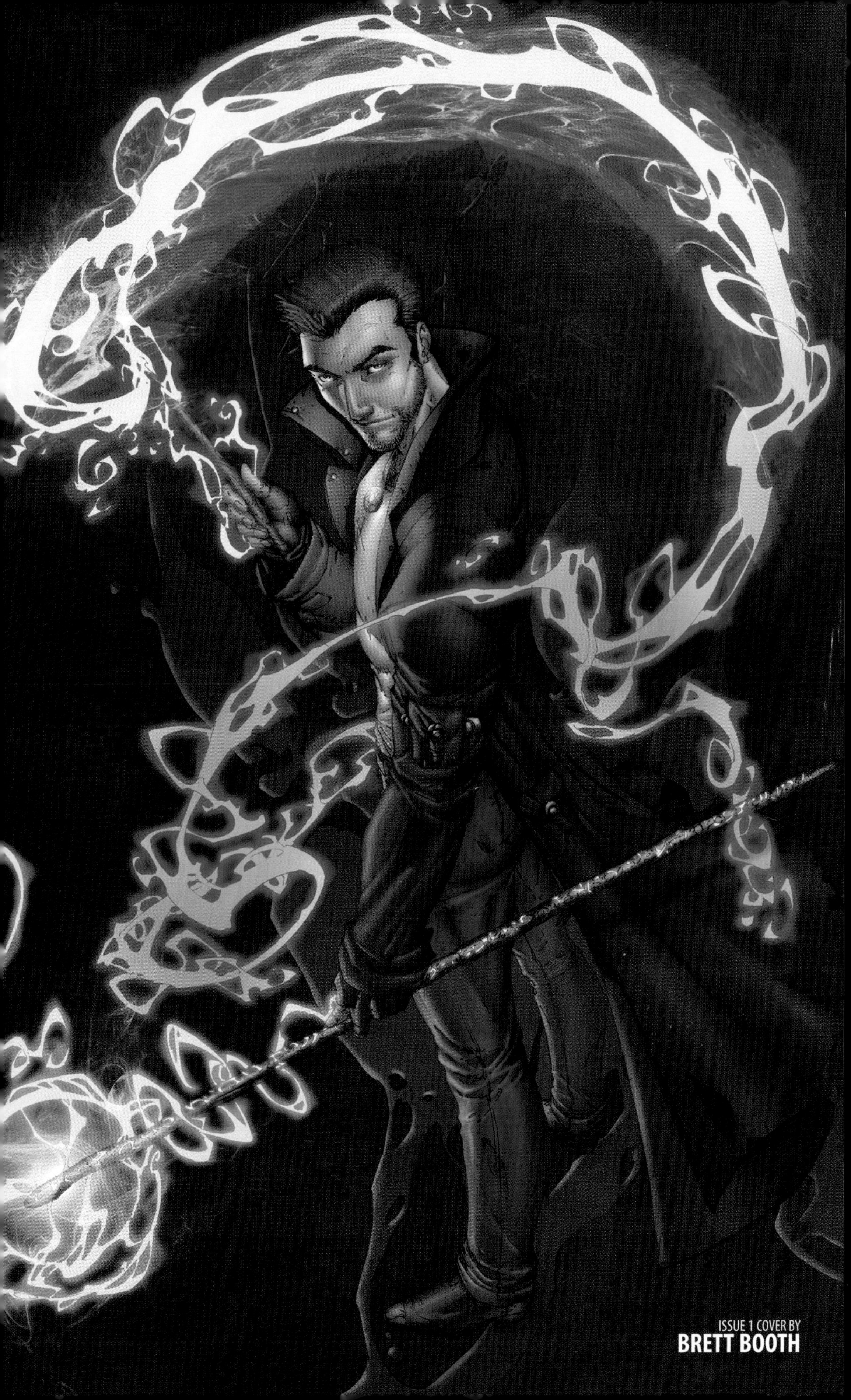

ISSUE 1 COVER BY
BRETT BOOTH

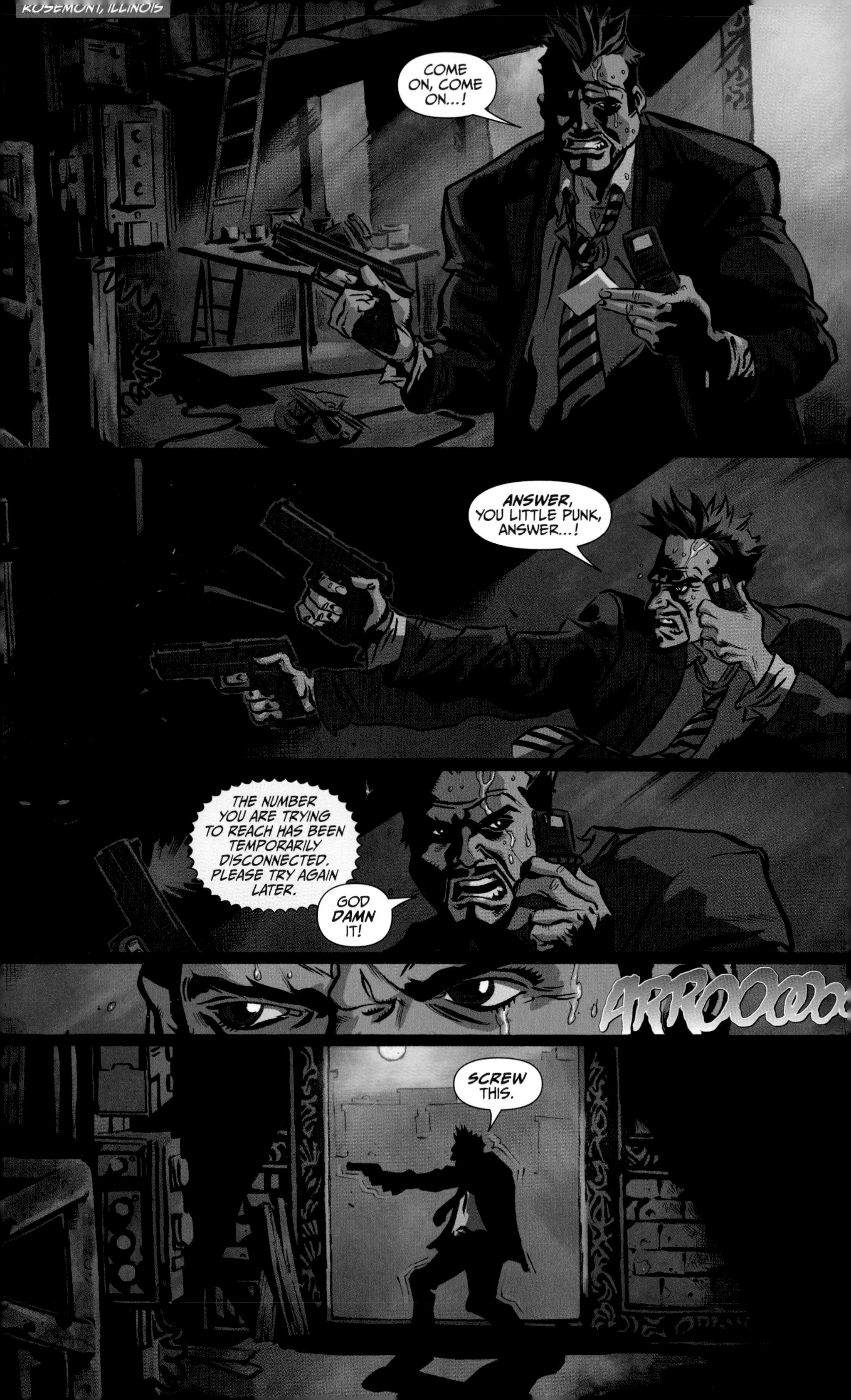
ROSEMONT, ILLINOIS
COME ON, COME ON...!
ANSWER, YOU LITTLE PUNK, ANSWER...!
THE NUMBER YOU ARE TRYING TO REACH HAS BEEN TEMPORARILY DISCONNECTED. PLEASE TRY AGAIN LATER.
GOD DAMN IT!
ARROOOOO
SCREW THIS.

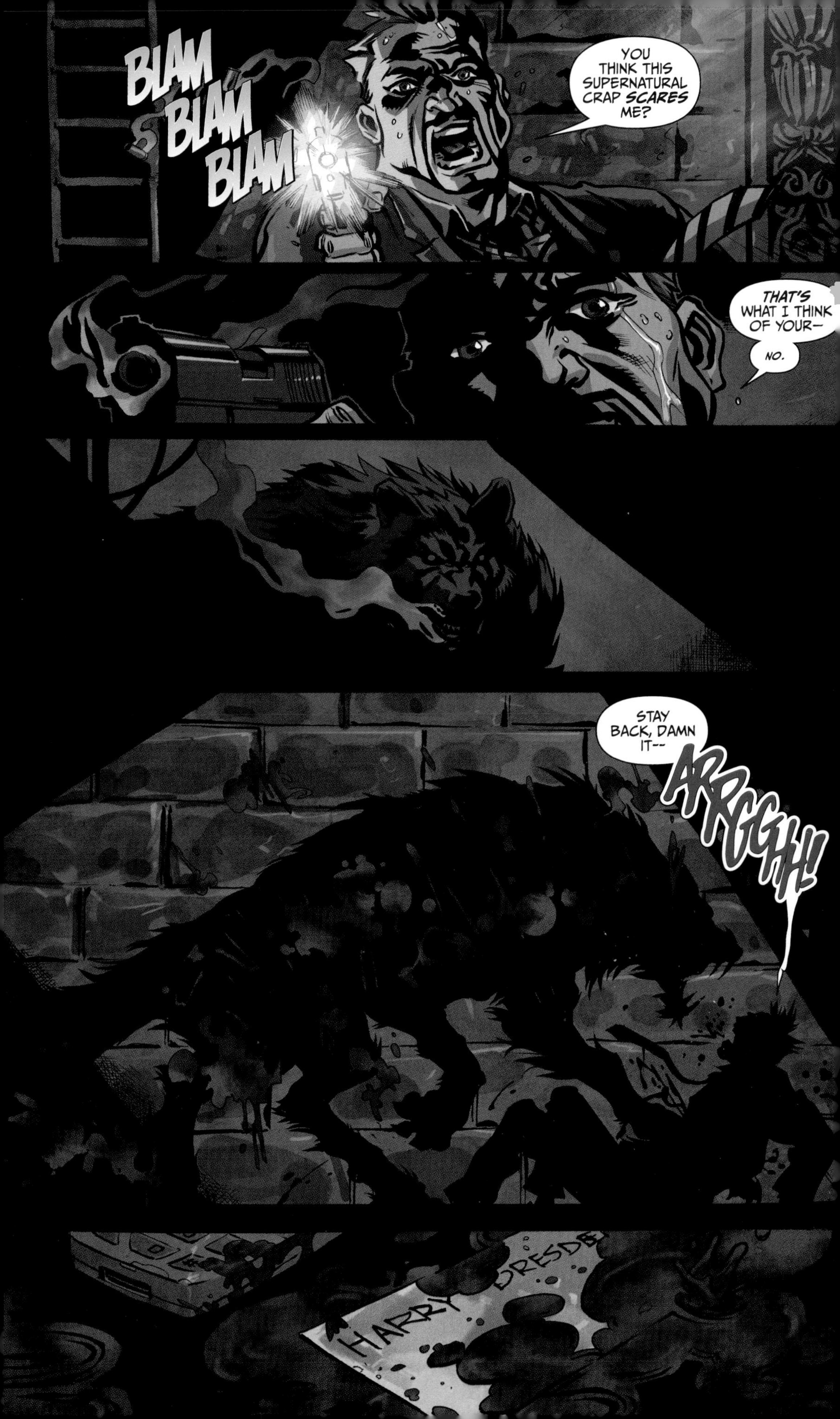
BLAM BLAM BLAM
YOU THINK THIS SUPERNATURAL CRAP *SCARES* ME?
THAT'S WHAT I THINK OF YOUR—
NO.
STAY BACK, DAMN IT--
ARRGGHH!!
HARRY DRESDE

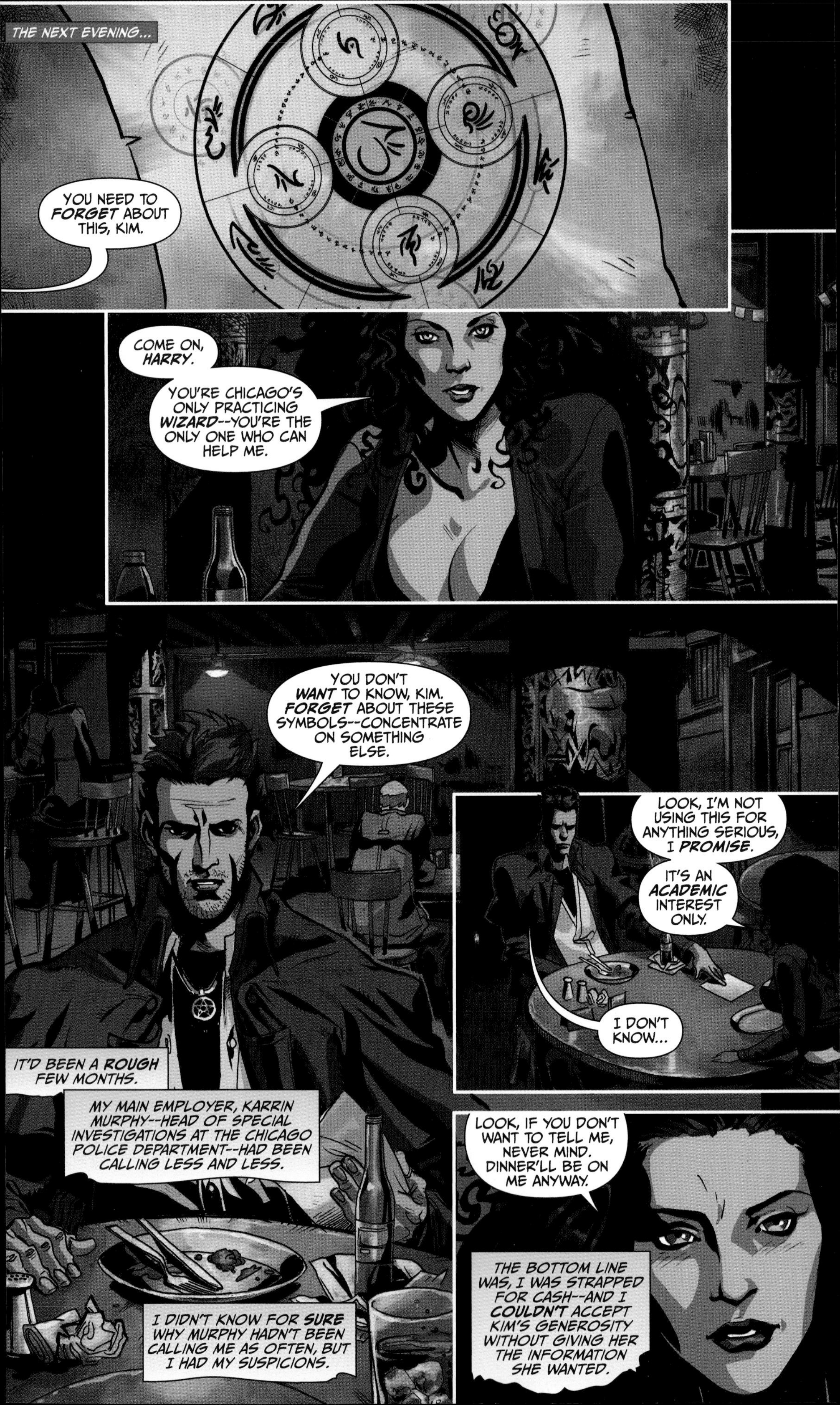
THE NEXT EVENING...
YOU NEED TO FORGET ABOUT THIS, KIM.
COME ON, HARRY.
YOU'RE CHICAGO'S ONLY PRACTICING WIZARD--YOU'RE THE ONLY ONE WHO CAN HELP ME.
YOU DON'T WANT TO KNOW, KIM. FORGET ABOUT THESE SYMBOLS--CONCENTRATE ON SOMETHING ELSE.
IT'D BEEN A ROUGH FEW MONTHS.
MY MAIN EMPLOYER, KARRIN MURPHY--HEAD OF SPECIAL INVESTIGATIONS AT THE CHICAGO POLICE DEPARTMENT--HAD BEEN CALLING LESS AND LESS.
I DIDN'T KNOW FOR SURE WHY MURPHY HADN'T BEEN CALLING ME AS OFTEN, BUT I HAD MY SUSPICIONS.
LOOK, I'M NOT USING THIS FOR ANYTHING SERIOUS, I PROMISE.
IT'S AN ACADEMIC INTEREST ONLY.
I DON'T KNOW...
LOOK, IF YOU DON'T WANT TO TELL ME, NEVER MIND. DINNER'LL BE ON ME ANYWAY.
THE BOTTOM LINE WAS, I WAS STRAPPED FOR CASH--AND I COULDN'T ACCEPT KIM'S GENEROSITY WITHOUT GIVING HER THE INFORMATION SHE WANTED.

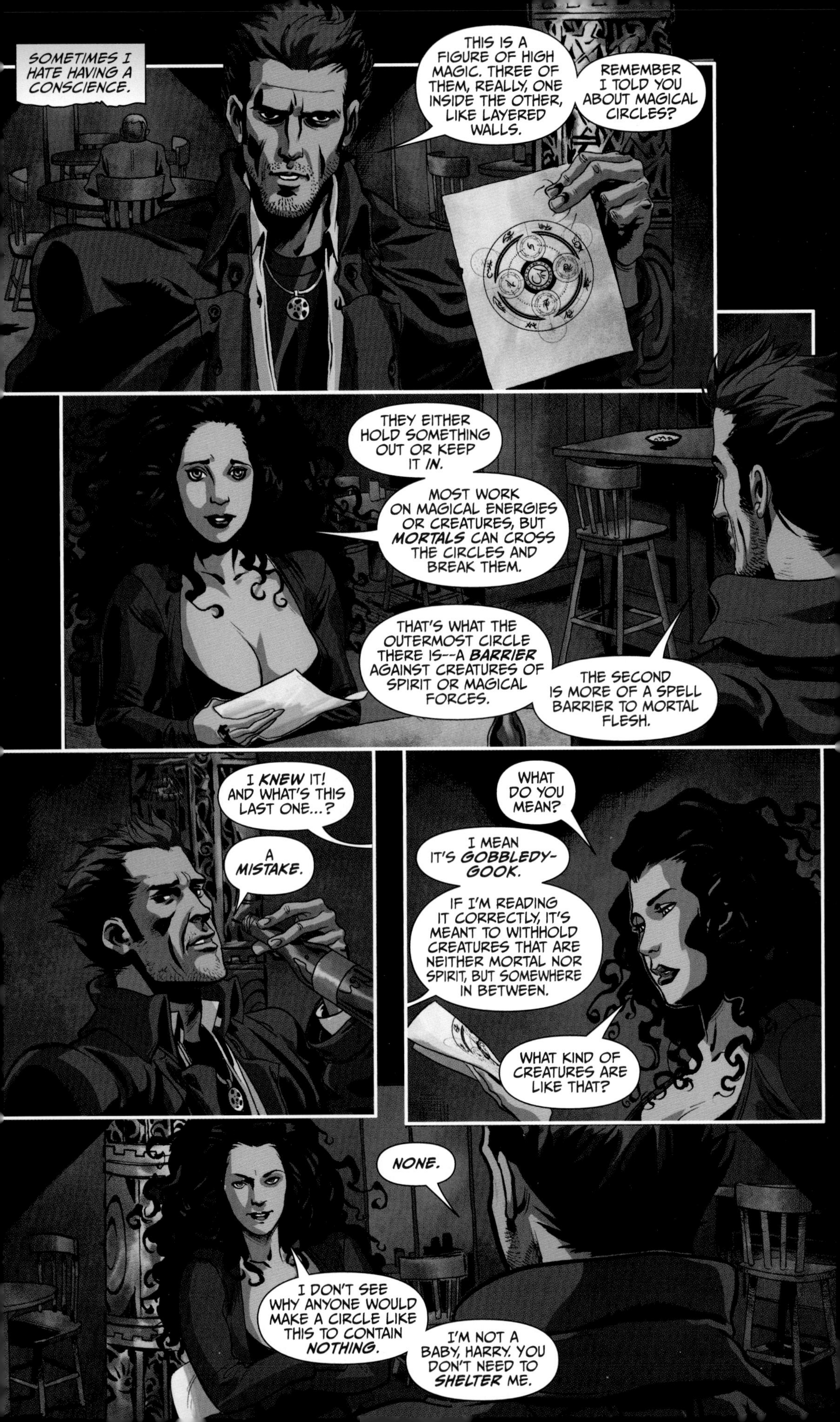
SOMETIMES I HATE HAVING A CONSCIENCE.
THIS IS A FIGURE OF HIGH MAGIC. THREE OF THEM, REALLY, ONE INSIDE THE OTHER, LIKE LAYERED WALLS.
REMEMBER I TOLD YOU ABOUT MAGICAL CIRCLES?
THEY EITHER HOLD SOMETHING OUT OR KEEP IT IN.
MOST WORK ON MAGICAL ENERGIES OR CREATURES, BUT MORTALS CAN CROSS THE CIRCLES AND BREAK THEM.
THAT'S WHAT THE OUTERMOST CIRCLE THERE IS--A BARRIER AGAINST CREATURES OF SPIRIT OR MAGICAL FORCES.
THE SECOND IS MORE OF A SPELL BARRIER TO MORTAL FLESH.
I KNEW IT! AND WHAT'S THIS LAST ONE...?
A MISTAKE.
WHAT DO YOU MEAN?
I MEAN IT'S GOBBLEDY-GOOK.
IF I'M READING IT CORRECTLY, IT'S MEANT TO WITHHOLD CREATURES THAT ARE NEITHER MORTAL NOR SPIRIT, BUT SOMEWHERE IN BETWEEN.
WHAT KIND OF CREATURES ARE LIKE THAT?
NONE.
I DON'T SEE WHY ANYONE WOULD MAKE A CIRCLE LIKE THIS TO CONTAIN NOTHING.
I'M NOT A BABY, HARRY. YOU DON'T NEED TO SHELTER ME.

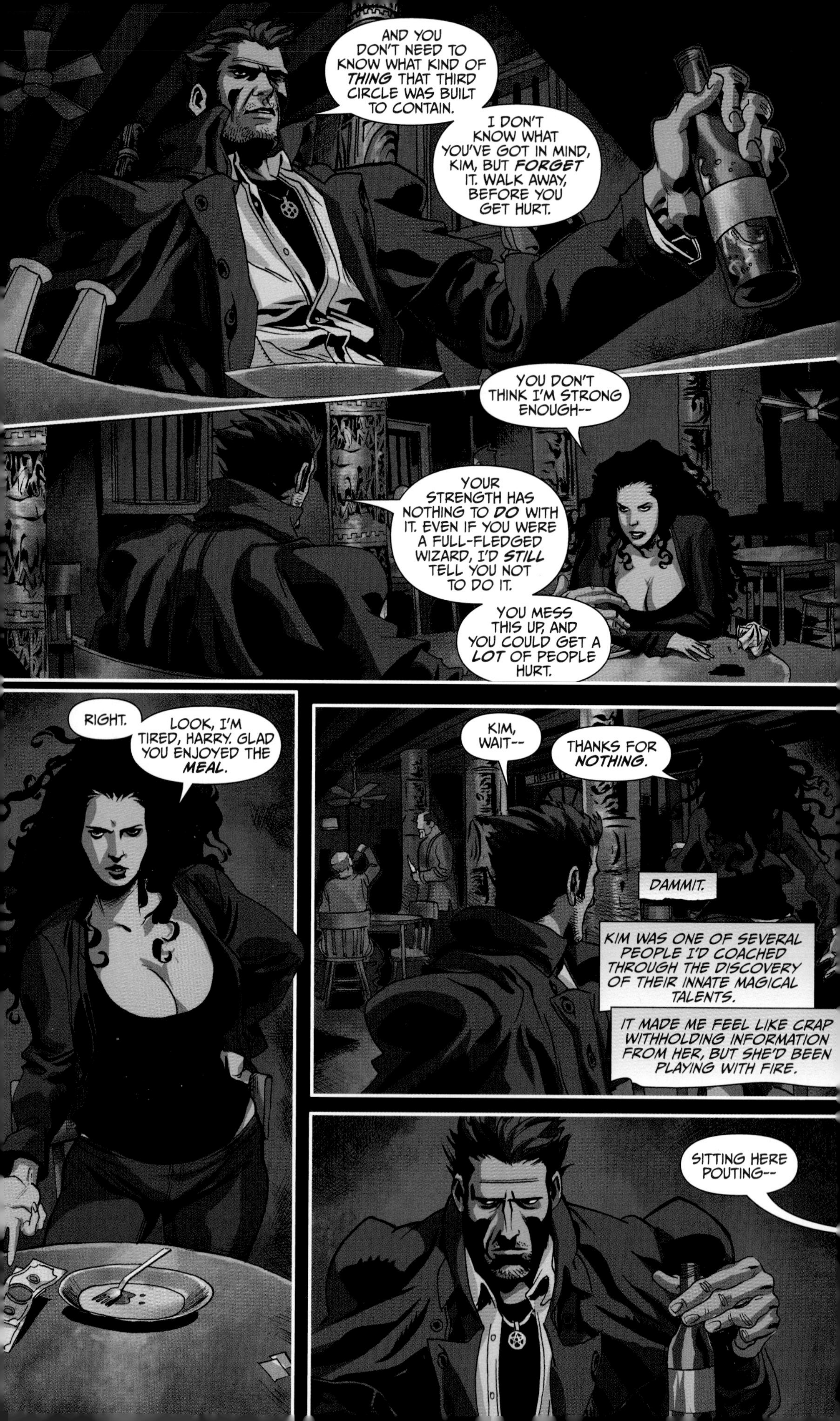
AND YOU DON'T NEED TO KNOW WHAT KIND OF THING THAT THIRD CIRCLE WAS BUILT TO CONTAIN.
I DON'T KNOW WHAT YOU'VE GOT IN MIND, KIM, BUT FORGET IT. WALK AWAY, BEFORE YOU GET HURT.
YOU DON'T THINK I'M STRONG ENOUGH--
YOUR STRENGTH HAS NOTHING TO DO WITH IT. EVEN IF YOU WERE A FULL-FLEDGED WIZARD, I'D STILL TELL YOU NOT TO DO IT.
YOU MESS THIS UP, AND YOU COULD GET A LOT OF PEOPLE HURT.
RIGHT.
LOOK, I'M TIRED, HARRY. GLAD YOU ENJOYED THE MEAL.
KIM, WAIT--
THANKS FOR NOTHING.
DAMMIT.
KIM WAS ONE OF SEVERAL PEOPLE I'D COACHED THROUGH THE DISCOVERY OF THEIR INNATE MAGICAL TALENTS.
IT MADE ME FEEL LIKE CRAP WITHHOLDING INFORMATION FROM HER, BUT SHE'D BEEN PLAYING WITH FIRE.
SITTING HERE POUTING--

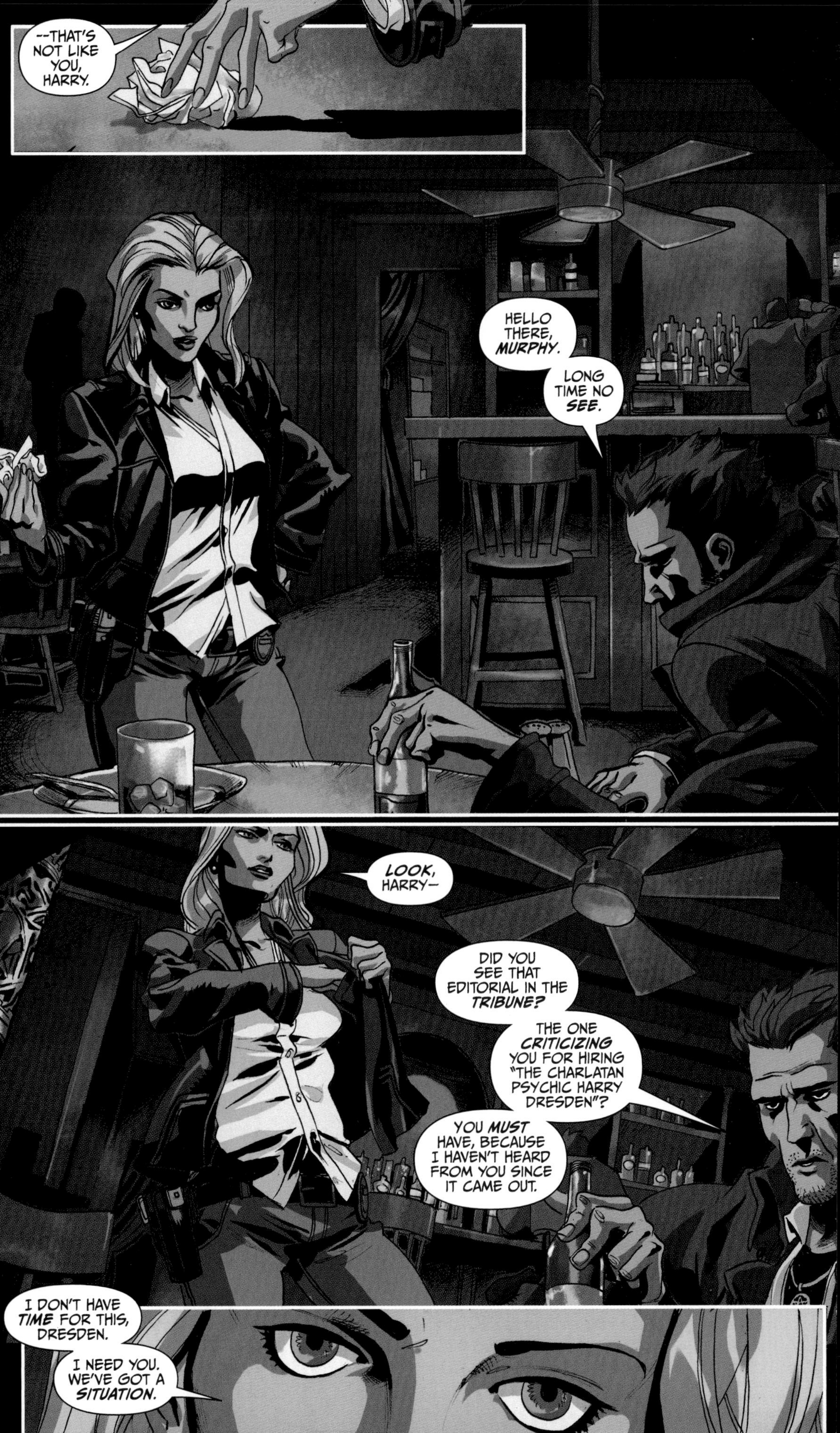
--THAT'S NOT LIKE YOU, HARRY.
HELLO THERE, *MURPHY*.
LONG TIME NO *SEE*.
LOOK, HARRY--
DID YOU SEE THAT EDITORIAL IN THE *TRIBUNE?*
THE ONE *CRITICIZING* YOU FOR HIRING "THE CHARLATAN PSYCHIC HARRY DRESDEN"?
YOU *MUST* HAVE, BECAUSE I HAVEN'T HEARD FROM YOU SINCE IT CAME OUT.
I DON'T HAVE *TIME* FOR THIS, DRESDEN.
I NEED YOU. WE'VE GOT A *SITUATION*.

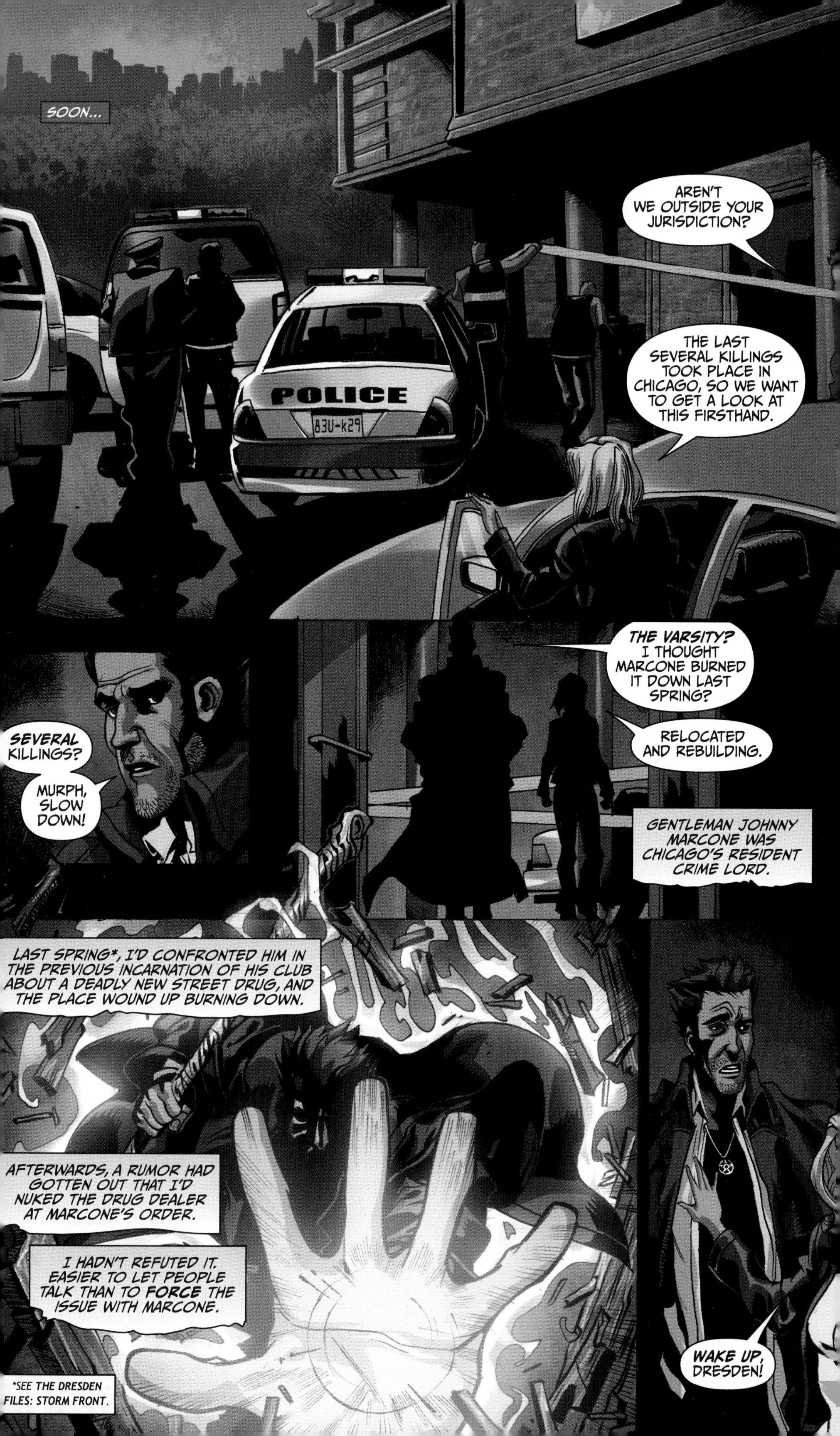
SOON...
AREN'T WE OUTSIDE YOUR JURISDICTION?
THE LAST SEVERAL KILLINGS TOOK PLACE IN CHICAGO, SO WE WANT TO GET A LOOK AT THIS FIRSTHAND.
POLICE
83U-k29
SEVERAL KILLINGS?
MURPH, SLOW DOWN!
THE VARSITY? I THOUGHT MARCONE BURNED IT DOWN LAST SPRING?
RELOCATED AND REBUILDING.
GENTLEMAN JOHNNY MARCONE WAS CHICAGO'S RESIDENT CRIME LORD.
LAST SPRING*, I'D CONFRONTED HIM IN THE PREVIOUS INCARNATION OF HIS CLUB ABOUT A DEADLY NEW STREET DRUG, AND THE PLACE WOUND UP BURNING DOWN.
AFTERWARDS, A RUMOR HAD GOTTEN OUT THAT I'D NUKED THE DRUG DEALER AT MARCONE'S ORDER.
I HADN'T REFUTED IT. EASIER TO LET PEOPLE TALK THAN TO FORCE THE ISSUE WITH MARCONE.
*SEE THE DRESDEN FILES: STORM FRONT.
WAKE UP, DRESDEN!

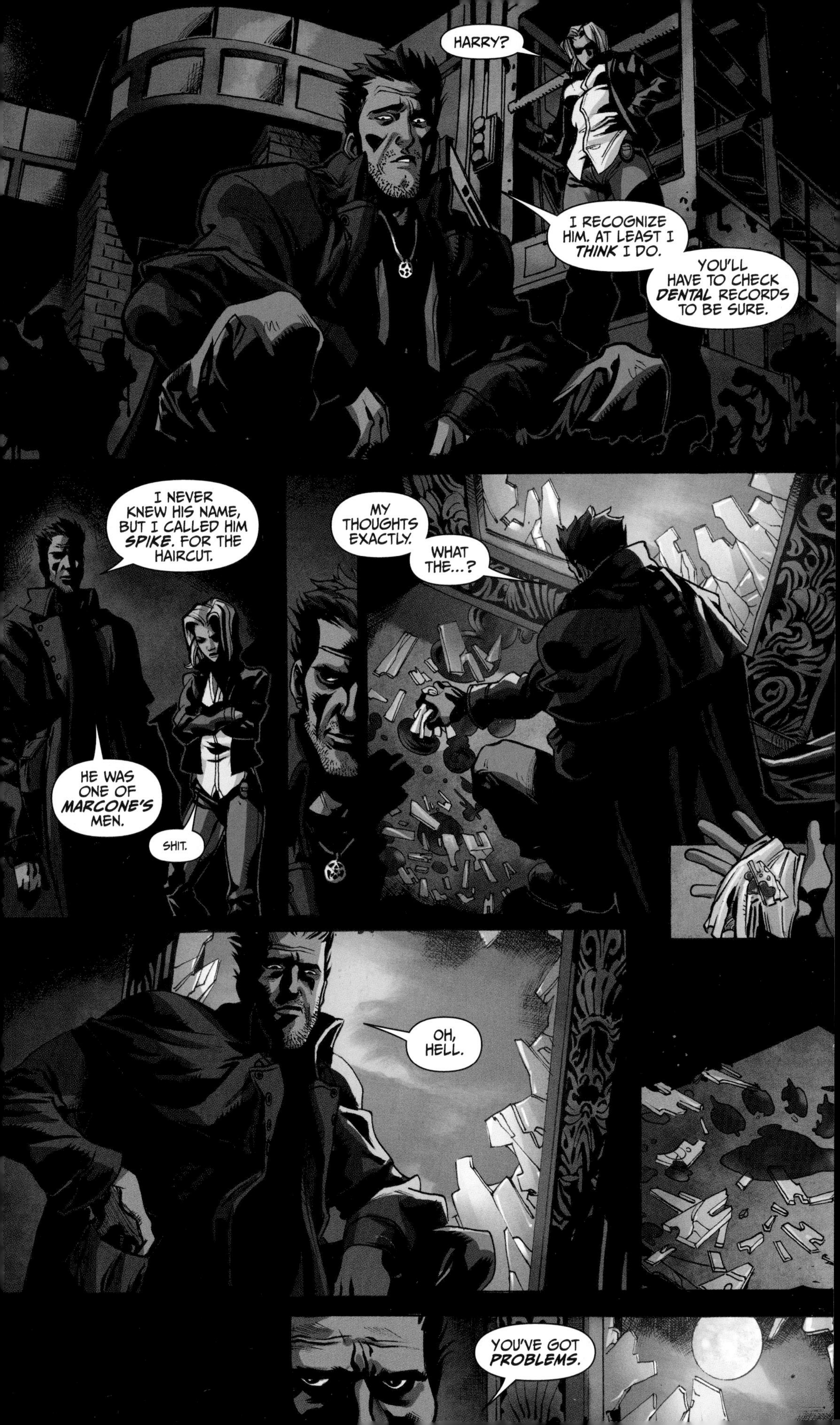
HARRY?
I RECOGNIZE HIM. AT LEAST I *THINK* I DO.
YOU'LL HAVE TO CHECK ***DENTAL*** RECORDS TO BE SURE.
I NEVER KNEW HIS NAME, BUT I CALLED HIM ***SPIKE***. FOR THE HAIRCUT.
HE WAS ONE OF ***MARCONE'S*** MEN.
SHIT.
MY THOUGHTS EXACTLY.
WHAT THE...?
OH, HELL.
YOU'VE GOT ***PROBLEMS***.

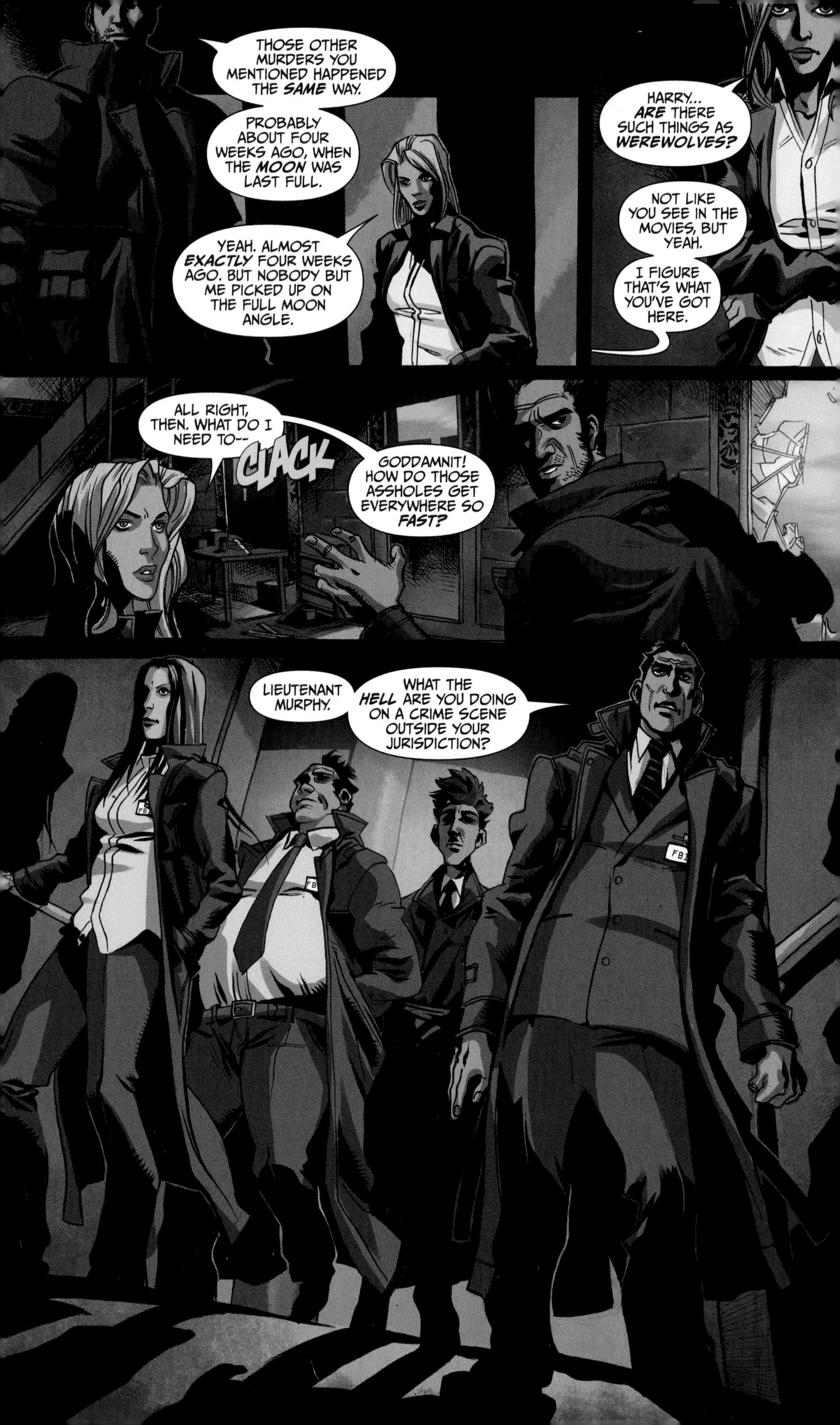
THOSE OTHER MURDERS YOU MENTIONED HAPPENED THE *SAME* WAY.
PROBABLY ABOUT FOUR WEEKS AGO, WHEN THE *MOON* WAS LAST FULL.
YEAH. ALMOST *EXACTLY* FOUR WEEKS AGO. BUT NOBODY BUT ME PICKED UP ON THE FULL MOON ANGLE.
HARRY... *ARE* THERE SUCH THINGS AS *WEREWOLVES?*
NOT LIKE YOU SEE IN THE MOVIES, BUT YEAH.
I FIGURE THAT'S WHAT YOU'VE GOT HERE.
ALL RIGHT, THEN. WHAT DO I NEED TO--
CLACK
GODDAMNIT! HOW DO THOSE ASSHOLES GET EVERYWHERE SO *FAST?*
LIEUTENANT MURPHY.
WHAT THE *HELL* ARE YOU DOING ON A CRIME SCENE OUTSIDE YOUR JURISDICTION?

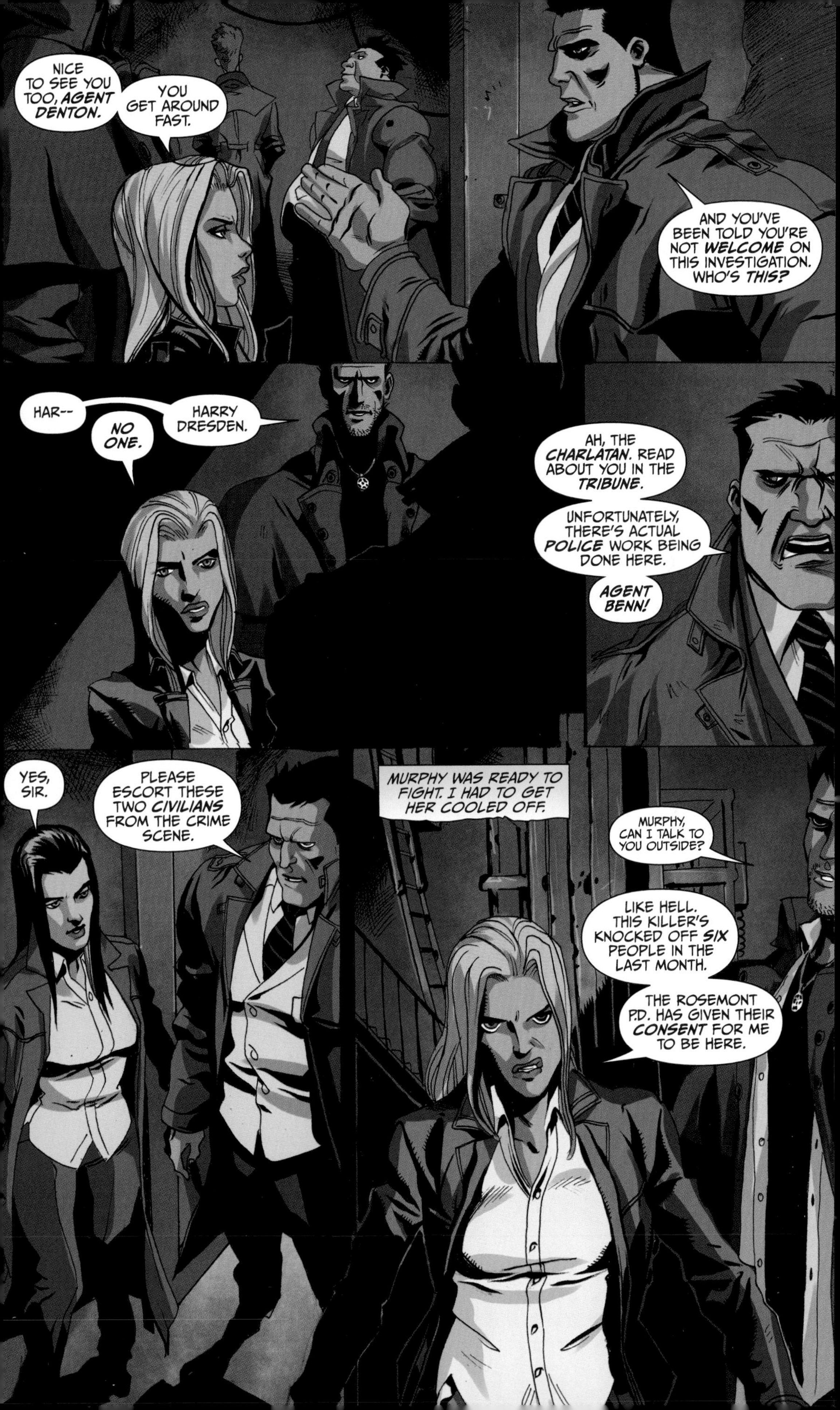
NICE TO SEE YOU TOO, AGENT DENTON.
YOU GET AROUND FAST.
AND YOU'VE BEEN TOLD YOU'RE NOT WELCOME ON THIS INVESTIGATION. WHO'S THIS?
HAR--
NO ONE.
HARRY DRESDEN.
AH, THE CHARLATAN. READ ABOUT YOU IN THE TRIBUNE.
UNFORTUNATELY, THERE'S ACTUAL POLICE WORK BEING DONE HERE.
AGENT BENN!
YES, SIR.
PLEASE ESCORT THESE TWO CIVILIANS FROM THE CRIME SCENE.
MURPHY WAS READY TO FIGHT. I HAD TO GET HER COOLED OFF.
MURPHY, CAN I TALK TO YOU OUTSIDE?
LIKE HELL. THIS KILLER'S KNOCKED OFF SIX PEOPLE IN THE LAST MONTH.
THE ROSEMONT P.D. HAS GIVEN THEIR CONSENT FOR ME TO BE HERE.

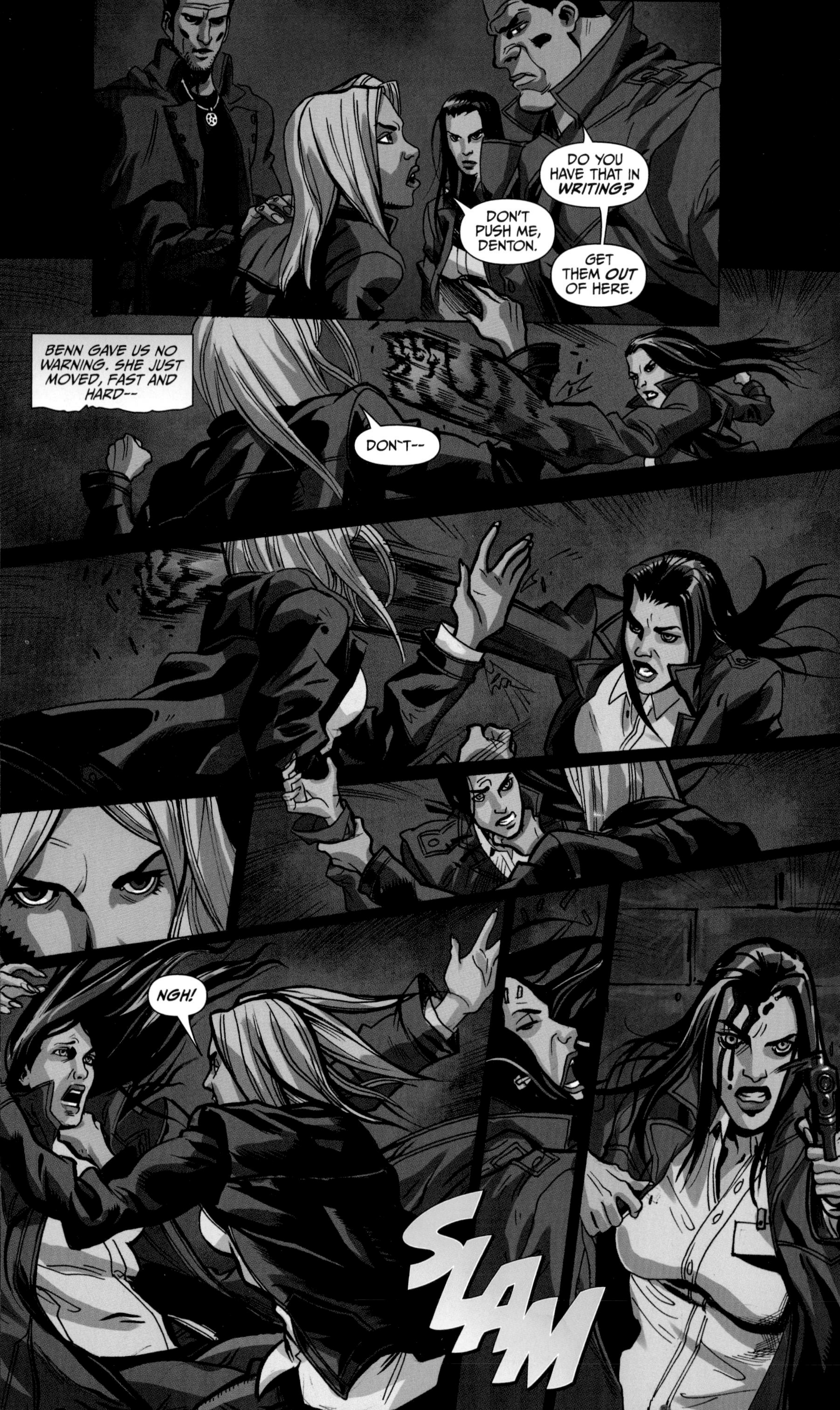
DO YOU HAVE THAT IN *WRITING?*
DON'T PUSH ME, DENTON.
GET THEM *OUT* OF HERE.
BENN GAVE US NO WARNING. SHE JUST MOVED, FAST AND HARD--
DON'T--
NGH!
SLAM

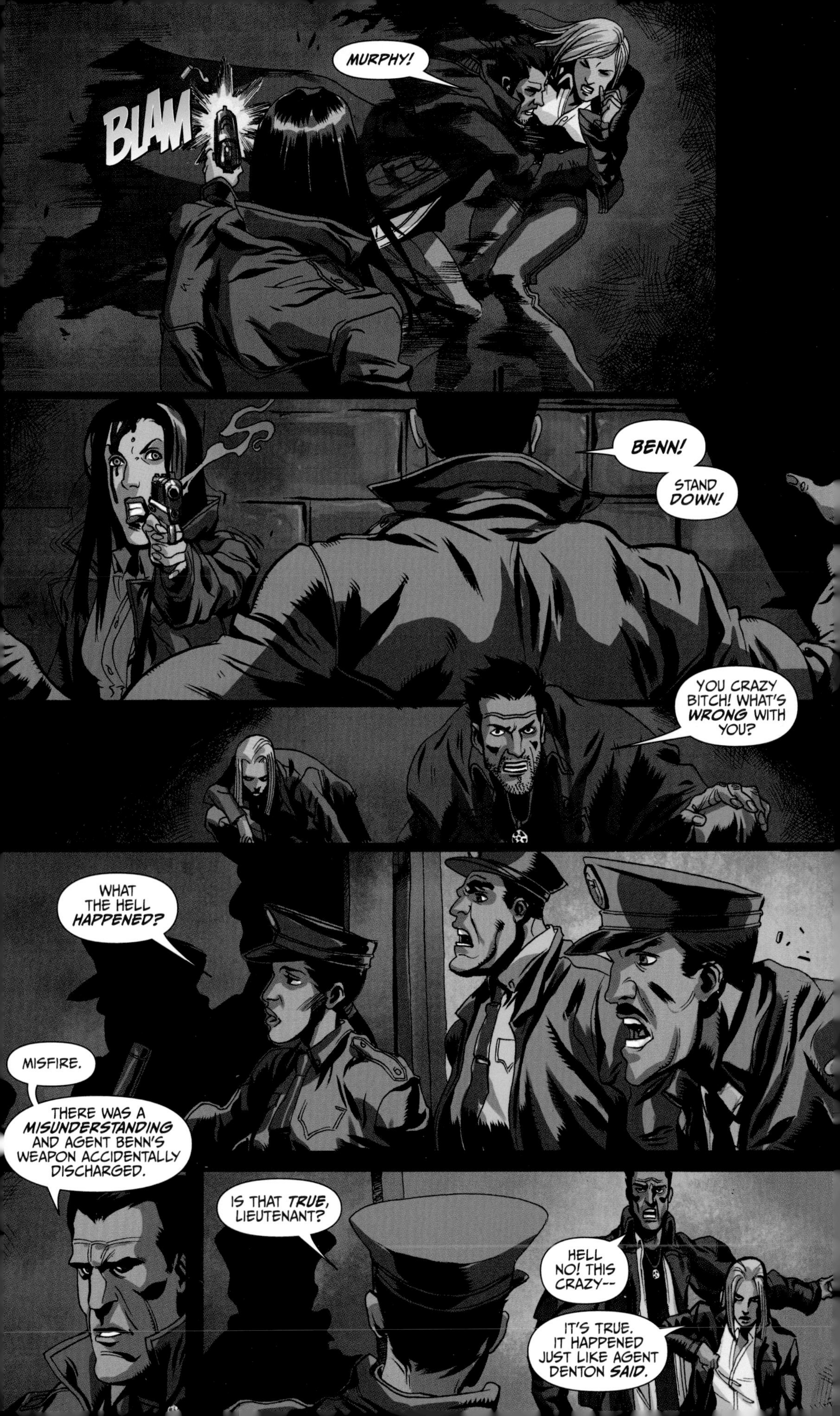
MURPHY!
BLAM
BENN!
STAND DOWN!
YOU CRAZY BITCH! WHAT'S WRONG WITH YOU?
WHAT THE HELL HAPPENED?
MISFIRE.
THERE WAS A MISUNDERSTANDING AND AGENT BENN'S WEAPON ACCIDENTALLY DISCHARGED.
IS THAT TRUE, LIEUTENANT?
HELL NO! THIS CRAZY--
IT'S TRUE. IT HAPPENED JUST LIKE AGENT DENTON SAID.

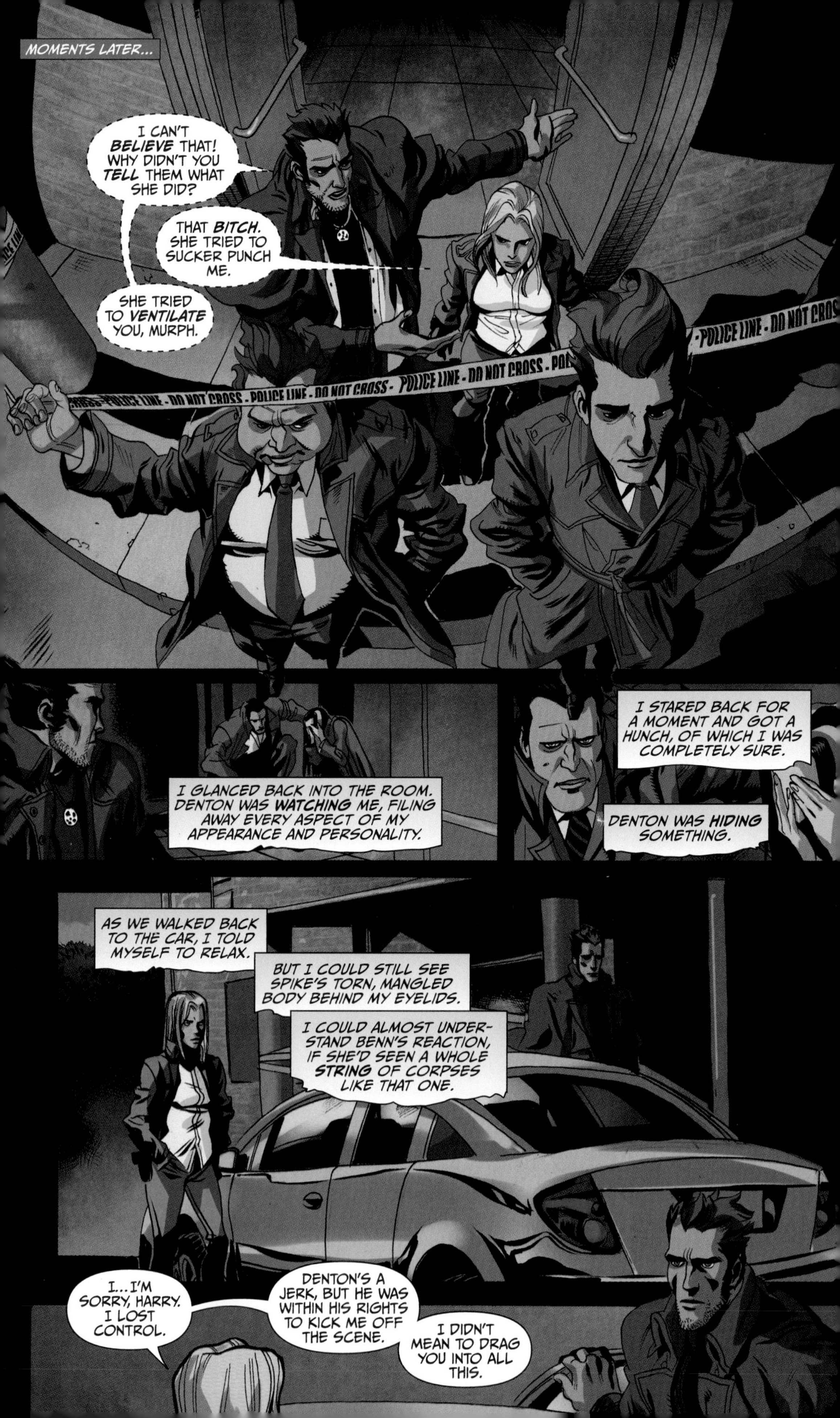
MOMENTS LATER...
I CAN'T BELIEVE THAT! WHY DIDN'T YOU TELL THEM WHAT SHE DID?
SHE TRIED TO VENTILATE YOU, MURPH.
THAT BITCH. SHE TRIED TO SUCKER PUNCH ME.
POLICE LINE - DO NOT CROSS
I GLANCED BACK INTO THE ROOM. DENTON WAS WATCHING ME, FILING AWAY EVERY ASPECT OF MY APPEARANCE AND PERSONALITY.
I STARED BACK FOR A MOMENT AND GOT A HUNCH, OF WHICH I WAS COMPLETELY SURE.
DENTON WAS HIDING SOMETHING.
AS WE WALKED BACK TO THE CAR, I TOLD MYSELF TO RELAX.
BUT I COULD STILL SEE SPIKE'S TORN, MANGLED BODY BEHIND MY EYELIDS.
I COULD ALMOST UNDERSTAND BENN'S REACTION, IF SHE'D SEEN A WHOLE STRING OF CORPSES LIKE THAT ONE.
I...I'M SORRY, HARRY. I LOST CONTROL.
DENTON'S A JERK, BUT HE WAS WITHIN HIS RIGHTS TO KICK ME OFF THE SCENE.
I DIDN'T MEAN TO DRAG YOU INTO ALL THIS.

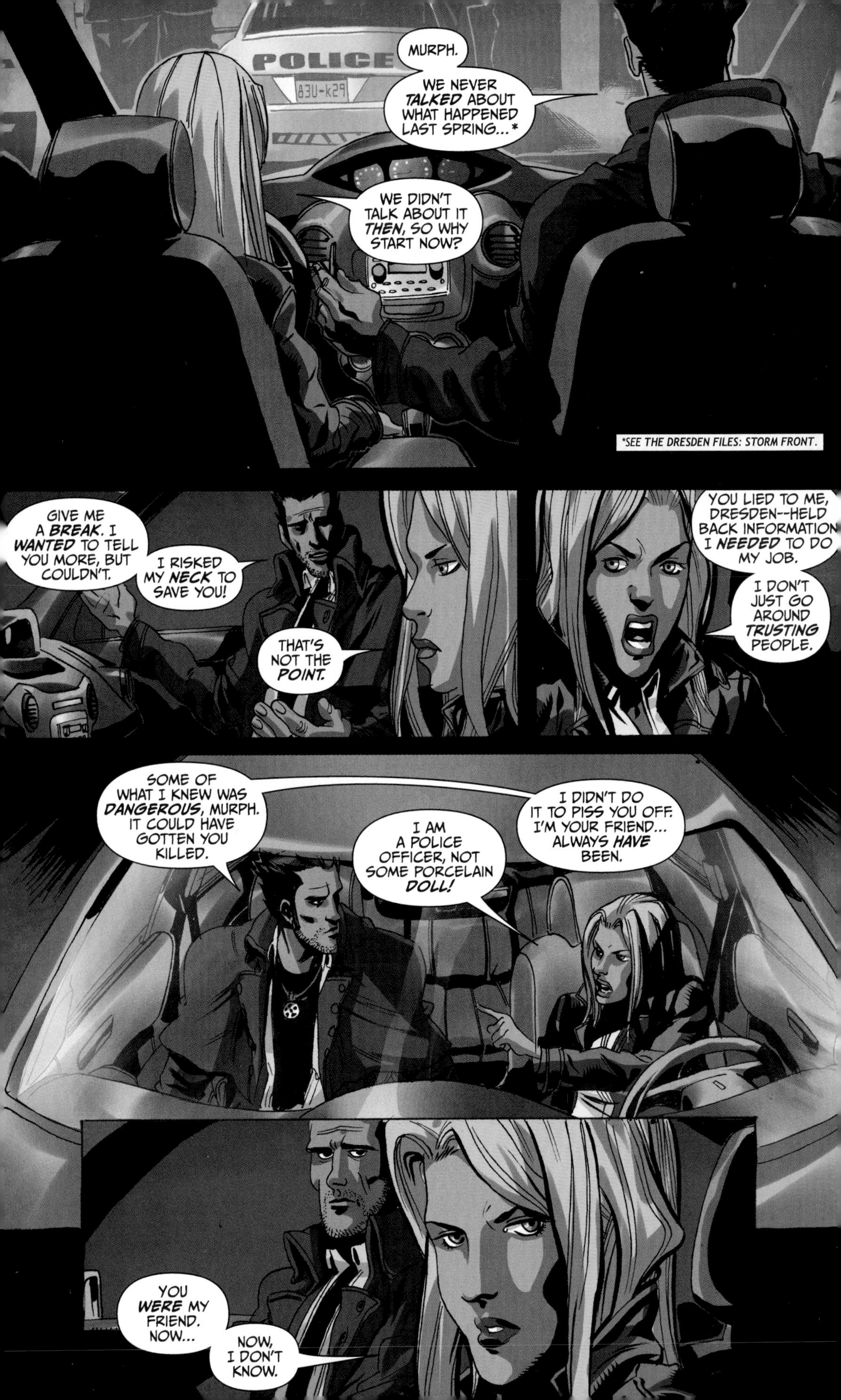
POLICE
83U-K29
MURPH.
WE NEVER TALKED ABOUT WHAT HAPPENED LAST SPRING...*
WE DIDN'T TALK ABOUT IT THEN, SO WHY START NOW?
*SEE THE DRESDEN FILES: STORM FRONT.
GIVE ME A BREAK. I WANTED TO TELL YOU MORE, BUT COULDN'T.
I RISKED MY NECK TO SAVE YOU!
THAT'S NOT THE POINT.
YOU LIED TO ME, DRESDEN--HELD BACK INFORMATION I NEEDED TO DO MY JOB.
I DON'T JUST GO AROUND TRUSTING PEOPLE.
SOME OF WHAT I KNEW WAS DANGEROUS, MURPH. IT COULD HAVE GOTTEN YOU KILLED.
I AM A POLICE OFFICER, NOT SOME PORCELAIN DOLL!
I DIDN'T DO IT TO PISS YOU OFF. I'M YOUR FRIEND... ALWAYS HAVE BEEN.
YOU WERE MY FRIEND. NOW...
NOW, I DON'T KNOW.

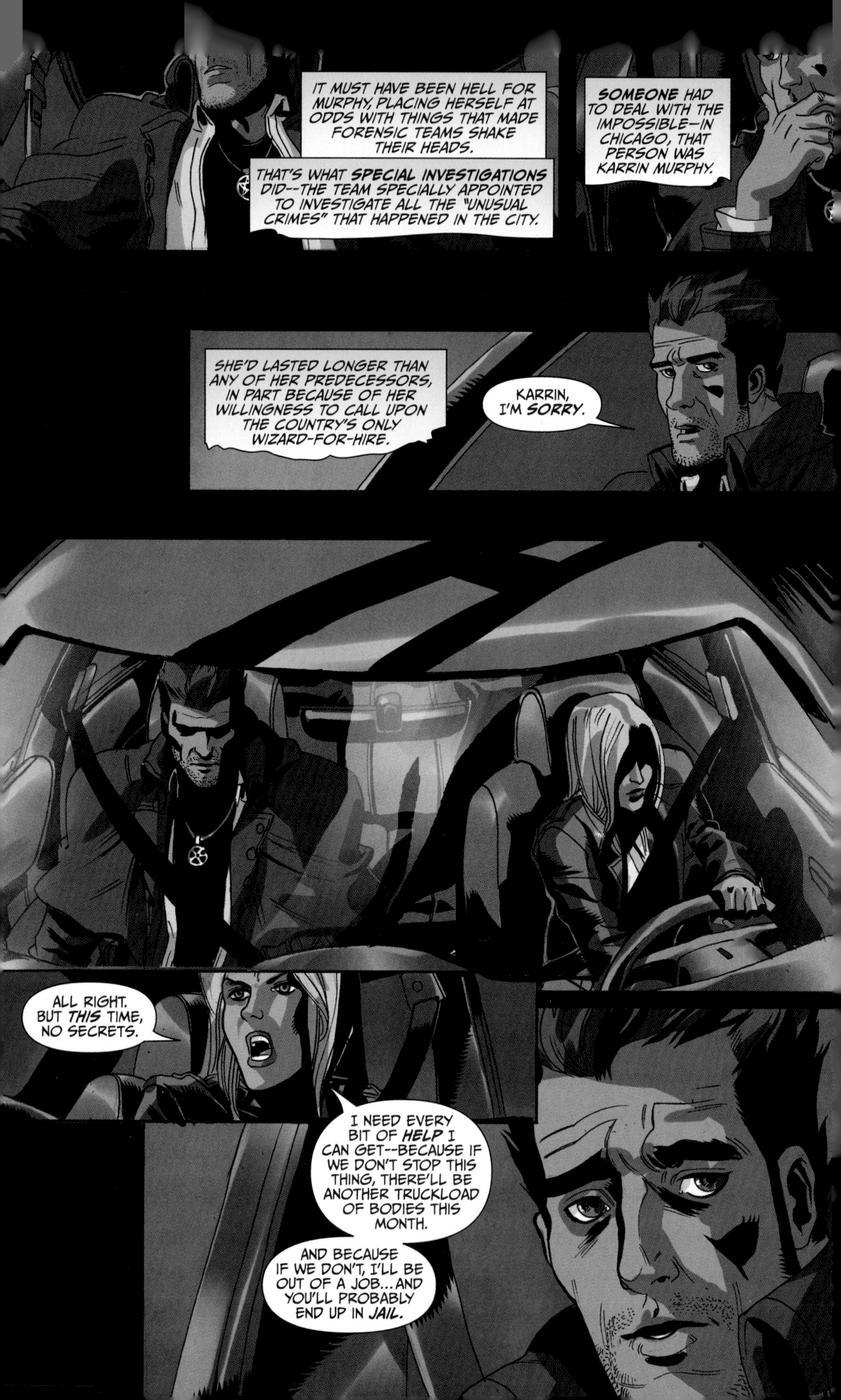
IT MUST HAVE BEEN HELL FOR MURPHY, PLACING HERSELF AT ODDS WITH THINGS THAT MADE FORENSIC TEAMS SHAKE THEIR HEADS.
THAT'S WHAT SPECIAL INVESTIGATIONS DID--THE TEAM SPECIALLY APPOINTED TO INVESTIGATE ALL THE "UNUSUAL CRIMES" THAT HAPPENED IN THE CITY.
SOMEONE HAD TO DEAL WITH THE IMPOSSIBLE—IN CHICAGO, THAT PERSON WAS KARRIN MURPHY.
SHE'D LASTED LONGER THAN ANY OF HER PREDECESSORS, IN PART BECAUSE OF HER WILLINGNESS TO CALL UPON THE COUNTRY'S ONLY WIZARD-FOR-HIRE.
KARRIN, I'M SORRY.
ALL RIGHT. BUT THIS TIME, NO SECRETS.
I NEED EVERY BIT OF HELP I CAN GET--BECAUSE IF WE DON'T STOP THIS THING, THERE'LL BE ANOTHER TRUCKLOAD OF BODIES THIS MONTH.
AND BECAUSE IF WE DON'T, I'LL BE OUT OF A JOB...AND YOU'LL PROBABLY END UP IN JAIL.

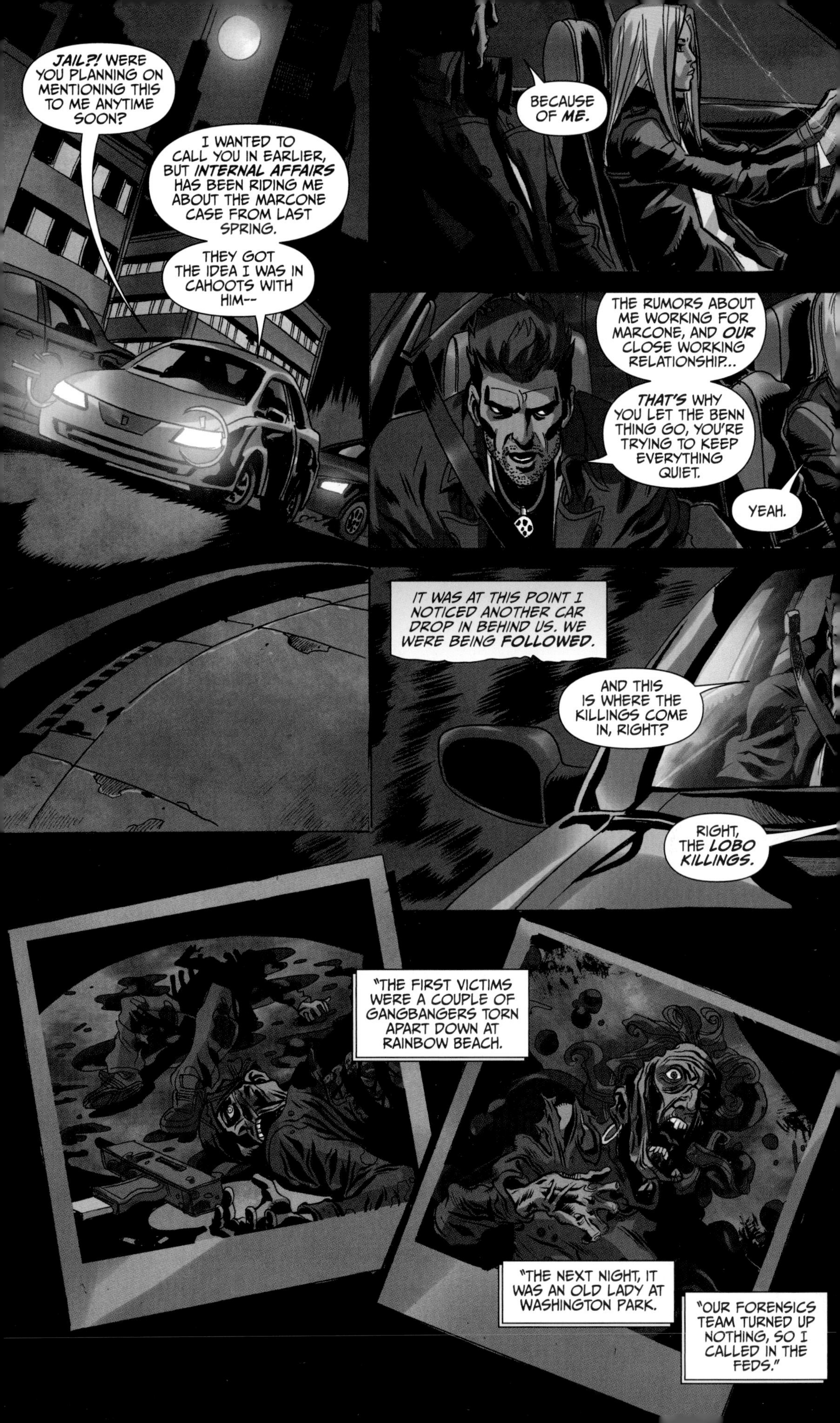
JAIL?! WERE YOU PLANNING ON MENTIONING THIS TO ME ANYTIME SOON?
I WANTED TO CALL YOU IN EARLIER, BUT INTERNAL AFFAIRS HAS BEEN RIDING ME ABOUT THE MARCONE CASE FROM LAST SPRING.
THEY GOT THE IDEA I WAS IN CAHOOTS WITH HIM--
BECAUSE OF ME.
THE RUMORS ABOUT ME WORKING FOR MARCONE, AND OUR CLOSE WORKING RELATIONSHIP...
THAT'S WHY YOU LET THE BENN THING GO, YOU'RE TRYING TO KEEP EVERYTHING QUIET.
YEAH.
IT WAS AT THIS POINT I NOTICED ANOTHER CAR DROP IN BEHIND US. WE WERE BEING FOLLOWED.
AND THIS IS WHERE THE KILLINGS COME IN, RIGHT?
RIGHT, THE LOBO KILLINGS.
"THE FIRST VICTIMS WERE A COUPLE OF GANGBANGERS TORN APART DOWN AT RAINBOW BEACH.
"THE NEXT NIGHT, IT WAS AN OLD LADY AT WASHINGTON PARK.
"OUR FORENSICS TEAM TURNED UP NOTHING, SO I CALLED IN THE FEDS."

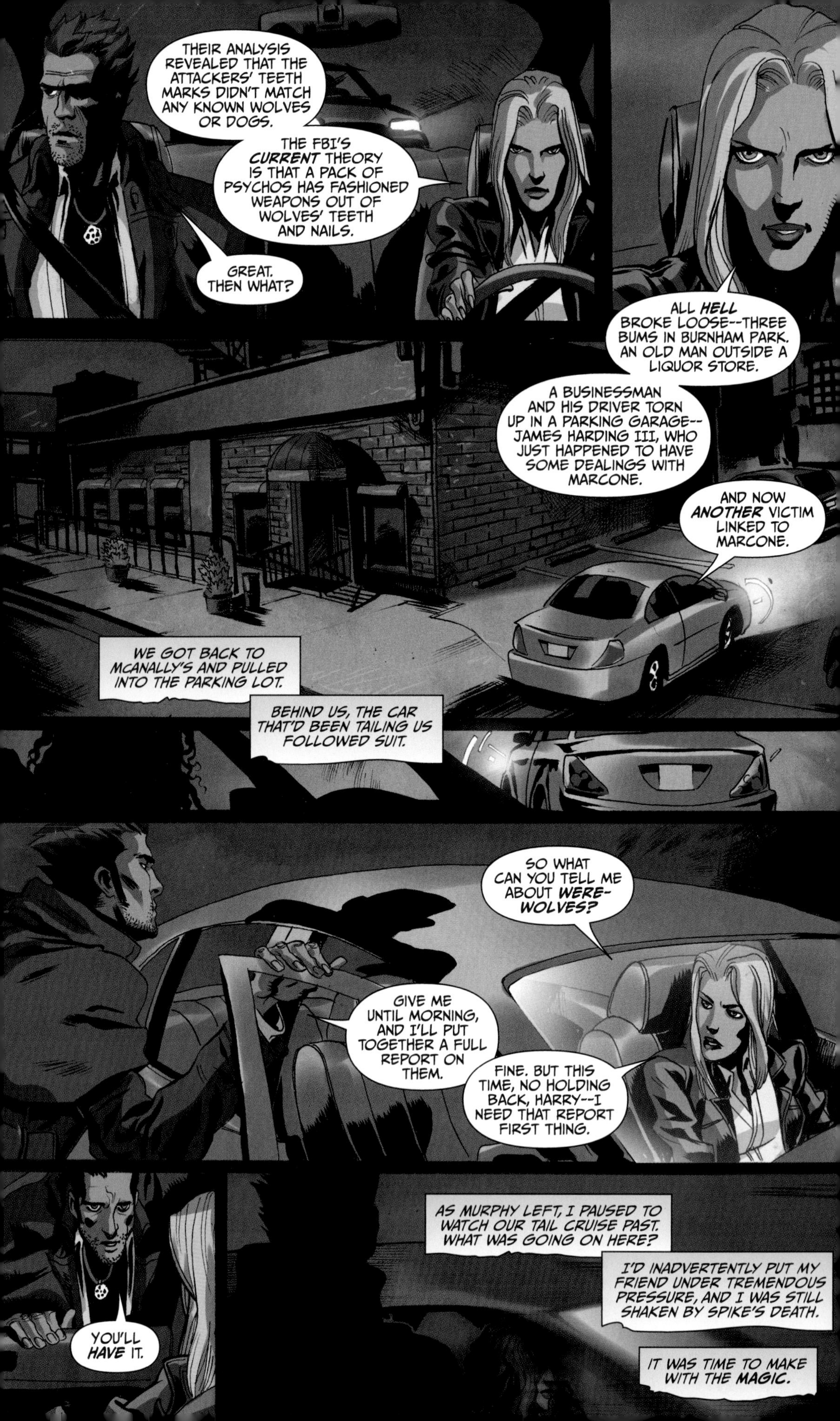
THEIR ANALYSIS REVEALED THAT THE ATTACKERS' TEETH MARKS DIDN'T MATCH ANY KNOWN WOLVES OR DOGS.
THE FBI'S *CURRENT* THEORY IS THAT A PACK OF PSYCHOS HAS FASHIONED WEAPONS OUT OF WOLVES' TEETH AND NAILS.
GREAT. THEN WHAT?
ALL *HELL* BROKE LOOSE--THREE BUMS IN BURNHAM PARK. AN OLD MAN OUTSIDE A LIQUOR STORE.
A BUSINESSMAN AND HIS DRIVER TORN UP IN A PARKING GARAGE--JAMES HARDING III, WHO JUST HAPPENED TO HAVE SOME DEALINGS WITH MARCONE.
AND NOW *ANOTHER* VICTIM LINKED TO MARCONE.
WE GOT BACK TO MCANALLY'S AND PULLED INTO THE PARKING LOT.
BEHIND US, THE CAR THAT'D BEEN TAILING US FOLLOWED SUIT.
SO WHAT CAN YOU TELL ME ABOUT *WERE-WOLVES?*
GIVE ME UNTIL MORNING, AND I'LL PUT TOGETHER A FULL REPORT ON THEM.
FINE. BUT THIS TIME, NO HOLDING BACK, HARRY--I NEED THAT REPORT FIRST THING.
YOU'LL *HAVE* IT.
AS MURPHY LEFT, I PAUSED TO WATCH OUR TAIL CRUISE PAST. WHAT WAS GOING ON HERE?
I'D INADVERTENTLY PUT MY FRIEND UNDER TREMENDOUS PRESSURE, AND I WAS STILL SHAKEN BY SPIKE'S DEATH.
IT WAS TIME TO MAKE WITH THE *MAGIC.*

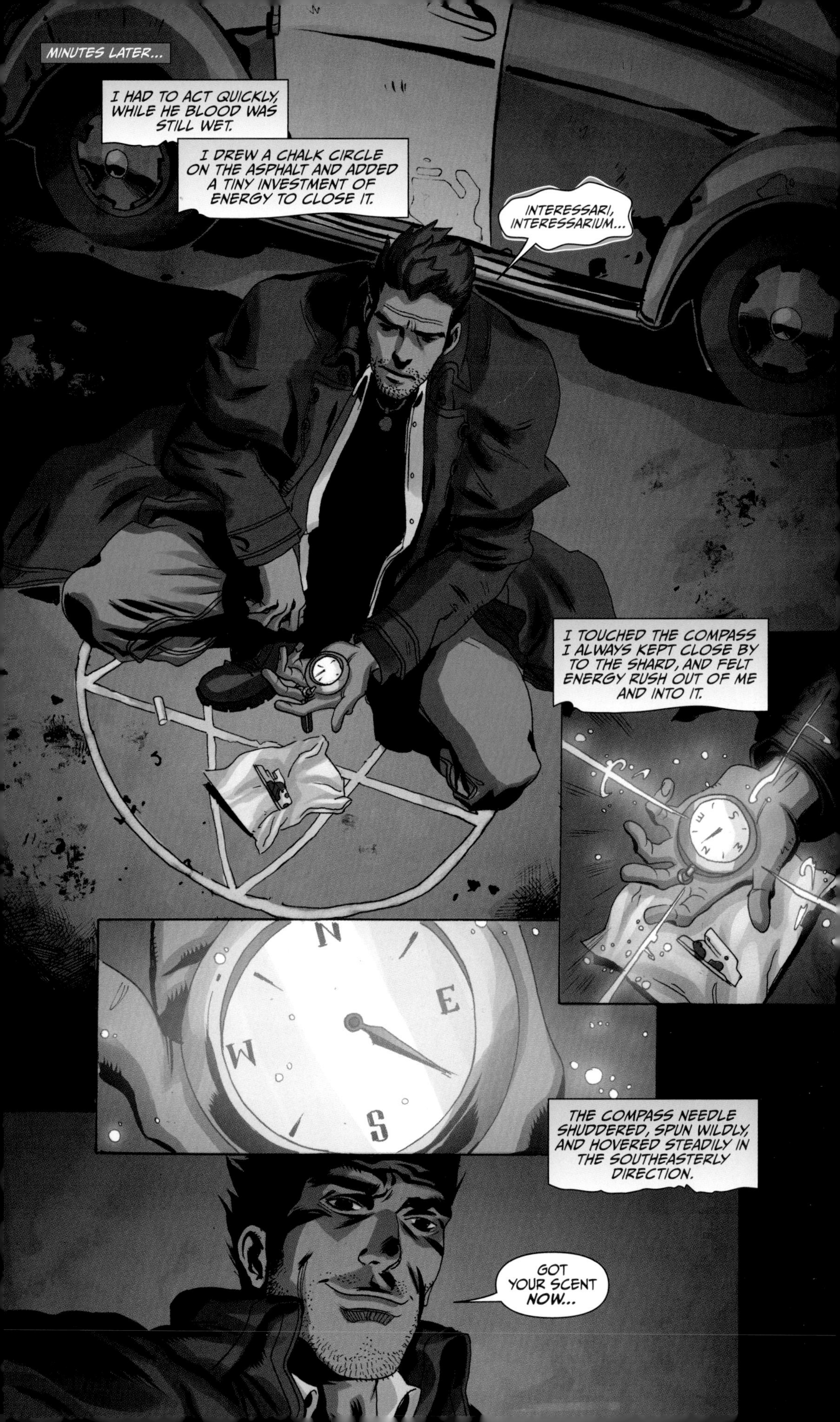
MINUTES LATER...
I HAD TO ACT QUICKLY, WHILE HE BLOOD WAS STILL WET.
I DREW A CHALK CIRCLE ON THE ASPHALT AND ADDED A TINY INVESTMENT OF ENERGY TO CLOSE IT.
INTERESSARI, INTERESSARIUM...
I TOUCHED THE COMPASS I ALWAYS KEPT CLOSE BY TO THE SHARD, AND FELT ENERGY RUSH OUT OF ME AND INTO IT.
N
E
W
S
THE COMPASS NEEDLE SHUDDERED, SPUN WILDLY, AND HOVERED STEADILY IN THE SOUTHEASTERLY DIRECTION.
GOT YOUR SCENT NOW...

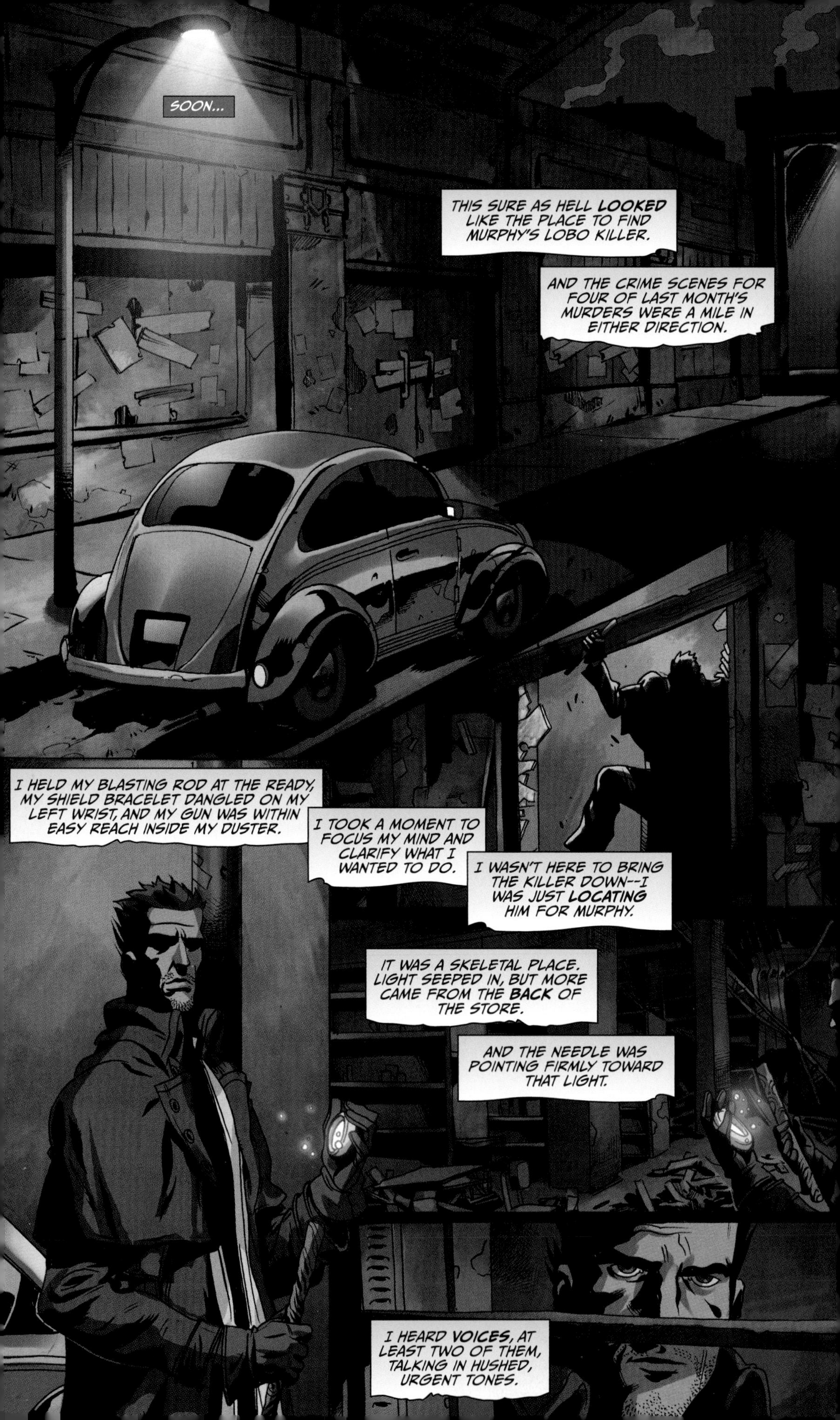
SOON...
THIS SURE AS HELL LOOKED LIKE THE PLACE TO FIND MURPHY'S LOBO KILLER.
AND THE CRIME SCENES FOR FOUR OF LAST MONTH'S MURDERS WERE A MILE IN EITHER DIRECTION.
I HELD MY BLASTING ROD AT THE READY, MY SHIELD BRACELET DANGLED ON MY LEFT WRIST, AND MY GUN WAS WITHIN EASY REACH INSIDE MY DUSTER.
I TOOK A MOMENT TO FOCUS MY MIND AND CLARIFY WHAT I WANTED TO DO.
I WASN'T HERE TO BRING THE KILLER DOWN--I WAS JUST LOCATING HIM FOR MURPHY.
IT WAS A SKELETAL PLACE. LIGHT SEEPED IN, BUT MORE CAME FROM THE BACK OF THE STORE.
AND THE NEEDLE WAS POINTING FIRMLY TOWARD THAT LIGHT.
I HEARD VOICES, AT LEAST TWO OF THEM, TALKING IN HUSHED, URGENT TONES.

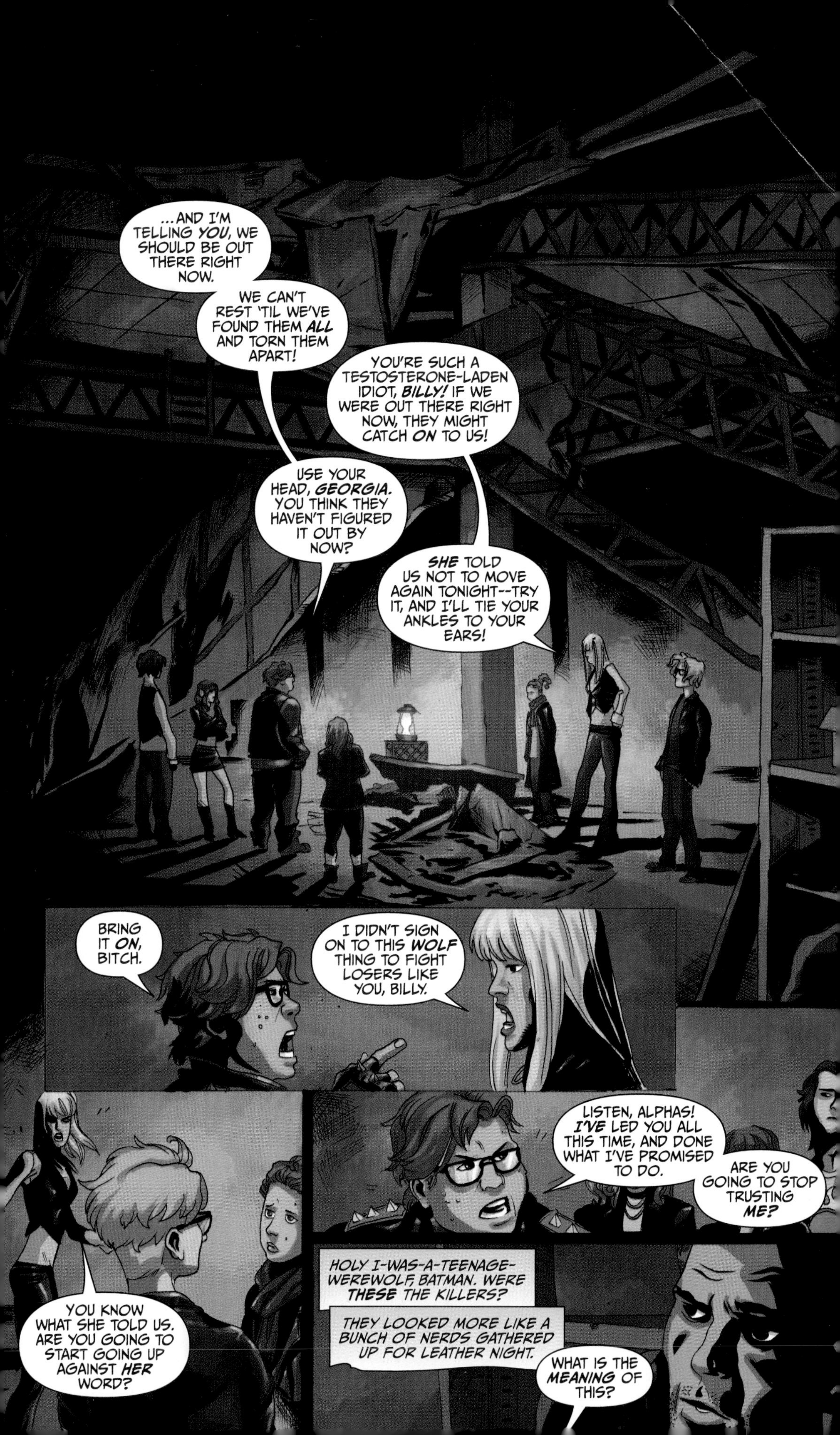
...AND I'M TELLING *YOU*, WE SHOULD BE OUT THERE RIGHT NOW.
WE CAN'T REST 'TIL WE'VE FOUND THEM *ALL* AND TORN THEM APART!
YOU'RE SUCH A TESTOSTERONE-LADEN IDIOT, *BILLY!* IF WE WERE OUT THERE RIGHT NOW, THEY MIGHT CATCH *ON* TO US!
USE YOUR HEAD, *GEORGIA.* YOU THINK THEY HAVEN'T FIGURED IT OUT BY NOW?
SHE TOLD US NOT TO MOVE AGAIN TONIGHT--TRY IT, AND I'LL TIE YOUR ANKLES TO YOUR EARS!
BRING IT *ON*, BITCH.
I DIDN'T SIGN ON TO THIS *WOLF* THING TO FIGHT LOSERS LIKE YOU, BILLY.
YOU KNOW WHAT SHE TOLD US. ARE YOU GOING TO START GOING UP AGAINST *HER* WORD?
LISTEN, ALPHAS! *I'VE* LED YOU ALL THIS TIME, AND DONE WHAT I'VE PROMISED TO DO.
ARE YOU GOING TO STOP TRUSTING *ME?*
*HOLY I-WAS-A-TEENAGE-WEREWOLF, BATMAN. WERE **THESE** THE KILLERS?*
THEY LOOKED MORE LIKE A BUNCH OF NERDS GATHERED UP FOR LEATHER NIGHT.
WHAT IS THE *MEANING* OF THIS?

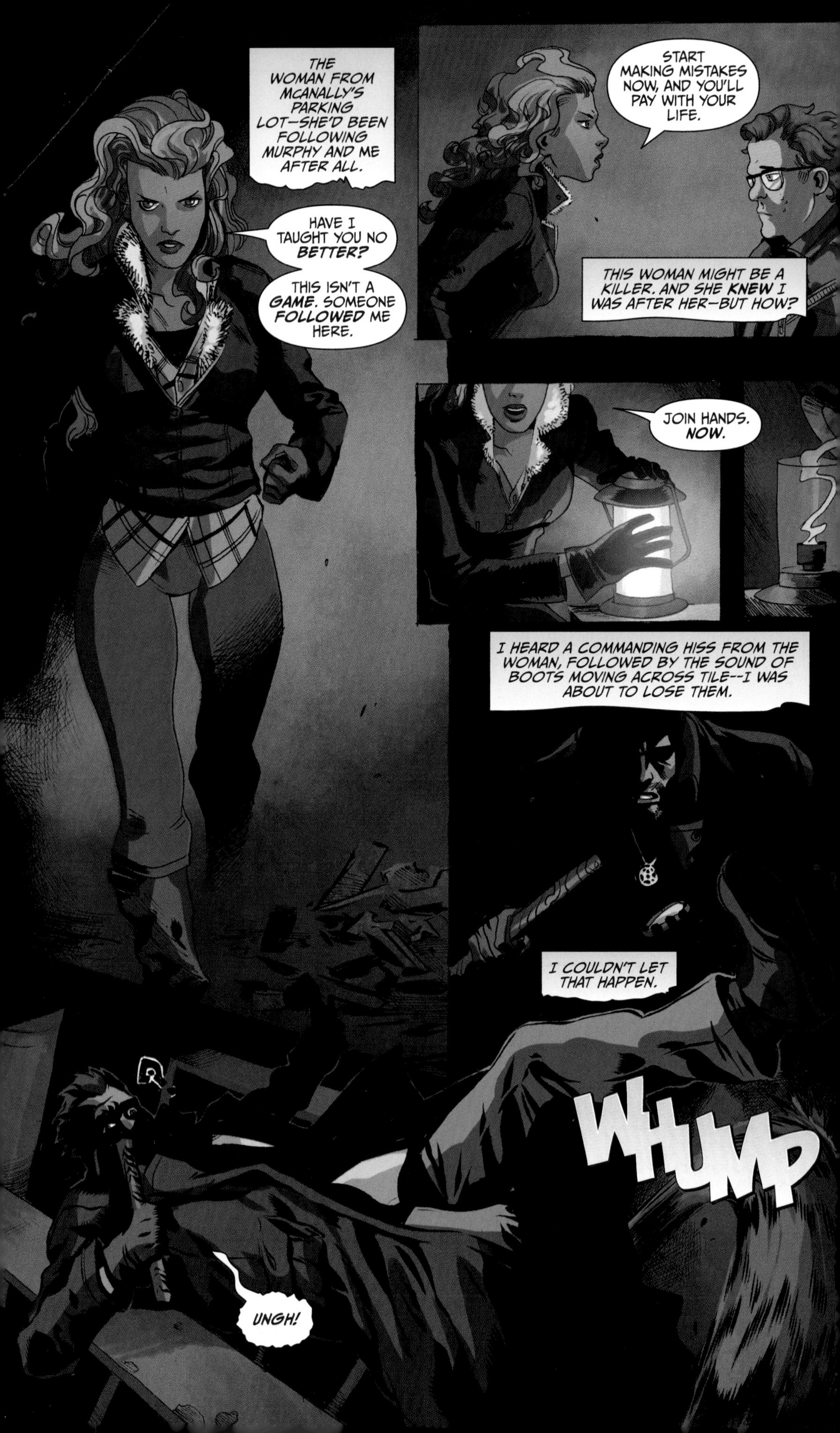
THE WOMAN FROM McANALLY'S PARKING LOT—SHE'D BEEN FOLLOWING MURPHY AND ME AFTER ALL.
HAVE I TAUGHT YOU NO BETTER?
THIS ISN'T A GAME. SOMEONE FOLLOWED ME HERE.
START MAKING MISTAKES NOW, AND YOU'LL PAY WITH YOUR LIFE.
THIS WOMAN MIGHT BE A KILLER. AND SHE KNEW I WAS AFTER HER—BUT HOW?
JOIN HANDS. NOW.
I HEARD A COMMANDING HISS FROM THE WOMAN, FOLLOWED BY THE SOUND OF BOOTS MOVING ACROSS TILE--I WAS ABOUT TO LOSE THEM.
I COULDN'T LET THAT HAPPEN.
WHUMP
UNGH!

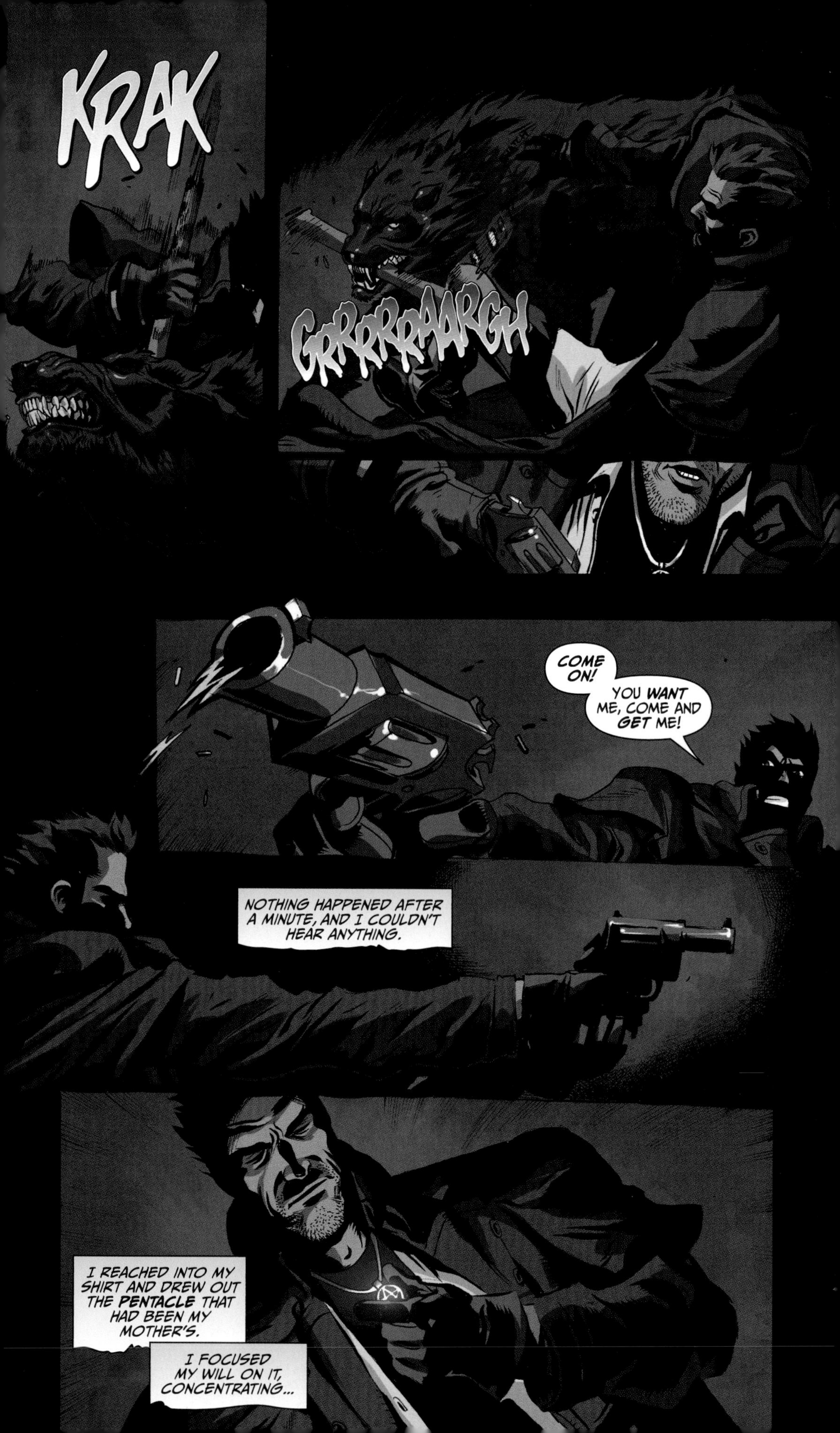
KRAK
GRRRRAARGH
COME ON!
YOU WANT ME, COME AND GET ME!
NOTHING HAPPENED AFTER A MINUTE, AND I COULDN'T HEAR ANYTHING.
I REACHED INTO MY SHIRT AND DREW OUT THE PENTACLE THAT HAD BEEN MY MOTHER'S.
I FOCUSED MY WILL ON IT, CONCENTRATING...

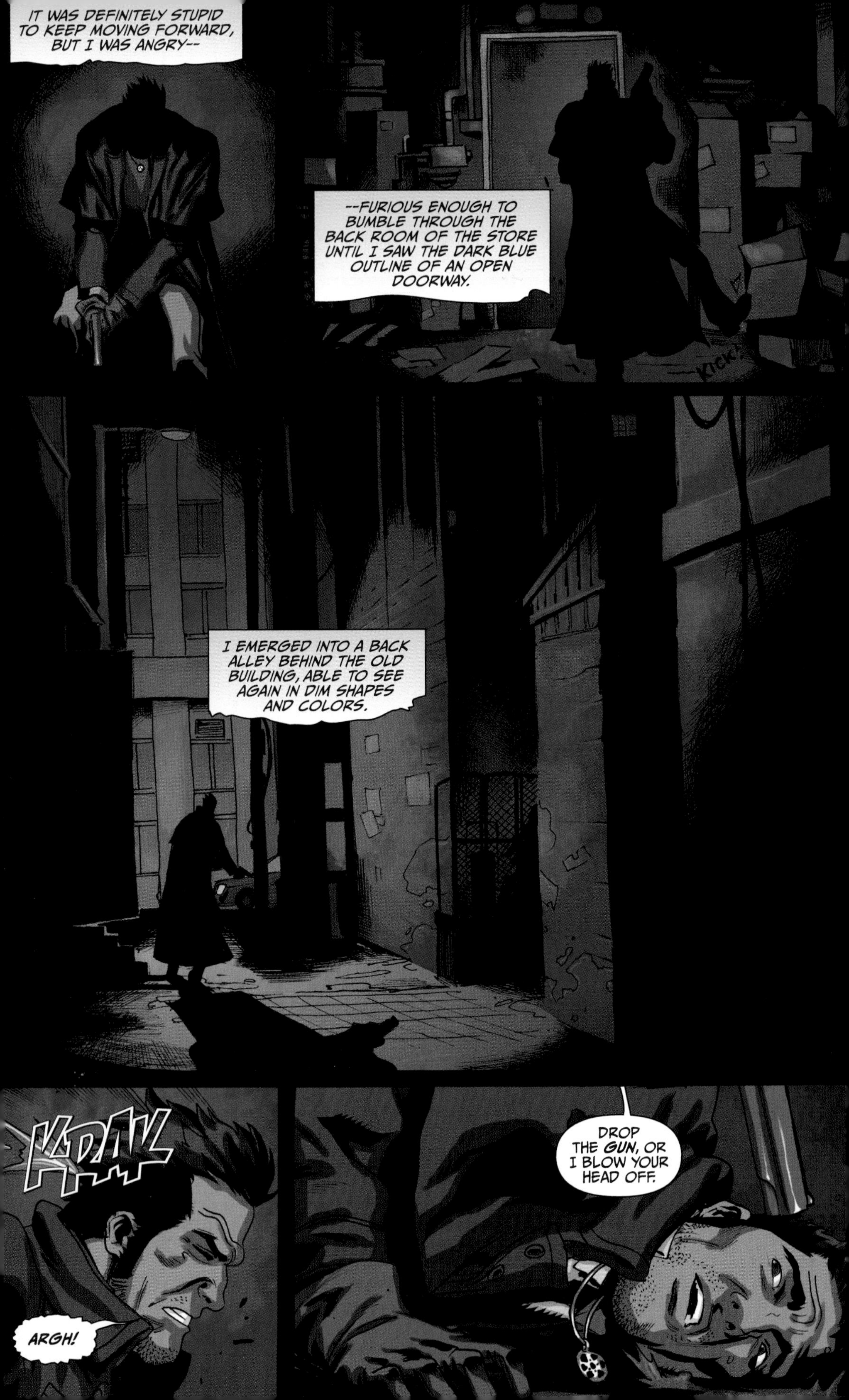
IT WAS DEFINITELY STUPID TO KEEP MOVING FORWARD, BUT I WAS ANGRY--
--FURIOUS ENOUGH TO BUMBLE THROUGH THE BACK ROOM OF THE STORE UNTIL I SAW THE DARK BLUE OUTLINE OF AN OPEN DOORWAY.
KICK!
I EMERGED INTO A BACK ALLEY BEHIND THE OLD BUILDING, ABLE TO SEE AGAIN IN DIM SHAPES AND COLORS.
KRAK
ARGH!
DROP THE GUN, OR I BLOW YOUR HEAD OFF.

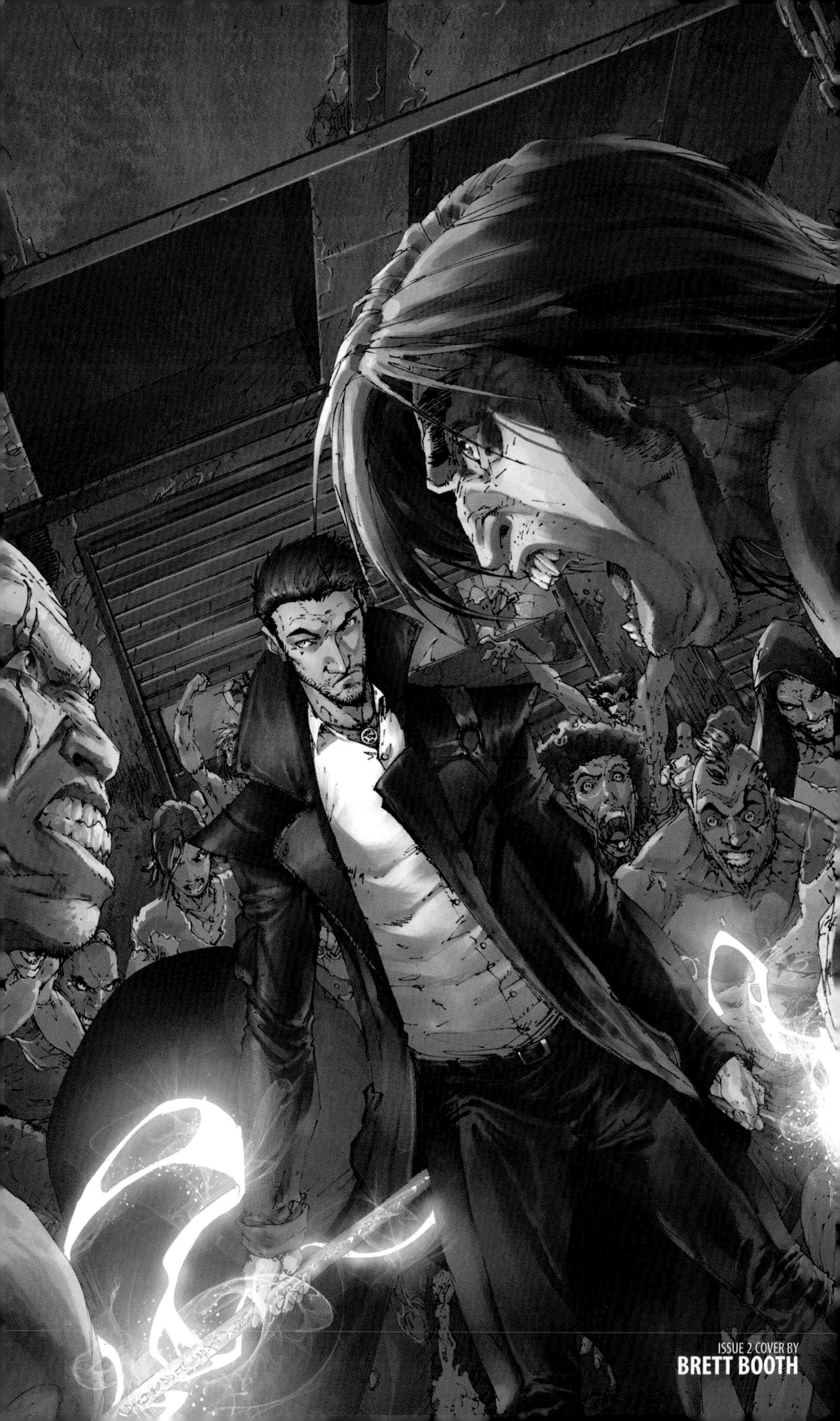

ISSUE 2 COVER BY
BRETT BOOTH

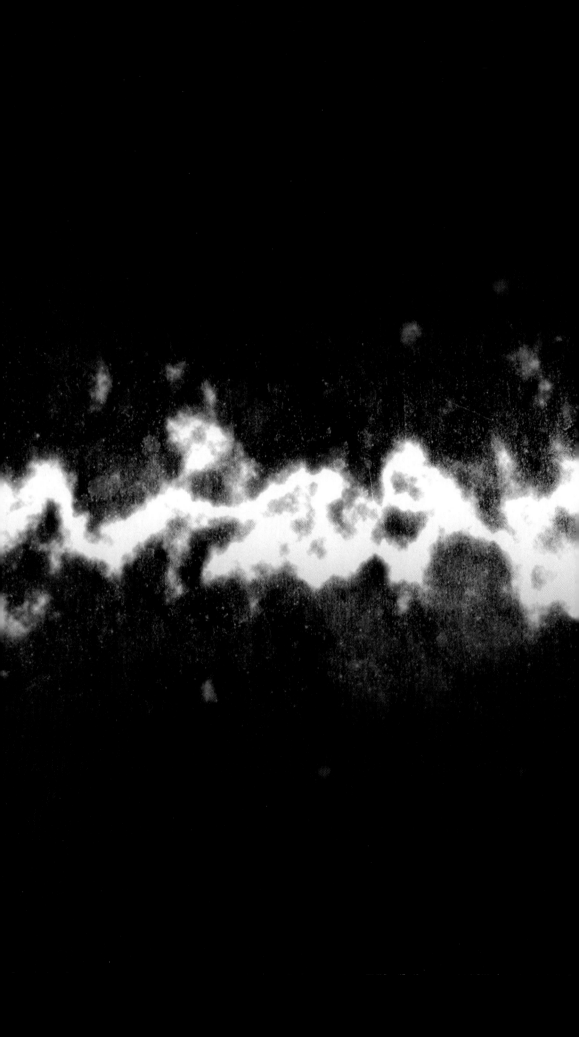

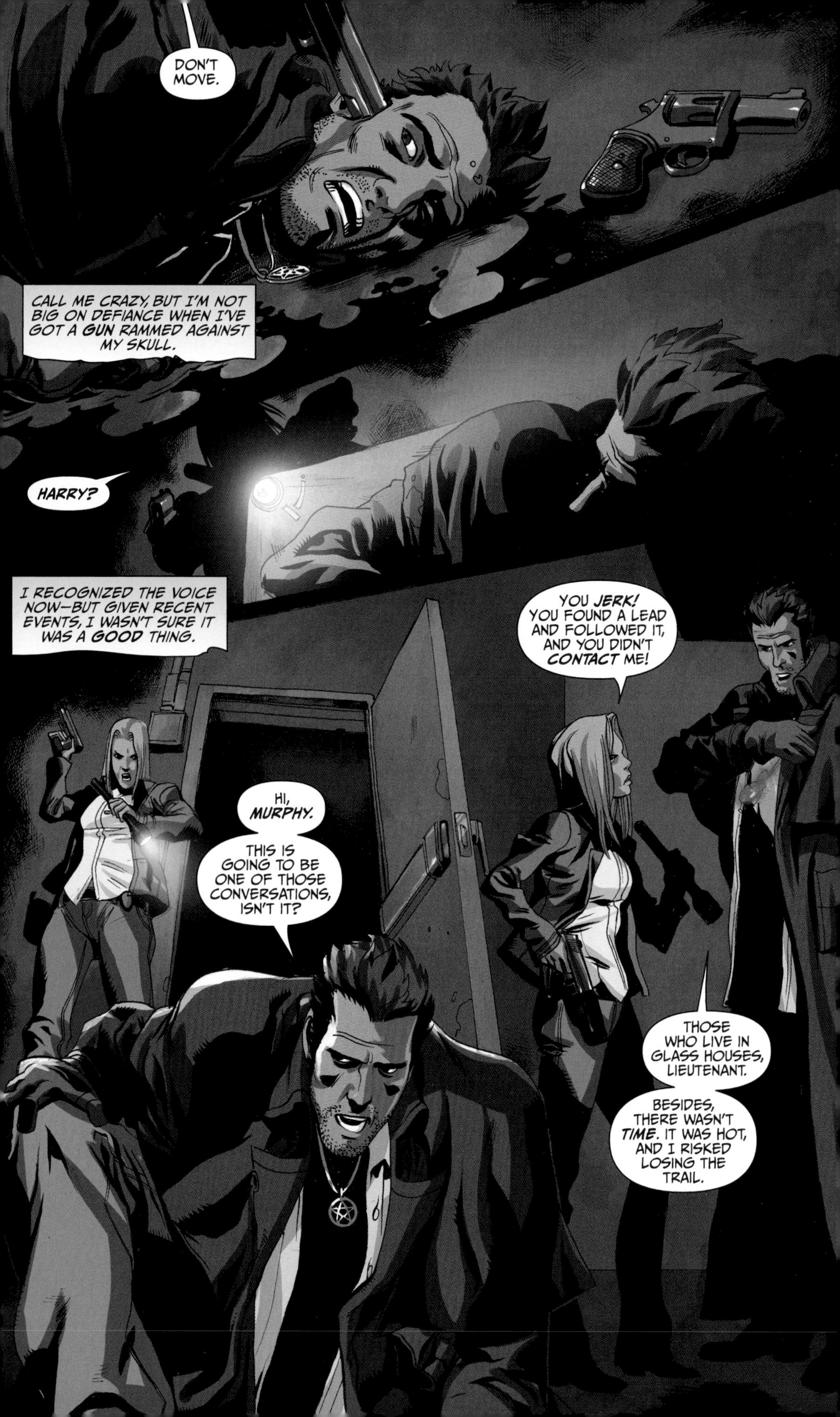
DON'T MOVE.
CALL ME CRAZY, BUT I'M NOT BIG ON DEFIANCE WHEN I'VE GOT A **GUN** RAMMED AGAINST MY SKULL.
HARRY?
I RECOGNIZED THE VOICE NOW—BUT GIVEN RECENT EVENTS, I WASN'T SURE IT WAS A **GOOD** THING.
HI, **MURPHY.**
THIS IS GOING TO BE ONE OF THOSE CONVERSATIONS, ISN'T IT?
YOU **JERK!** YOU FOUND A LEAD AND FOLLOWED IT, AND YOU DIDN'T **CONTACT** ME!
THOSE WHO LIVE IN GLASS HOUSES, LIEUTENANT.
BESIDES, THERE WASN'T **TIME**. IT WAS HOT, AND I RISKED LOSING THE TRAIL.

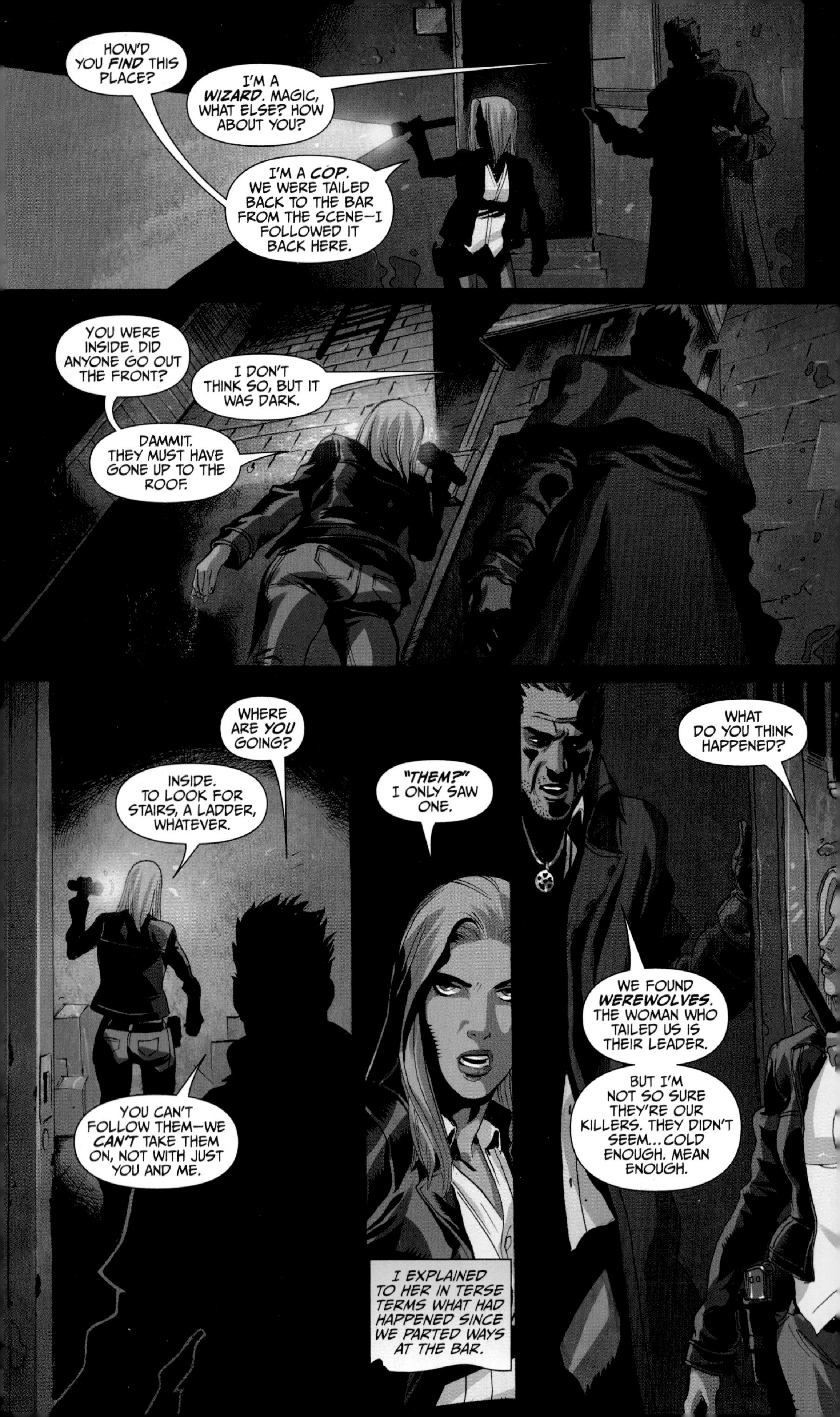
HOW'D YOU *FIND* THIS PLACE?
I'M A *WIZARD*. MAGIC, WHAT ELSE? HOW ABOUT YOU?
I'M A *COP*. WE WERE TAILED BACK TO THE BAR FROM THE SCENE—I FOLLOWED IT BACK HERE.
YOU WERE INSIDE. DID ANYONE GO OUT THE FRONT?
I DON'T THINK SO, BUT IT WAS DARK.
DAMMIT. THEY MUST HAVE GONE UP TO THE ROOF.
WHERE ARE *YOU* GOING?
INSIDE. TO LOOK FOR STAIRS, A LADDER, WHATEVER.
YOU CAN'T FOLLOW THEM—WE *CAN'T* TAKE THEM ON, NOT WITH JUST YOU AND ME.
"THEM?" I ONLY SAW ONE.
WHAT DO YOU THINK HAPPENED?
WE FOUND *WEREWOLVES*. THE WOMAN WHO TAILED US IS THEIR LEADER.
BUT I'M NOT SO SURE THEY'RE OUR KILLERS. THEY DIDN'T SEEM...COLD ENOUGH. MEAN ENOUGH.
I EXPLAINED TO HER IN TERSE TERMS WHAT HAD HAPPENED SINCE WE PARTED WAYS AT THE BAR.

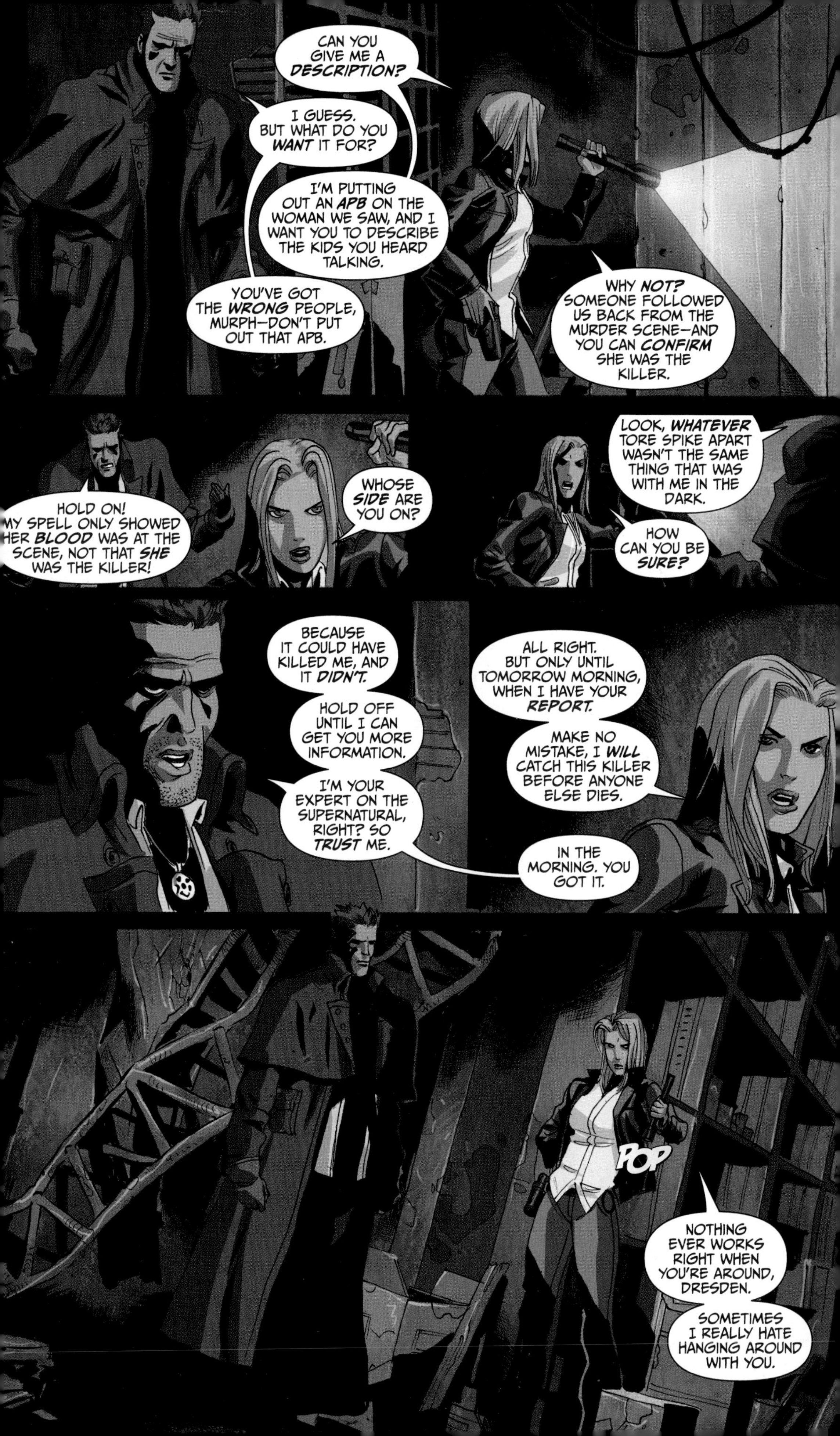

CAN YOU GIVE ME A DESCRIPTION?
I GUESS. BUT WHAT DO YOU WANT IT FOR?
I'M PUTTING OUT AN APB ON THE WOMAN WE SAW, AND I WANT YOU TO DESCRIBE THE KIDS YOU HEARD TALKING.
YOU'VE GOT THE WRONG PEOPLE, MURPH—DON'T PUT OUT THAT APB.
WHY NOT? SOMEONE FOLLOWED US BACK FROM THE MURDER SCENE—AND YOU CAN CONFIRM SHE WAS THE KILLER.
HOLD ON! MY SPELL ONLY SHOWED HER BLOOD WAS AT THE SCENE, NOT THAT SHE WAS THE KILLER!
WHOSE SIDE ARE YOU ON?
LOOK, WHATEVER TORE SPIKE APART WASN'T THE SAME THING THAT WAS WITH ME IN THE DARK.
HOW CAN YOU BE SURE?
BECAUSE IT COULD HAVE KILLED ME, AND IT DIDN'T.
HOLD OFF UNTIL I CAN GET YOU MORE INFORMATION.
I'M YOUR EXPERT ON THE SUPERNATURAL, RIGHT? SO TRUST ME.
ALL RIGHT. BUT ONLY UNTIL TOMORROW MORNING, WHEN I HAVE YOUR REPORT.
MAKE NO MISTAKE, I WILL CATCH THIS KILLER BEFORE ANYONE ELSE DIES.
IN THE MORNING. YOU GOT IT.
POP
NOTHING EVER WORKS RIGHT WHEN YOU'RE AROUND, DRESDEN.
SOMETIMES I REALLY HATE HANGING AROUND WITH YOU.

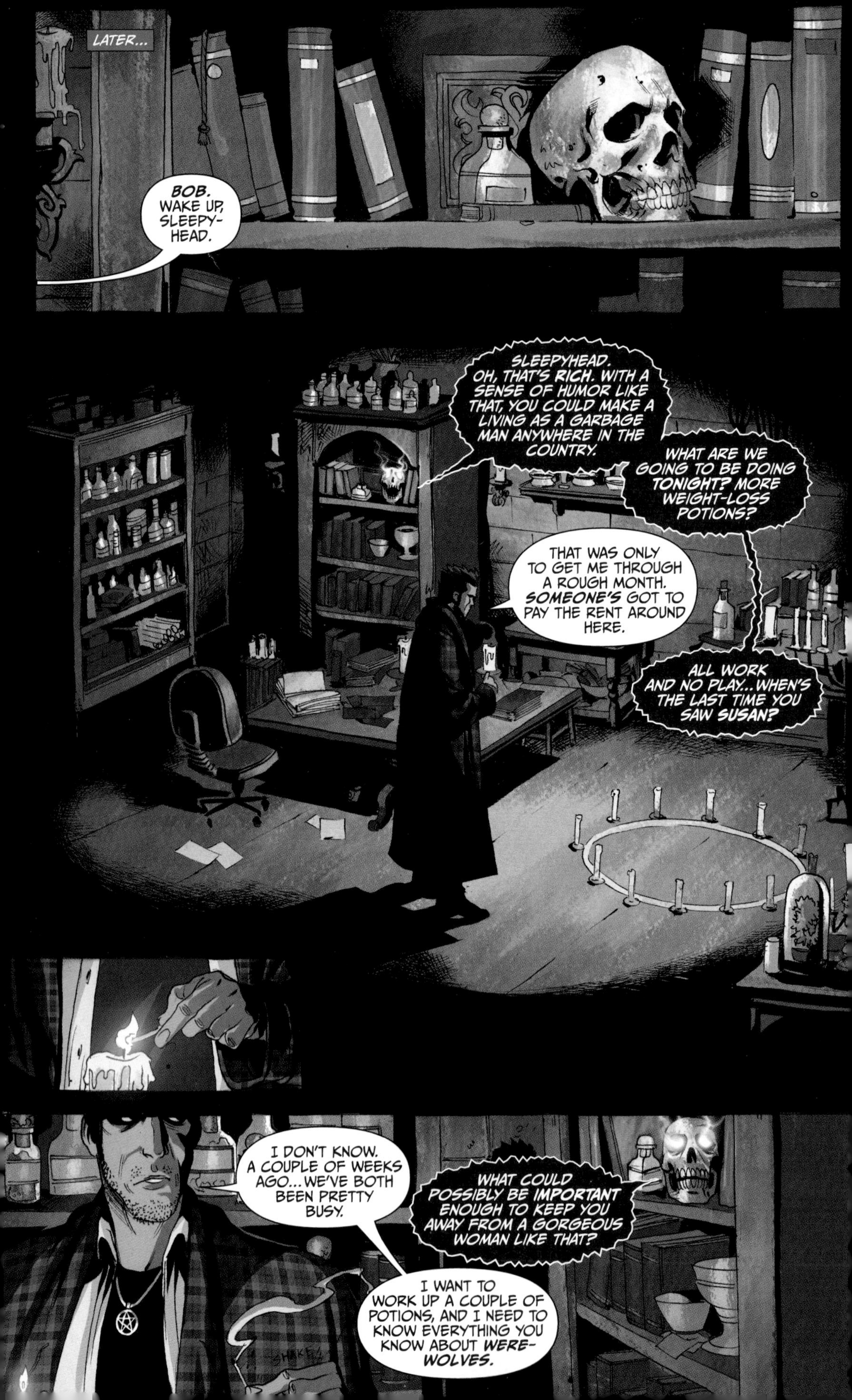
LATER...
BOB. WAKE UP, SLEEPY-HEAD.
SLEEPYHEAD. OH, THAT'S RICH. WITH A SENSE OF HUMOR LIKE THAT, YOU COULD MAKE A LIVING AS A GARBAGE MAN ANYWHERE IN THE COUNTRY.
WHAT ARE WE GOING TO BE DOING TONIGHT? MORE WEIGHT-LOSS POTIONS?
THAT WAS ONLY TO GET ME THROUGH A ROUGH MONTH. SOMEONE'S GOT TO PAY THE RENT AROUND HERE.
ALL WORK AND NO PLAY...WHEN'S THE LAST TIME YOU SAW SUSAN?
I DON'T KNOW. A COUPLE OF WEEKS AGO...WE'VE BOTH BEEN PRETTY BUSY.
WHAT COULD POSSIBLY BE IMPORTANT ENOUGH TO KEEP YOU AWAY FROM A GORGEOUS WOMAN LIKE THAT?
I WANT TO WORK UP A COUPLE OF POTIONS, AND I NEED TO KNOW EVERYTHING YOU KNOW ABOUT WERE-WOLVES.

WHAT KIND OF POTIONS, AND WHAT KIND OF WEREWOLVES?

THERE'S MORE THAN ONE?

HELL, WE'VE MADE AT LEAST THREE DOZEN KINDS OF POTIONS—

NO, NO, NO! THERE'S MORE THAN ONE KIND OF WEREWOLF?

OF COURSE. HOW MUCH DO YOU KNOW?

EXACTLY NOTHING. MY TEACHER NEVER COVERED THAT WITH ME.

OLD JUSTIN HAD A LOUSY SENSE ABOUT PRETTY MUCH EVERYTHING.

HE GOT WHAT WAS COMING TO HIM.

A SUDDEN RUSH OF MIXED FEELINGS WASHED THROUGH ME.

I COULD STILL SEE HIM, MY TEACHER, DYING IN FLAMES BORN OF MY WILL AND ANGER.

WERE-WOLVES, BOB.

RIGHT, OKAY. AND, UH, WHICH POTIONS DID YOU WANT?

A PICK-ME-UP POTION. AND, SOMETHING THAT WILL MAKE ME IMPERCEPTIBLE TO WEREWOLVES.

OKAY ON THE FIRST ONE, BUT THE SECOND ONE CAN'T REALLY BE DONE.

BEST WE CAN DO IS A BLENDING BREW, SOMETHING TO MAKE YOU LOOK LIKE A PART OF THE BACKGROUND.

I'LL TAKE WHAT I CAN GET. NOW TELL ME WHAT YOU KNOW ABOUT WERE-WOLVES...

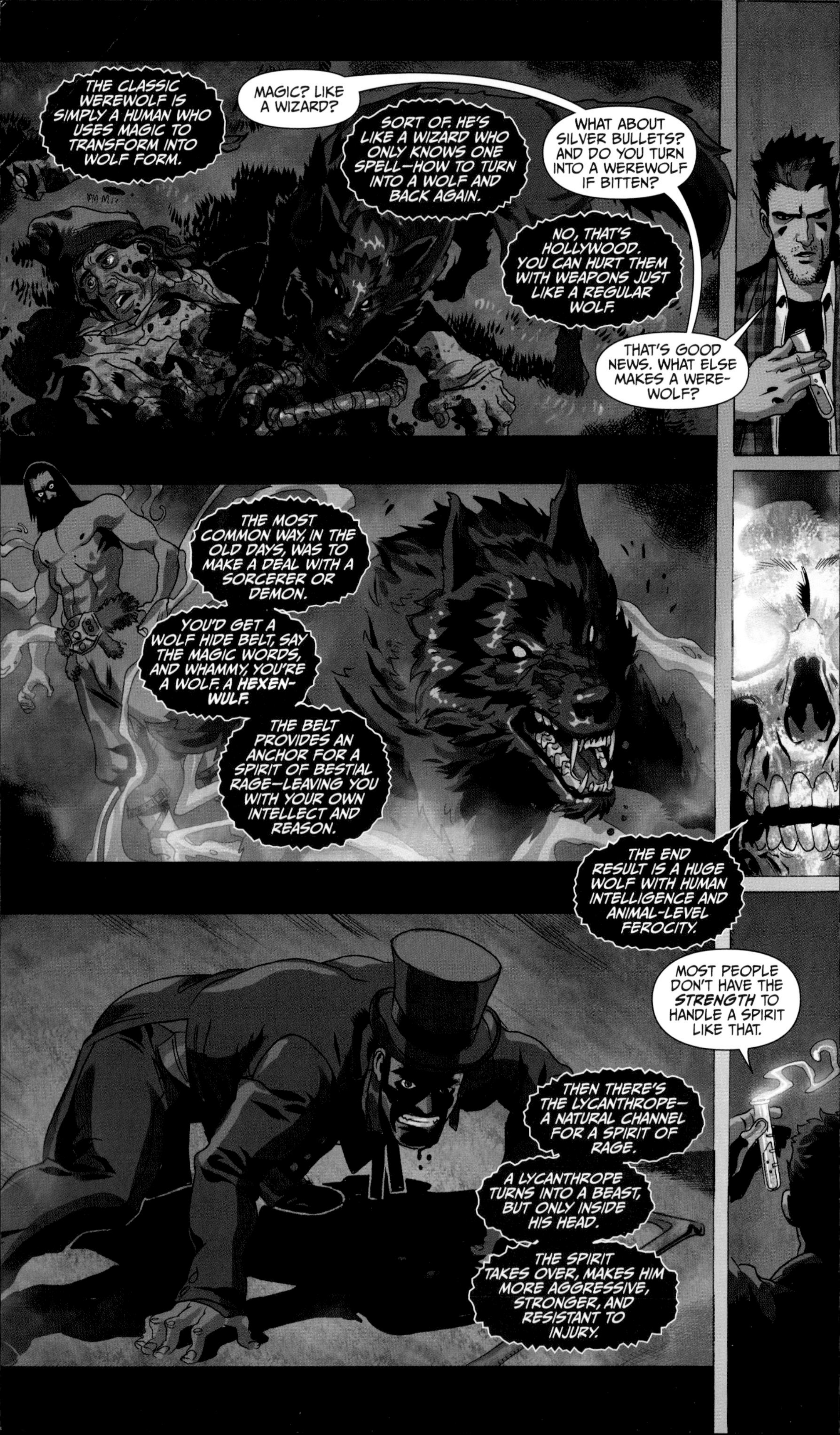
THE CLASSIC WEREWOLF IS SIMPLY A HUMAN WHO USES MAGIC TO TRANSFORM INTO WOLF FORM.
MAGIC? LIKE A WIZARD?
SORT OF. HE'S LIKE A WIZARD WHO ONLY KNOWS ONE SPELL—HOW TO TURN INTO A WOLF AND BACK AGAIN.
WHAT ABOUT SILVER BULLETS? AND DO YOU TURN INTO A WEREWOLF IF BITTEN?
NO, THAT'S HOLLYWOOD. YOU CAN HURT THEM WITH WEAPONS JUST LIKE A REGULAR WOLF.
THAT'S GOOD NEWS. WHAT ELSE MAKES A WERE-WOLF?
THE MOST COMMON WAY, IN THE OLD DAYS, WAS TO MAKE A DEAL WITH A SORCERER OR DEMON.
YOU'D GET A WOLF HIDE BELT, SAY THE MAGIC WORDS, AND WHAMMY, YOU'RE A WOLF. A **HEXEN-WULF.**
THE BELT PROVIDES AN ANCHOR FOR A SPIRIT OF BESTIAL RAGE—LEAVING YOU WITH YOUR OWN INTELLECT AND REASON.
THE END RESULT IS A HUGE WOLF WITH HUMAN INTELLIGENCE AND ANIMAL-LEVEL FEROCITY.
MOST PEOPLE DON'T HAVE THE ***STRENGTH*** TO HANDLE A SPIRIT LIKE THAT.
THEN THERE'S THE LYCANTHROPE—A NATURAL CHANNEL FOR A SPIRIT OF RAGE.
A LYCANTHROPE TURNS INTO A BEAST, BUT ONLY INSIDE HIS HEAD.
THE SPIRIT TAKES OVER, MAKES HIM MORE AGGRESSIVE, STRONGER, AND RESISTANT TO INJURY.

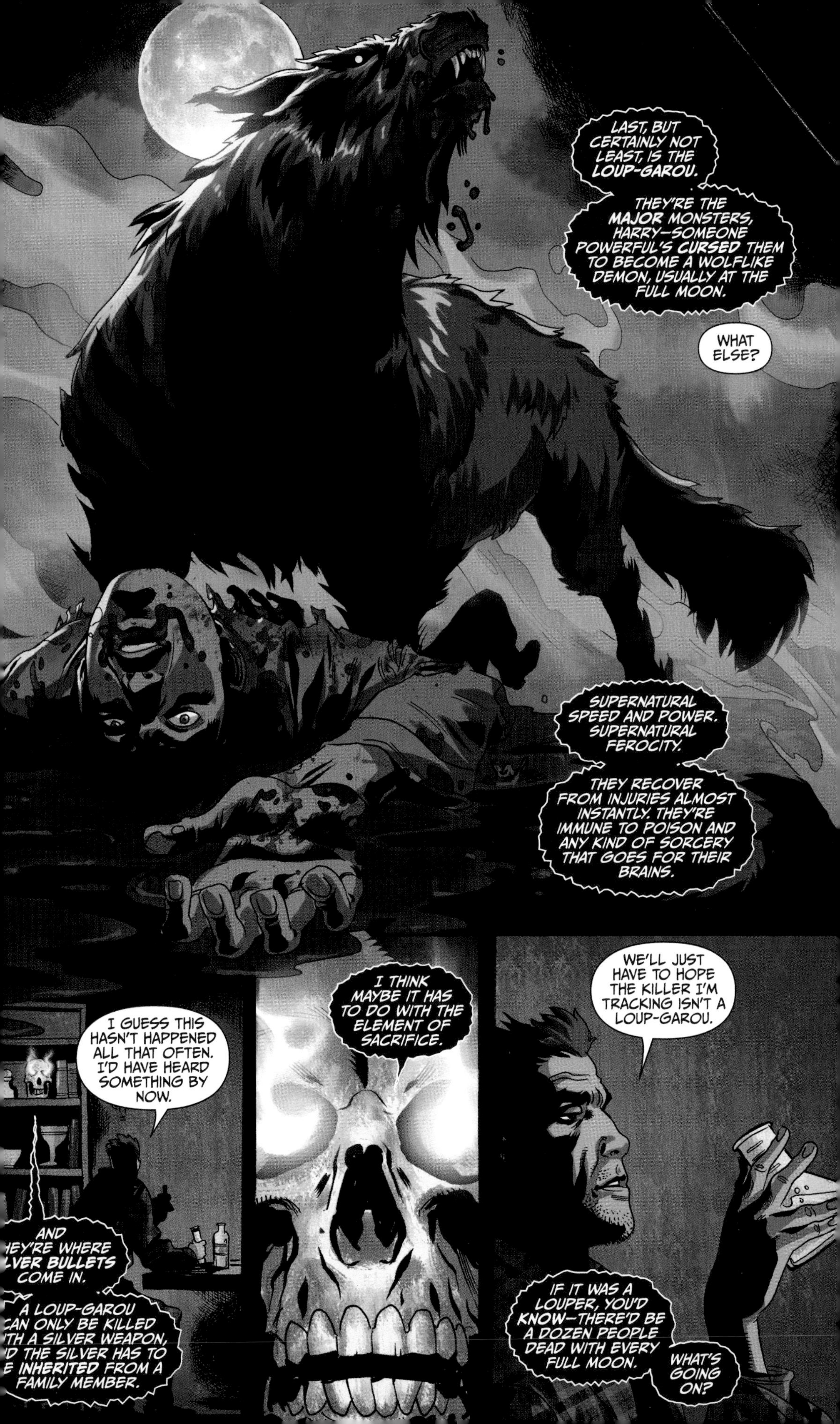
LAST, BUT CERTAINLY NOT LEAST, IS THE LOUP-GAROU.
THEY'RE THE MAJOR MONSTERS, HARRY—SOMEONE POWERFUL'S CURSED THEM TO BECOME A WOLFLIKE DEMON, USUALLY AT THE FULL MOON.
WHAT ELSE?
SUPERNATURAL SPEED AND POWER. SUPERNATURAL FEROCITY.
THEY RECOVER FROM INJURIES ALMOST INSTANTLY. THEY'RE IMMUNE TO POISON AND ANY KIND OF SORCERY THAT GOES FOR THEIR BRAINS.
I GUESS THIS HASN'T HAPPENED ALL THAT OFTEN. I'D HAVE HEARD SOMETHING BY NOW.
AND HEY'RE WHERE LVER BULLETS COME IN.
A LOUP-GAROU CAN ONLY BE KILLED TH A SILVER WEAPON, D THE SILVER HAS TO E INHERITED FROM A FAMILY MEMBER.
I THINK MAYBE IT HAS TO DO WITH THE ELEMENT OF SACRIFICE.
WE'LL JUST HAVE TO HOPE THE KILLER I'M TRACKING ISN'T A LOUP-GAROU.
IF IT WAS A LOUPER, YOU'D KNOW—THERE'D BE A DOZEN PEOPLE DEAD WITH EVERY FULL MOON.
WHAT'S GOING ON?

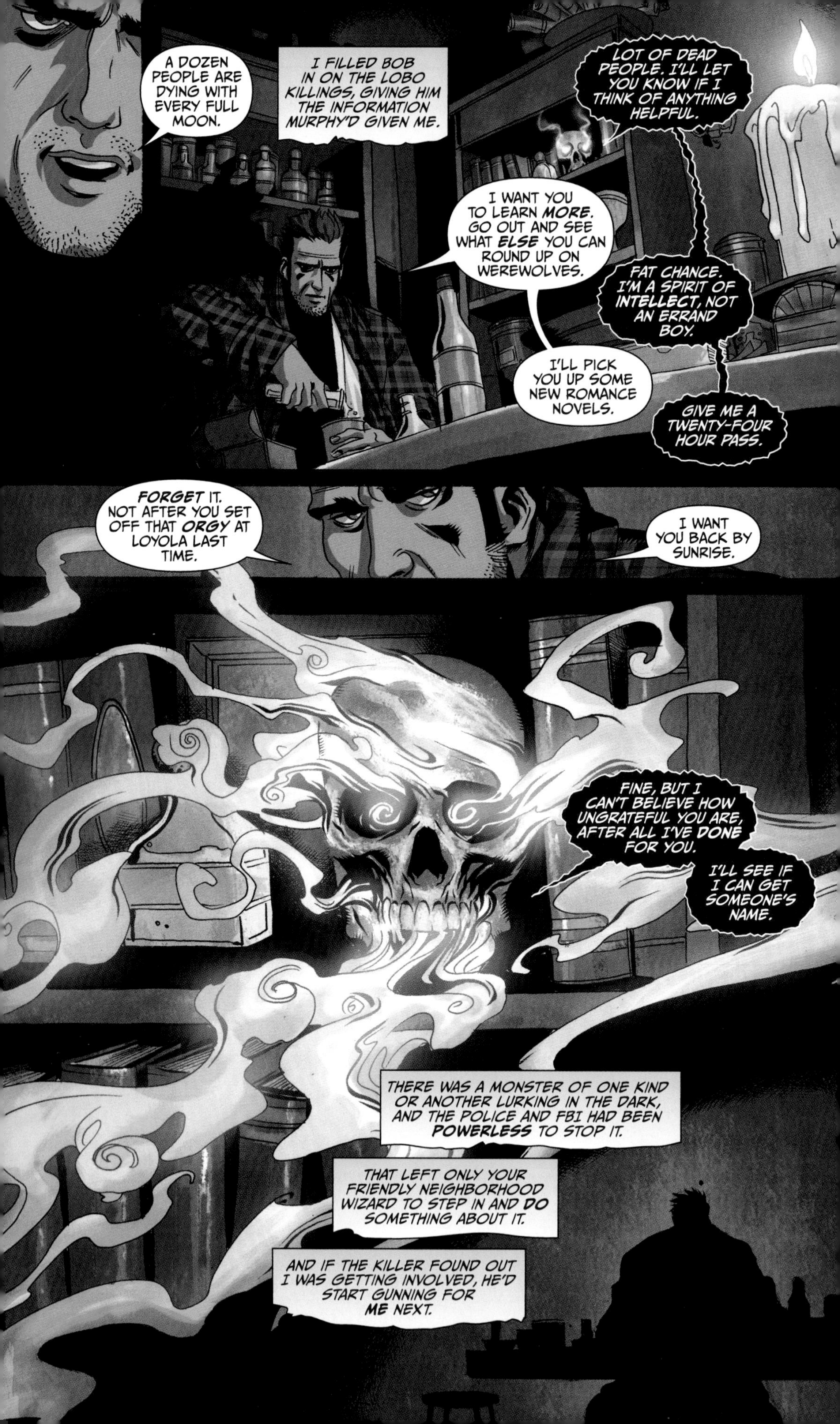
A DOZEN PEOPLE ARE DYING WITH EVERY FULL MOON.
I FILLED BOB IN ON THE LOBO KILLINGS, GIVING HIM THE INFORMATION MURPHY'D GIVEN ME.
LOT OF DEAD PEOPLE. I'LL LET YOU KNOW IF I THINK OF ANYTHING HELPFUL.
I WANT YOU TO LEARN MORE. GO OUT AND SEE WHAT ELSE YOU CAN ROUND UP ON WEREWOLVES.
FAT CHANCE. I'M A SPIRIT OF INTELLECT, NOT AN ERRAND BOY.
I'LL PICK YOU UP SOME NEW ROMANCE NOVELS.
GIVE ME A TWENTY-FOUR HOUR PASS.
FORGET IT. NOT AFTER YOU SET OFF THAT ORGY AT LOYOLA LAST TIME.
I WANT YOU BACK BY SUNRISE.
FINE, BUT I CAN'T BELIEVE HOW UNGRATEFUL YOU ARE, AFTER ALL I'VE DONE FOR YOU.
I'LL SEE IF I CAN GET SOMEONE'S NAME.
THERE WAS A MONSTER OF ONE KIND OR ANOTHER LURKING IN THE DARK, AND THE POLICE AND FBI HAD BEEN POWERLESS TO STOP IT.
THAT LEFT ONLY YOUR FRIENDLY NEIGHBORHOOD WIZARD TO STEP IN AND DO SOMETHING ABOUT IT.
AND IF THE KILLER FOUND OUT I WAS GETTING INVOLVED, HE'D START GUNNING FOR ME NEXT.

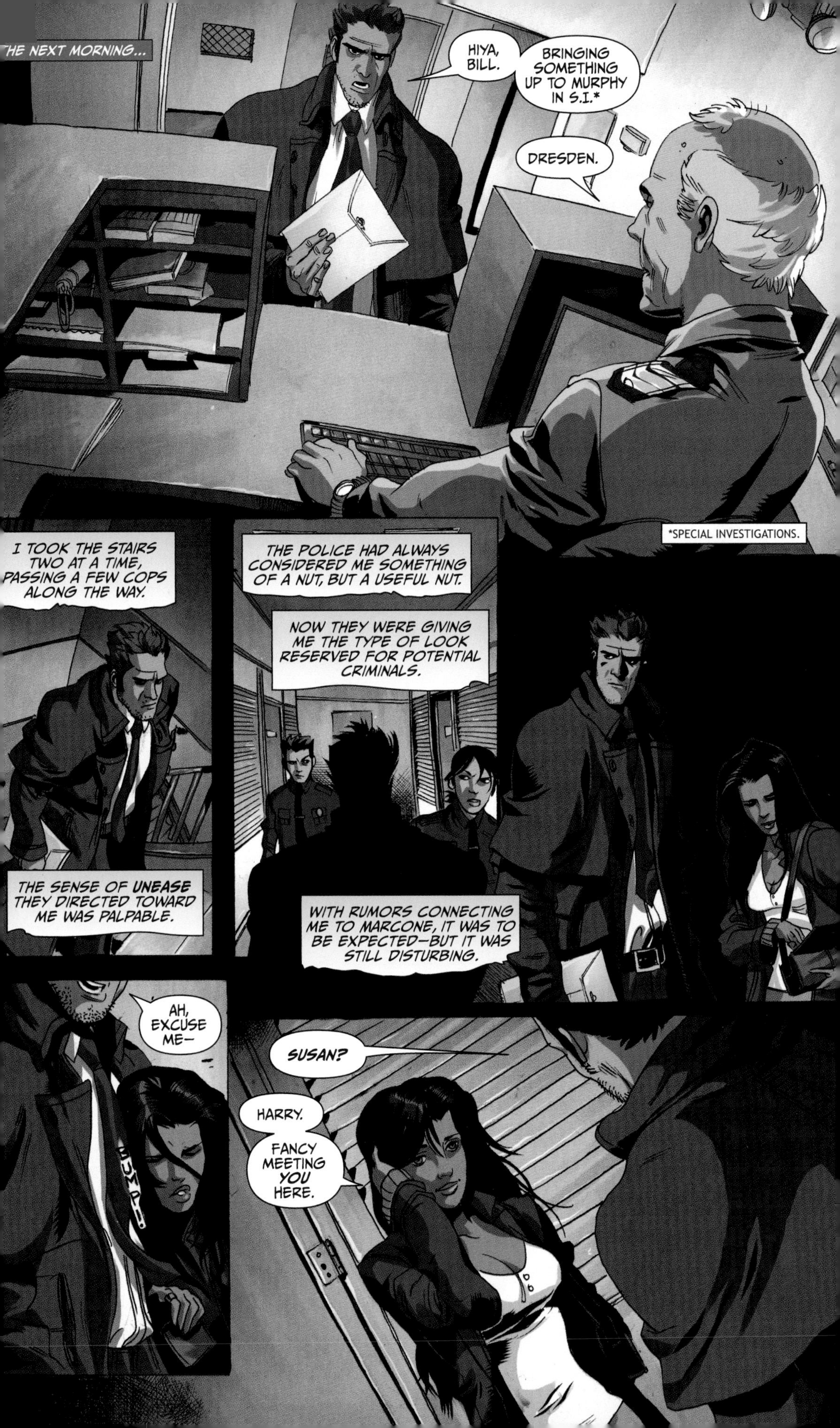
THE NEXT MORNING...
HIYA, BILL.
BRINGING SOMETHING UP TO MURPHY IN S.I.*
DRESDEN.
*SPECIAL INVESTIGATIONS.
I TOOK THE STAIRS TWO AT A TIME, PASSING A FEW COPS ALONG THE WAY.
THE SENSE OF UNEASE THEY DIRECTED TOWARD ME WAS PALPABLE.
THE POLICE HAD ALWAYS CONSIDERED ME SOMETHING OF A NUT, BUT A USEFUL NUT.
NOW THEY WERE GIVING ME THE TYPE OF LOOK RESERVED FOR POTENTIAL CRIMINALS.
WITH RUMORS CONNECTING ME TO MARCONE, IT WAS TO BE EXPECTED—BUT IT WAS STILL DISTURBING.
AH, EXCUSE ME—
BUMP!
SUSAN?
HARRY.
FANCY MEETING YOU HERE.

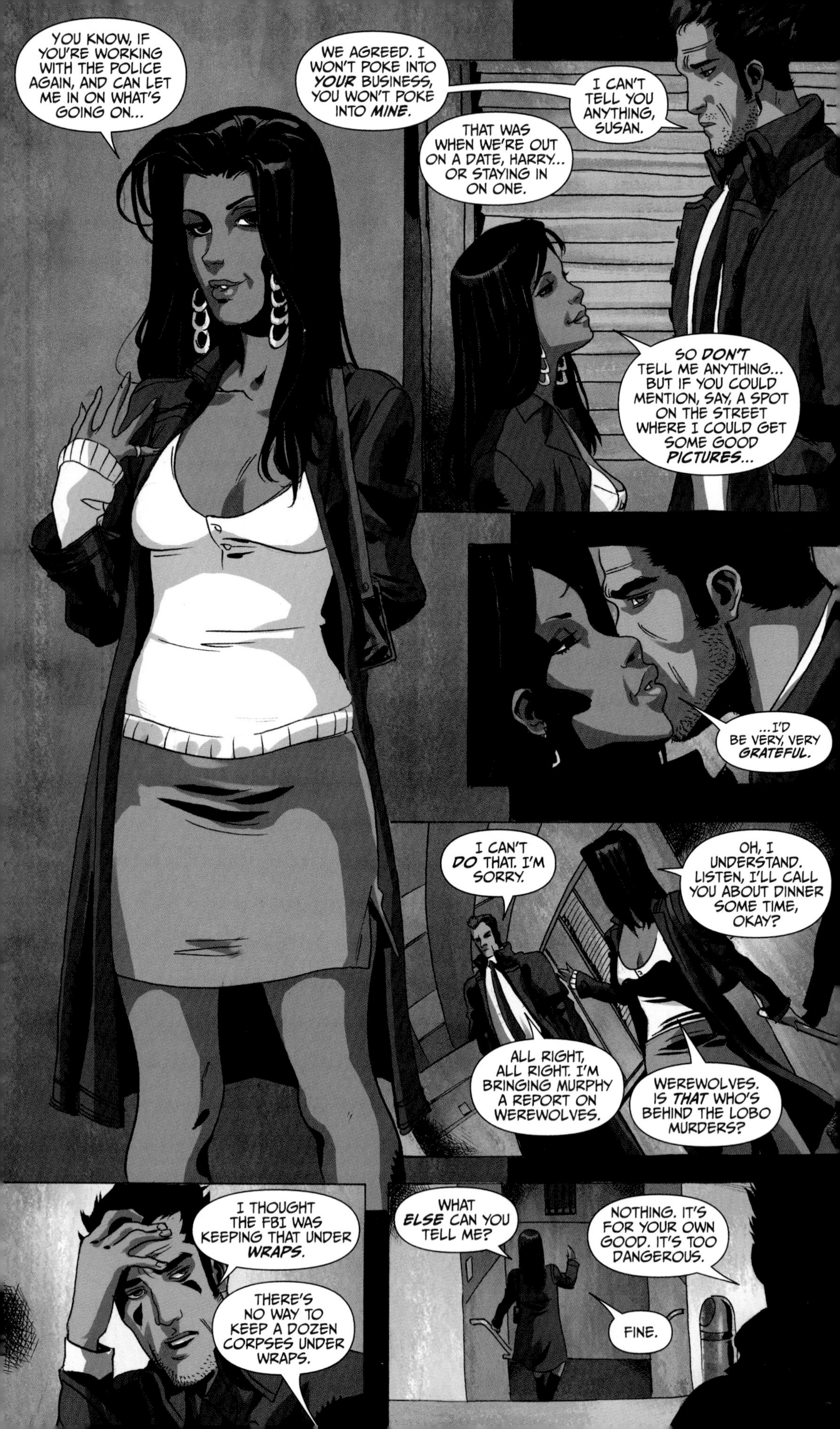
YOU KNOW, IF YOU'RE WORKING WITH THE POLICE AGAIN, AND CAN LET ME IN ON WHAT'S GOING ON...
I CAN'T TELL YOU ANYTHING, SUSAN.
WE AGREED. I WON'T POKE INTO *YOUR* BUSINESS, YOU WON'T POKE INTO *MINE*.
THAT WAS WHEN WE'RE OUT ON A DATE, HARRY... OR STAYING IN ON ONE.
SO *DON'T* TELL ME ANYTHING... BUT IF YOU COULD MENTION, SAY, A SPOT ON THE STREET WHERE I COULD GET SOME GOOD *PICTURES*...
...I'D BE VERY, VERY *GRATEFUL*.
I CAN'T *DO* THAT. I'M SORRY.
OH, I UNDERSTAND. LISTEN, I'LL CALL YOU ABOUT DINNER SOME TIME, OKAY?
ALL RIGHT, ALL RIGHT. I'M BRINGING MURPHY A REPORT ON WEREWOLVES.
WEREWOLVES. IS *THAT* WHO'S BEHIND THE LOBO MURDERS?
I THOUGHT THE FBI WAS KEEPING THAT UNDER *WRAPS*.
THERE'S NO WAY TO KEEP A DOZEN CORPSES UNDER WRAPS.
WHAT *ELSE* CAN YOU TELL ME?
NOTHING. IT'S FOR YOUR OWN GOOD. IT'S TOO DANGEROUS.
FINE.

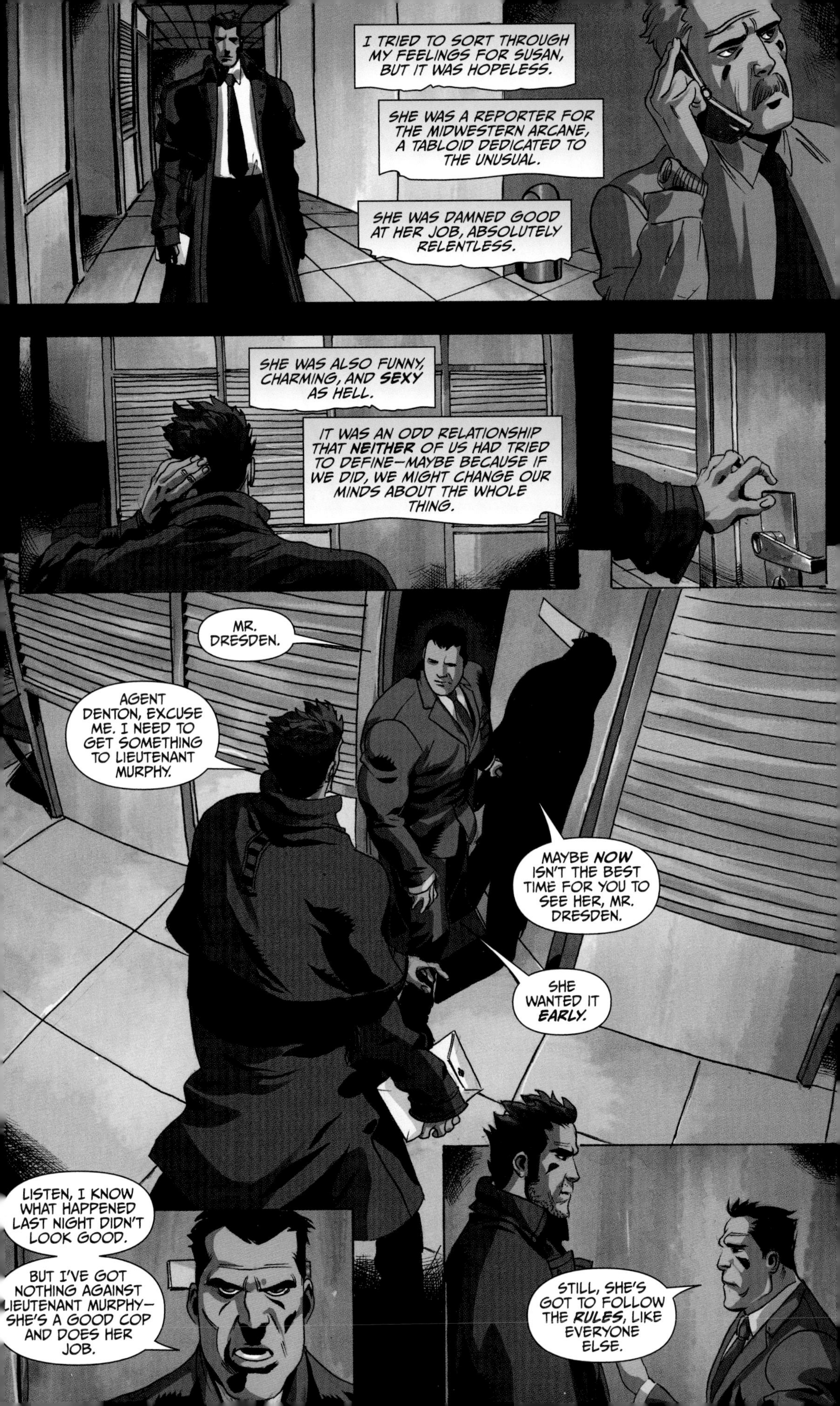

I TRIED TO SORT THROUGH MY FEELINGS FOR SUSAN, BUT IT WAS HOPELESS.
SHE WAS A REPORTER FOR THE MIDWESTERN ARCANE, A TABLOID DEDICATED TO THE UNUSUAL.
SHE WAS DAMNED GOOD AT HER JOB, ABSOLUTELY RELENTLESS.
SHE WAS ALSO FUNNY, CHARMING, AND SEXY AS HELL.
IT WAS AN ODD RELATIONSHIP THAT NEITHER OF US HAD TRIED TO DEFINE—MAYBE BECAUSE IF WE DID, WE MIGHT CHANGE OUR MINDS ABOUT THE WHOLE THING.
MR. DRESDEN.
AGENT DENTON, EXCUSE ME. I NEED TO GET SOMETHING TO LIEUTENANT MURPHY.
MAYBE NOW ISN'T THE BEST TIME FOR YOU TO SEE HER, MR. DRESDEN.
SHE WANTED IT EARLY.
LISTEN, I KNOW WHAT HAPPENED LAST NIGHT DIDN'T LOOK GOOD.
BUT I'VE GOT NOTHING AGAINST LIEUTENANT MURPHY—SHE'S A GOOD COP AND DOES HER JOB.
STILL, SHE'S GOT TO FOLLOW THE RULES, LIKE EVERYONE ELSE.

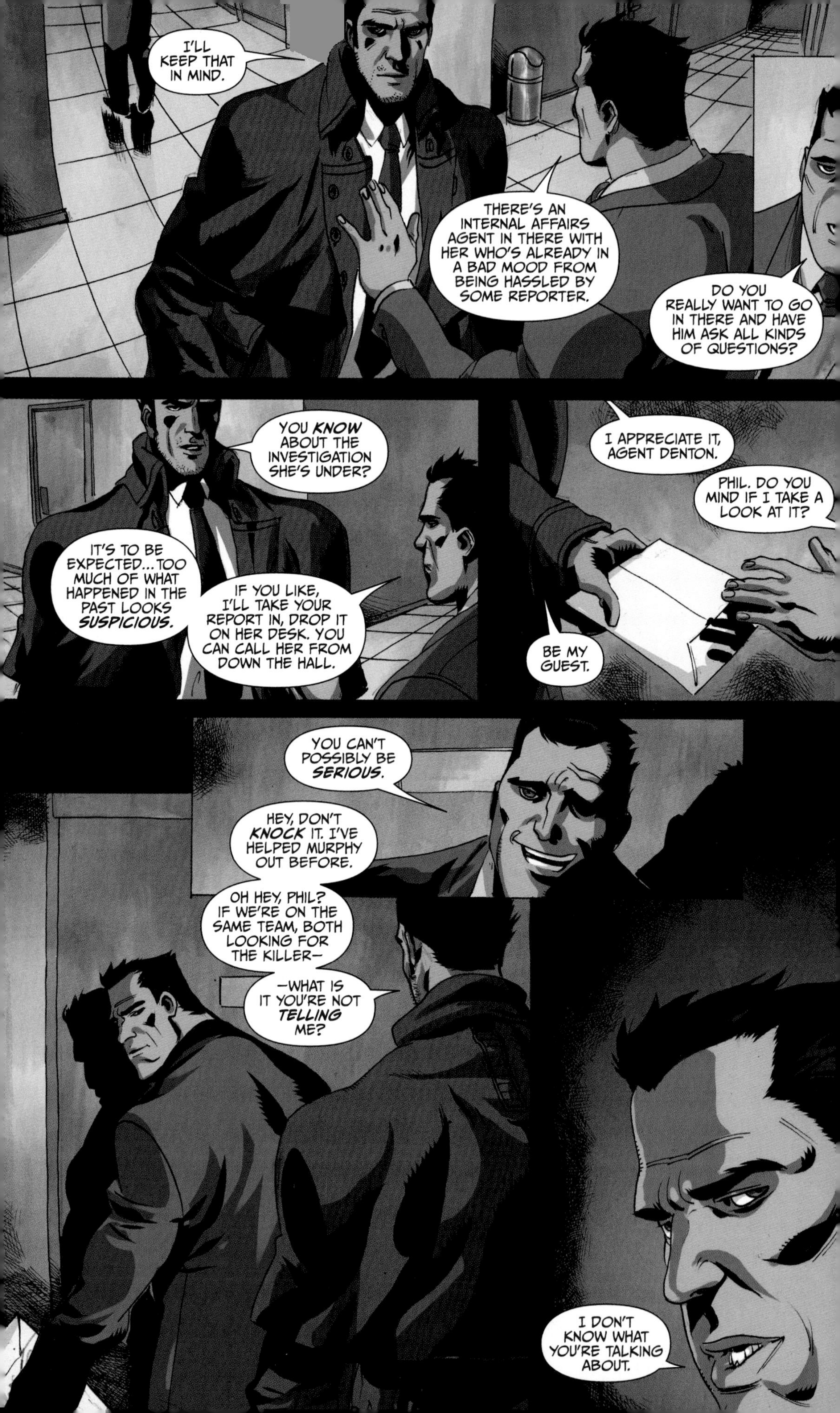
I'LL KEEP THAT IN MIND.
THERE'S AN INTERNAL AFFAIRS AGENT IN THERE WITH HER WHO'S ALREADY IN A BAD MOOD FROM BEING HASSLED BY SOME REPORTER.
DO YOU REALLY WANT TO GO IN THERE AND HAVE HIM ASK ALL KINDS OF QUESTIONS?
YOU **KNOW** ABOUT THE INVESTIGATION SHE'S UNDER?
IT'S TO BE EXPECTED...TOO MUCH OF WHAT HAPPENED IN THE PAST LOOKS **SUSPICIOUS.**
IF YOU LIKE, I'LL TAKE YOUR REPORT IN, DROP IT ON HER DESK. YOU CAN CALL HER FROM DOWN THE HALL.
I APPRECIATE IT, AGENT DENTON.
PHIL. DO YOU MIND IF I TAKE A LOOK AT IT?
BE MY GUEST.
YOU CAN'T POSSIBLY BE **SERIOUS**.
HEY, DON'T **KNOCK** IT. I'VE HELPED MURPHY OUT BEFORE.
OH HEY, PHIL? IF WE'RE ON THE SAME TEAM, BOTH LOOKING FOR THE KILLER—
—WHAT IS IT YOU'RE NOT **TELLING** ME?
I DON'T KNOW WHAT YOU'RE TALKING ABOUT.

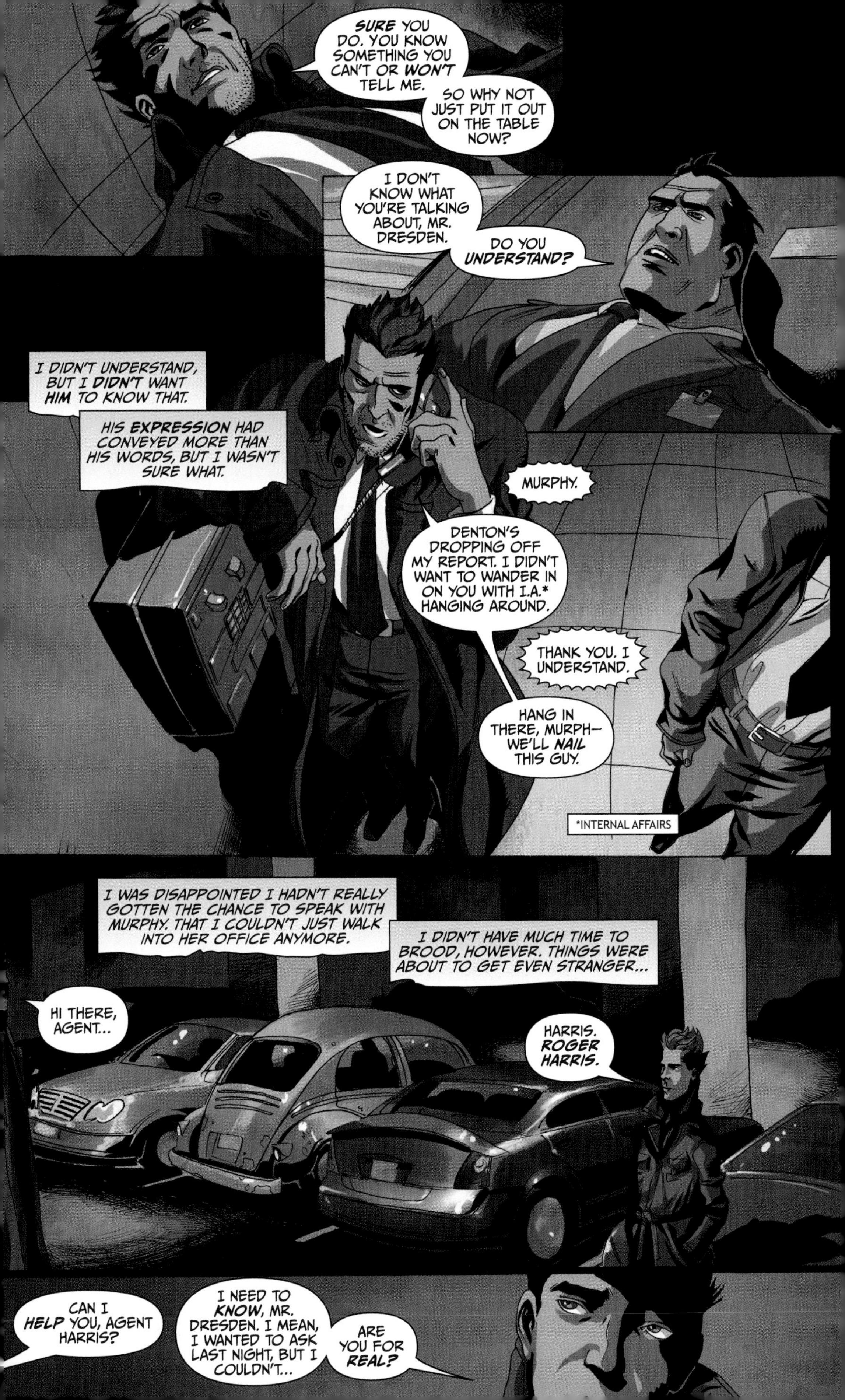
SURE YOU DO. YOU KNOW SOMETHING YOU CAN'T OR WON'T TELL ME.
SO WHY NOT JUST PUT IT OUT ON THE TABLE NOW?
I DON'T KNOW WHAT YOU'RE TALKING ABOUT, MR. DRESDEN.
DO YOU UNDERSTAND?
I DIDN'T UNDERSTAND, BUT I DIDN'T WANT HIM TO KNOW THAT.
HIS EXPRESSION HAD CONVEYED MORE THAN HIS WORDS, BUT I WASN'T SURE WHAT.
MURPHY.
DENTON'S DROPPING OFF MY REPORT. I DIDN'T WANT TO WANDER IN ON YOU WITH I.A.* HANGING AROUND.
THANK YOU. I UNDERSTAND.
HANG IN THERE, MURPH— WE'LL NAIL THIS GUY.
*INTERNAL AFFAIRS
I WAS DISAPPOINTED I HADN'T REALLY GOTTEN THE CHANCE TO SPEAK WITH MURPHY. THAT I COULDN'T JUST WALK INTO HER OFFICE ANYMORE.
I DIDN'T HAVE MUCH TIME TO BROOD, HOWEVER. THINGS WERE ABOUT TO GET EVEN STRANGER...
HI THERE, AGENT...
HARRIS. ROGER HARRIS.
CAN I HELP YOU, AGENT HARRIS?
I NEED TO KNOW, MR. DRESDEN. I MEAN, I WANTED TO ASK LAST NIGHT, BUT I COULDN'T...
ARE YOU FOR REAL?

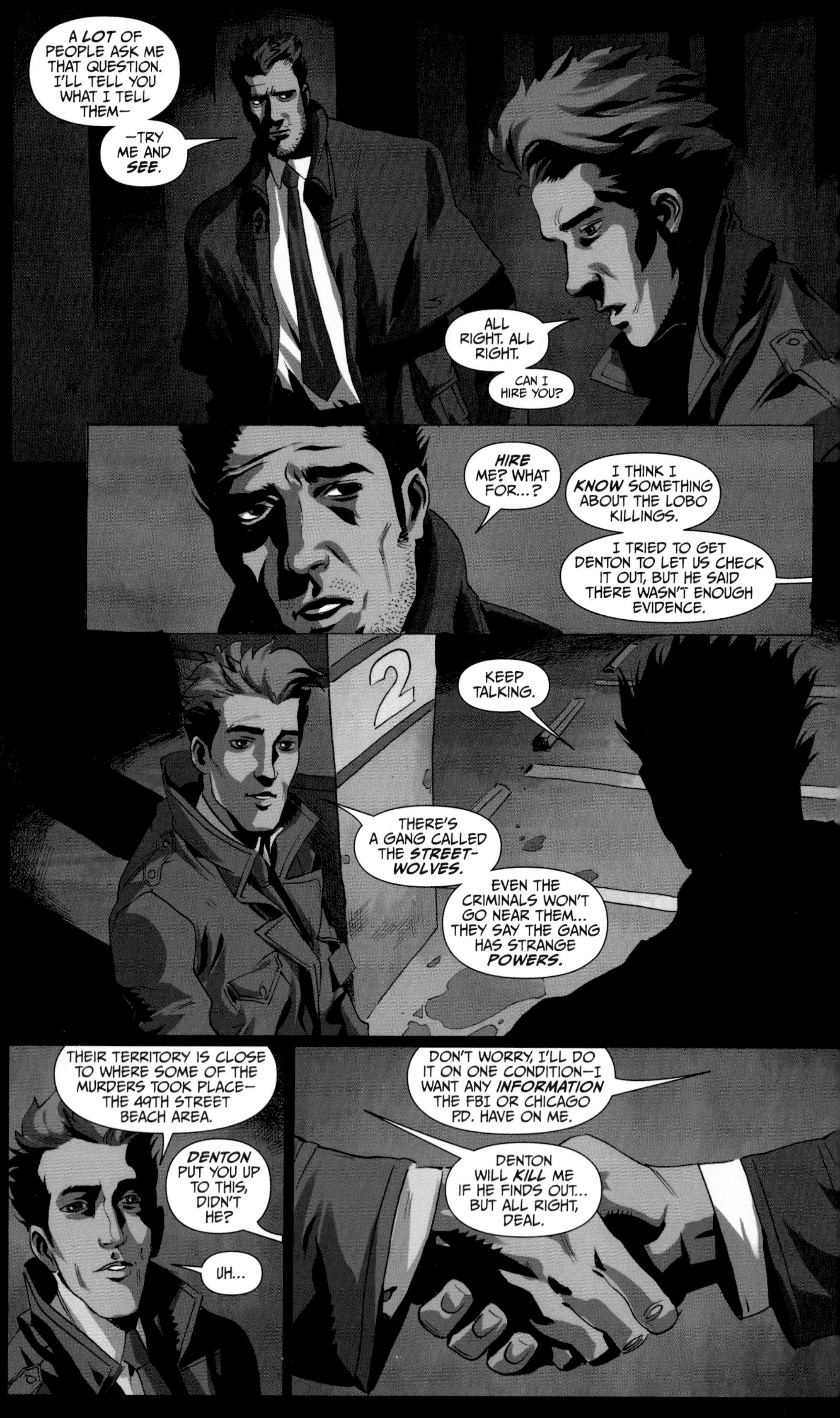
A LOT OF PEOPLE ASK ME THAT QUESTION. I'LL TELL YOU WHAT I TELL THEM—
—TRY ME AND SEE.
ALL RIGHT. ALL RIGHT.
CAN I HIRE YOU?
HIRE ME? WHAT FOR...?
I THINK I KNOW SOMETHING ABOUT THE LOBO KILLINGS.
I TRIED TO GET DENTON TO LET US CHECK IT OUT, BUT HE SAID THERE WASN'T ENOUGH EVIDENCE.
2
KEEP TALKING.
THERE'S A GANG CALLED THE STREET-WOLVES.
EVEN THE CRIMINALS WON'T GO NEAR THEM... THEY SAY THE GANG HAS STRANGE POWERS.
THEIR TERRITORY IS CLOSE TO WHERE SOME OF THE MURDERS TOOK PLACE— THE 49TH STREET BEACH AREA.
DENTON PUT YOU UP TO THIS, DIDN'T HE?
UH...
DON'T WORRY, I'LL DO IT ON ONE CONDITION—I WANT ANY INFORMATION THE FBI OR CHICAGO P.D. HAVE ON ME.
DENTON WILL KILL ME IF HE FINDS OUT... BUT ALL RIGHT, DEAL.

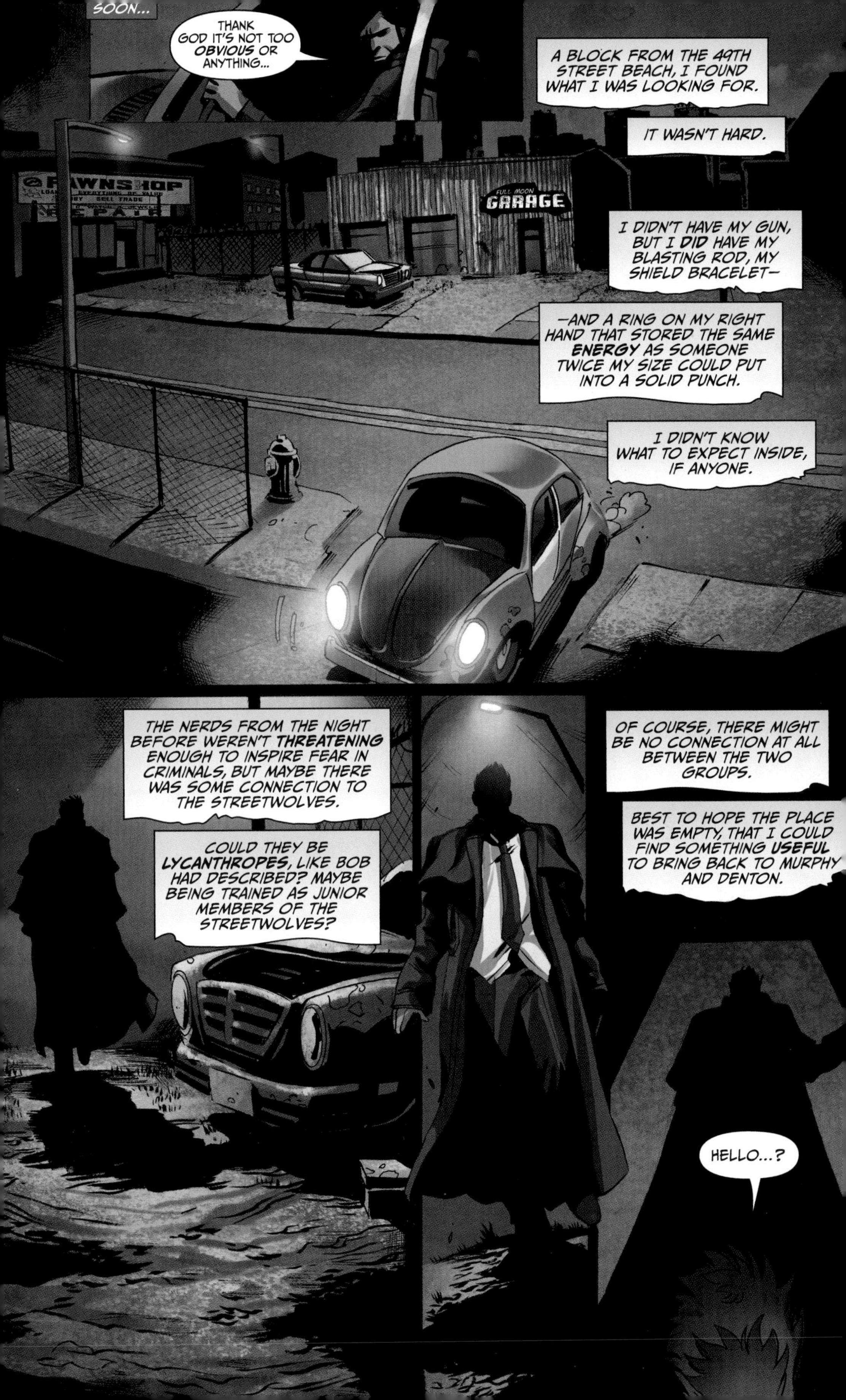
SOON...
THANK GOD IT'S NOT TOO OBVIOUS OR ANYTHING...
A BLOCK FROM THE 49TH STREET BEACH, I FOUND WHAT I WAS LOOKING FOR.
IT WASN'T HARD.
PAWNSHOP
FULL MOON GARAGE
I DIDN'T HAVE MY GUN, BUT I DID HAVE MY BLASTING ROD, MY SHIELD BRACELET—
—AND A RING ON MY RIGHT HAND THAT STORED THE SAME ENERGY AS SOMEONE TWICE MY SIZE COULD PUT INTO A SOLID PUNCH.
I DIDN'T KNOW WHAT TO EXPECT INSIDE, IF ANYONE.
THE NERDS FROM THE NIGHT BEFORE WEREN'T THREATENING ENOUGH TO INSPIRE FEAR IN CRIMINALS, BUT MAYBE THERE WAS SOME CONNECTION TO THE STREETWOLVES.
COULD THEY BE LYCANTHROPES, LIKE BOB HAD DESCRIBED? MAYBE BEING TRAINED AS JUNIOR MEMBERS OF THE STREETWOLVES?
OF COURSE, THERE MIGHT BE NO CONNECTION AT ALL BETWEEN THE TWO GROUPS.
BEST TO HOPE THE PLACE WAS EMPTY, THAT I COULD FIND SOMETHING USEFUL TO BRING BACK TO MURPHY AND DENTON.
HELLO...?

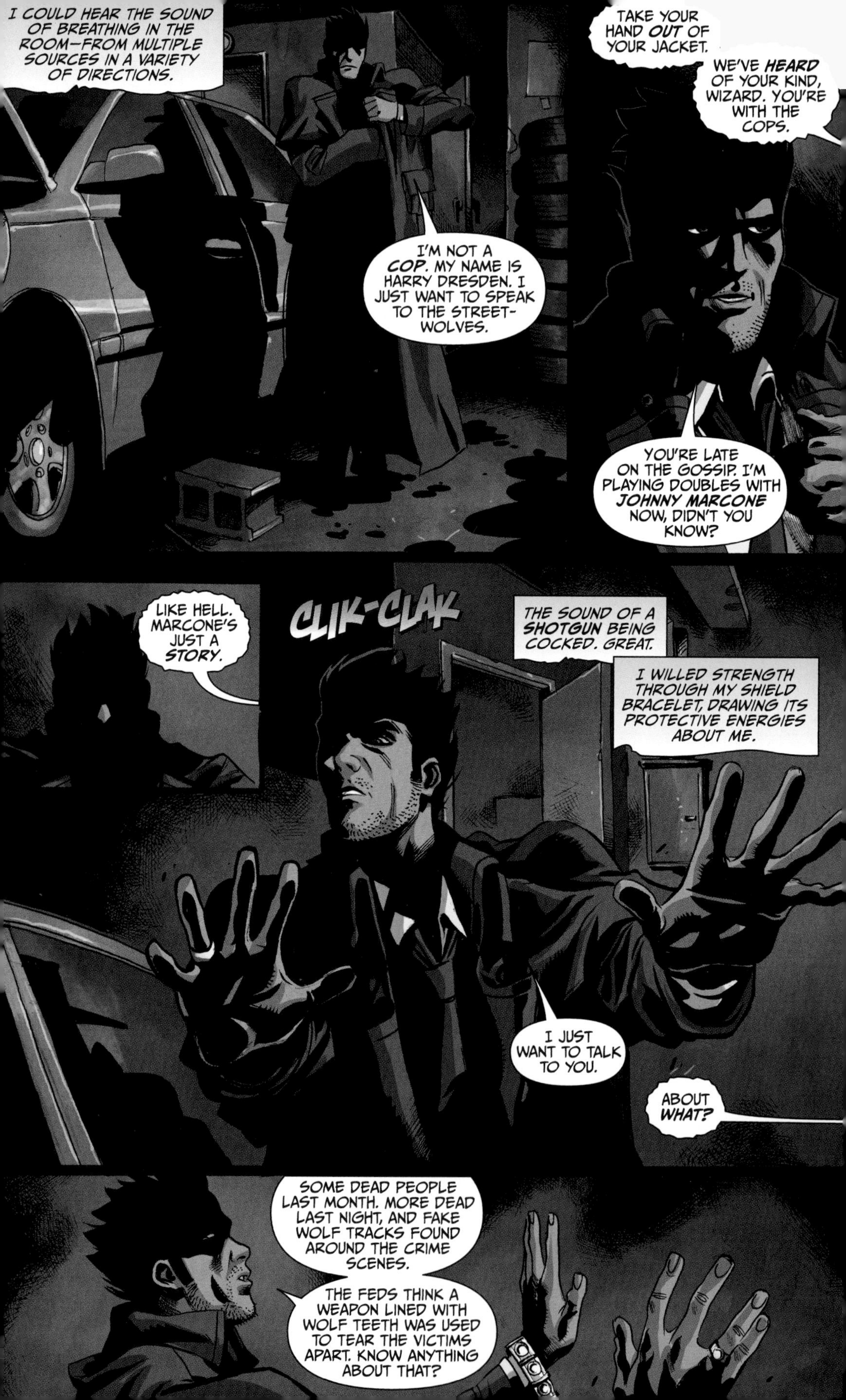

I COULD HEAR THE SOUND OF BREATHING IN THE ROOM—FROM MULTIPLE SOURCES IN A VARIETY OF DIRECTIONS.
I'M NOT A COP. MY NAME IS HARRY DRESDEN. I JUST WANT TO SPEAK TO THE STREET-WOLVES.
TAKE YOUR HAND OUT OF YOUR JACKET.
WE'VE HEARD OF YOUR KIND, WIZARD. YOU'RE WITH THE COPS.
YOU'RE LATE ON THE GOSSIP. I'M PLAYING DOUBLES WITH JOHNNY MARCONE NOW, DIDN'T YOU KNOW?
LIKE HELL. MARCONE'S JUST A STORY.
CLIK-CLAK
THE SOUND OF A SHOTGUN BEING COCKED. GREAT.
I WILLED STRENGTH THROUGH MY SHIELD BRACELET, DRAWING ITS PROTECTIVE ENERGIES ABOUT ME.
I JUST WANT TO TALK TO YOU.
ABOUT WHAT?
SOME DEAD PEOPLE LAST MONTH. MORE DEAD LAST NIGHT, AND FAKE WOLF TRACKS FOUND AROUND THE CRIME SCENES.
THE FEDS THINK A WEAPON LINED WITH WOLF TEETH WAS USED TO TEAR THE VICTIMS APART. KNOW ANYTHING ABOUT THAT?

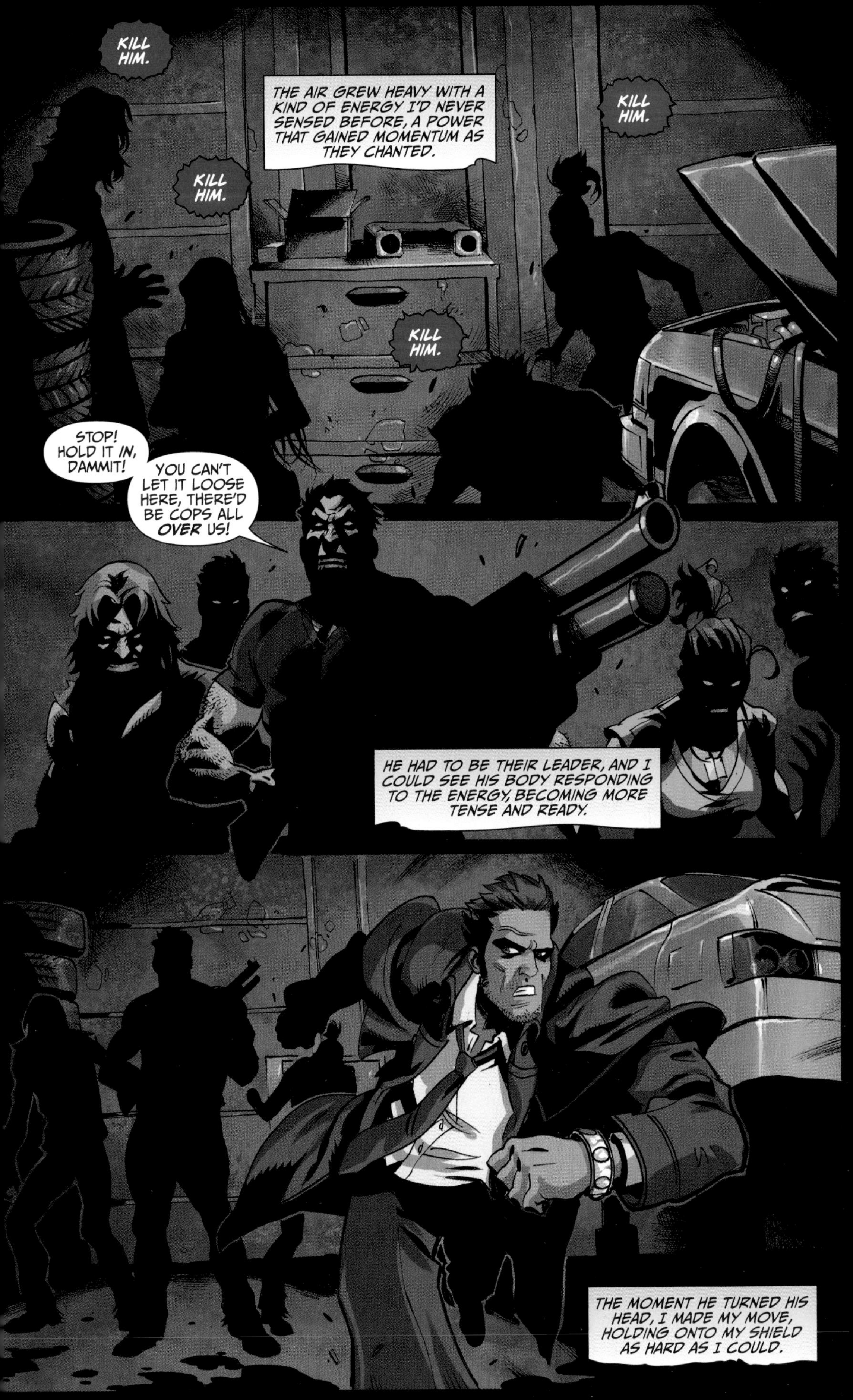
KILL HIM.
THE AIR GREW HEAVY WITH A KIND OF ENERGY I'D NEVER SENSED BEFORE, A POWER THAT GAINED MOMENTUM AS THEY CHANTED.
KILL HIM.
KILL HIM.
KILL HIM.
STOP! HOLD IT *IN*, DAMMIT!
YOU CAN'T LET IT LOOSE HERE, THERE'D BE COPS ALL **OVER** US!
HE HAD TO BE THEIR LEADER, AND I COULD SEE HIS BODY RESPONDING TO THE ENERGY, BECOMING MORE TENSE AND READY.
THE MOMENT HE TURNED HIS HEAD, I MADE MY MOVE, HOLDING ONTO MY SHIELD AS HARD AS I COULD.

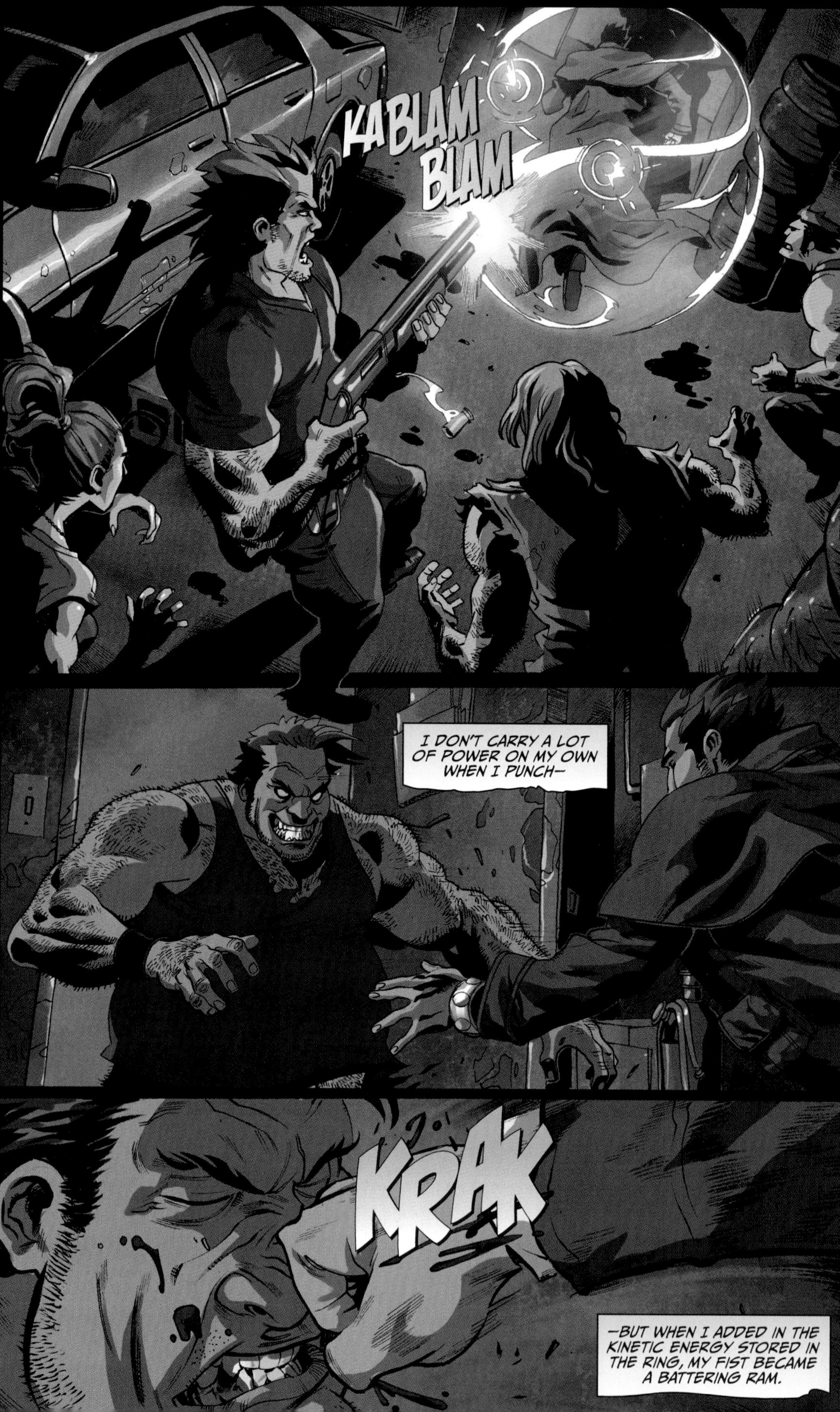
KA BLAM BLAM
I DON'T CARRY A LOT OF POWER ON MY OWN WHEN I PUNCH—
KRAK
—BUT WHEN I ADDED IN THE KINETIC ENERGY STORED IN THE RING, MY FIST BECAME A BATTERING RAM.

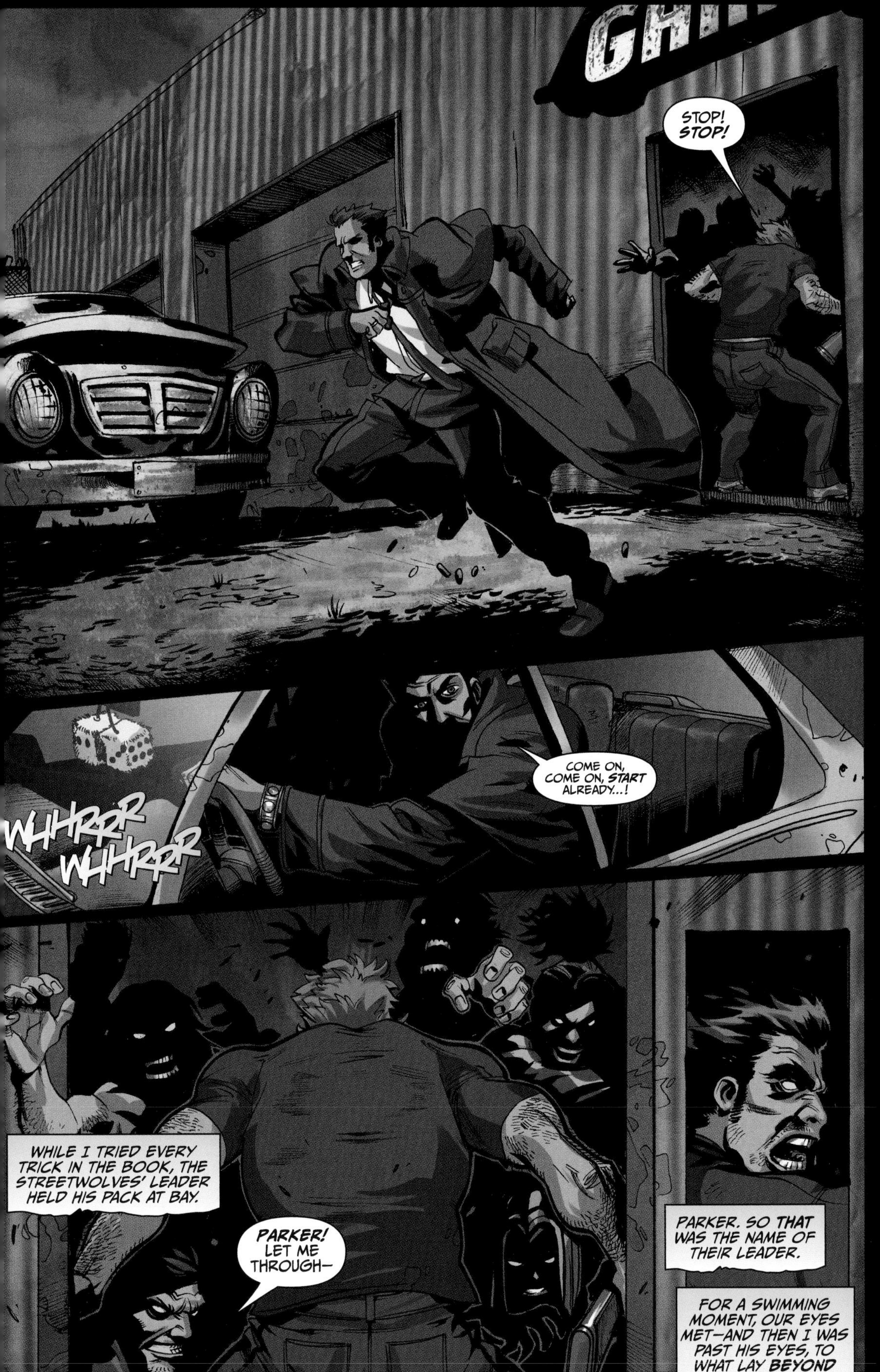

STOP! STOP!
COME ON, COME ON, START ALREADY...!
WHHRRR WHHRRR
WHILE I TRIED EVERY TRICK IN THE BOOK, THE STREETWOLVES' LEADER HELD HIS PACK AT BAY.
PARKER! LET ME THROUGH—
PARKER. SO THAT WAS THE NAME OF THEIR LEADER.
FOR A SWIMMING MOMENT, OUR EYES MET—AND THEN I WAS PAST HIS EYES, TO WHAT LAY BEYOND THEM.

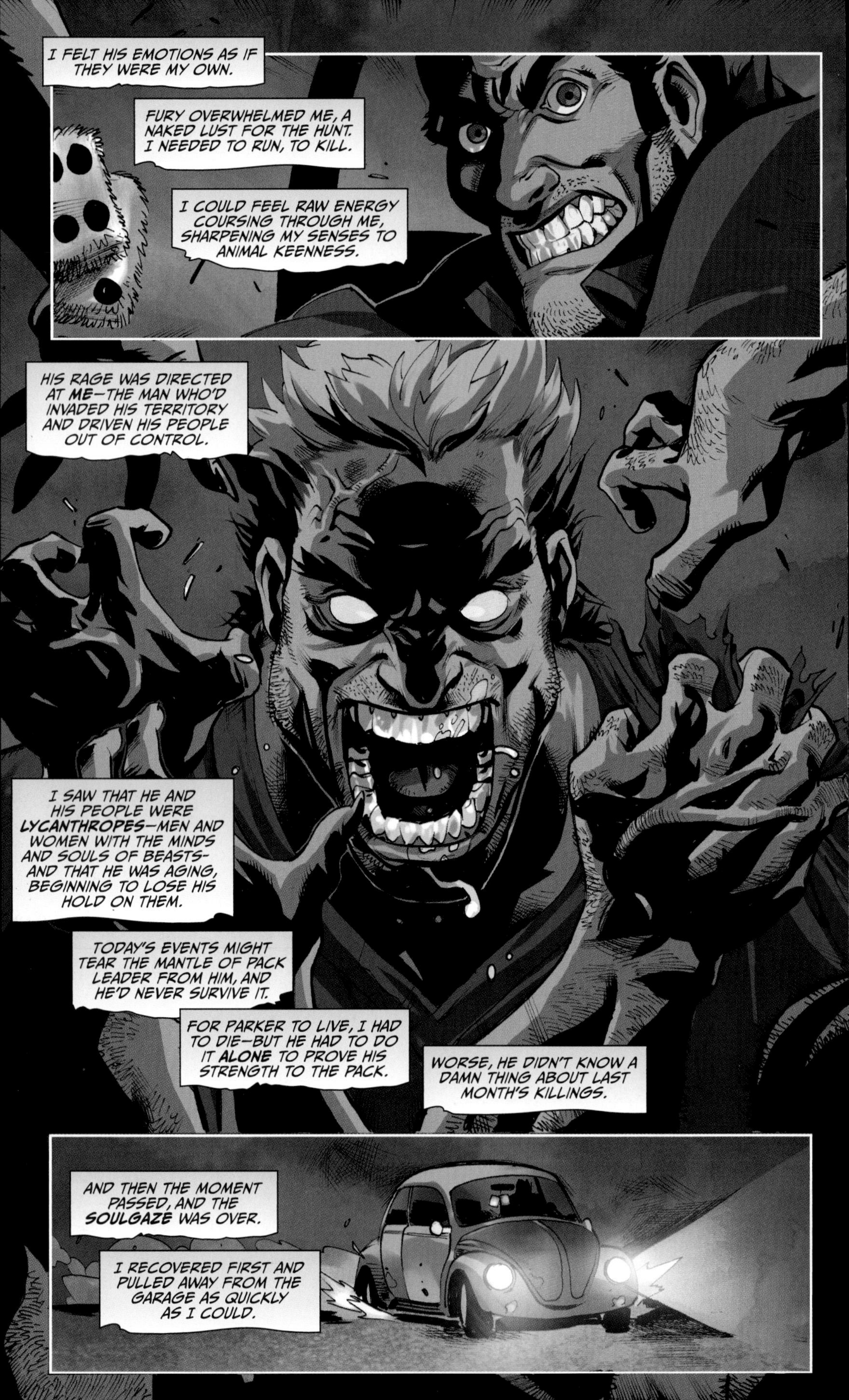
I FELT HIS EMOTIONS AS IF THEY WERE MY OWN.
FURY OVERWHELMED ME, A NAKED LUST FOR THE HUNT. I NEEDED TO RUN, TO KILL.
I COULD FEEL RAW ENERGY COURSING THROUGH ME, SHARPENING MY SENSES TO ANIMAL KEENNESS.
HIS RAGE WAS DIRECTED AT **ME**—THE MAN WHO'D INVADED HIS TERRITORY AND DRIVEN HIS PEOPLE OUT OF CONTROL.
I SAW THAT HE AND HIS PEOPLE WERE **LYCANTHROPES**—MEN AND WOMEN WITH THE MINDS AND SOULS OF BEASTS-AND THAT HE WAS AGING, BEGINNING TO LOSE HIS HOLD ON THEM.
TODAY'S EVENTS MIGHT TEAR THE MANTLE OF PACK LEADER FROM HIM, AND HE'D NEVER SURVIVE IT.
FOR PARKER TO LIVE, I HAD TO DIE—BUT HE HAD TO DO IT **ALONE** TO PROVE HIS STRENGTH TO THE PACK.
WORSE, HE DIDN'T KNOW A DAMN THING ABOUT LAST MONTH'S KILLINGS.
AND THEN THE MOMENT PASSED, AND THE **SOULGAZE** WAS OVER.
I RECOVERED FIRST AND PULLED AWAY FROM THE GARAGE AS QUICKLY AS I COULD.

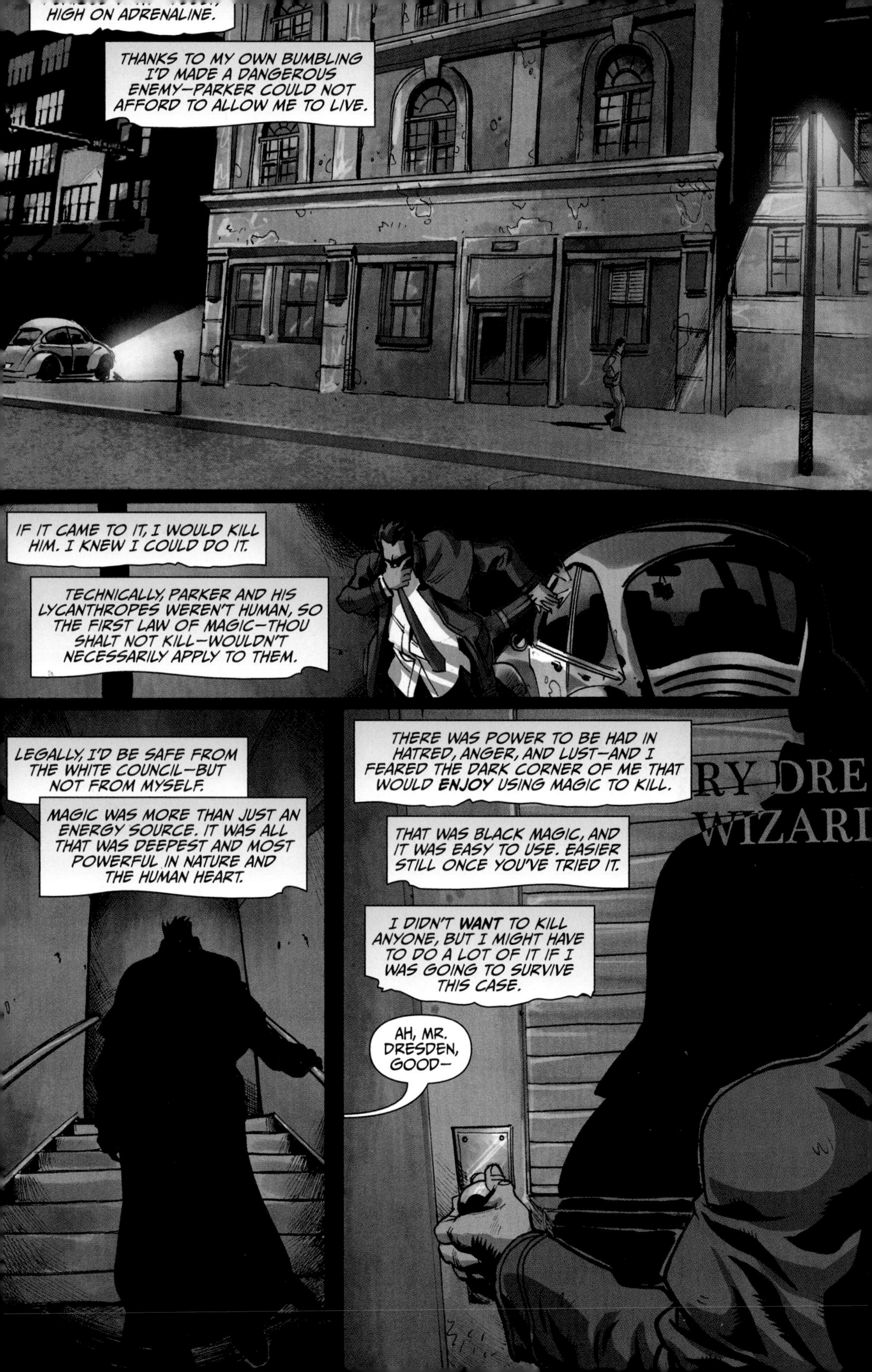
HIGH ON ADRENALINE.
THANKS TO MY OWN BUMBLING I'D MADE A DANGEROUS ENEMY—PARKER COULD NOT AFFORD TO ALLOW ME TO LIVE.
IF IT CAME TO IT, I WOULD KILL HIM. I KNEW I COULD DO IT.
TECHNICALLY, PARKER AND HIS LYCANTHROPES WEREN'T HUMAN, SO THE FIRST LAW OF MAGIC—THOU SHALT NOT KILL—WOULDN'T NECESSARILY APPLY TO THEM.
LEGALLY, I'D BE SAFE FROM THE WHITE COUNCIL—BUT NOT FROM MYSELF.
MAGIC WAS MORE THAN JUST AN ENERGY SOURCE. IT WAS ALL THAT WAS DEEPEST AND MOST POWERFUL IN NATURE AND THE HUMAN HEART.
THERE WAS POWER TO BE HAD IN HATRED, ANGER, AND LUST—AND I FEARED THE DARK CORNER OF ME THAT WOULD **ENJOY** USING MAGIC TO KILL.
THAT WAS BLACK MAGIC, AND IT WAS EASY TO USE. EASIER STILL ONCE YOU'VE TRIED IT.
I DIDN'T **WANT** TO KILL ANYONE, BUT I MIGHT HAVE TO DO A LOT OF IT IF I WAS GOING TO SURVIVE THIS CASE.
AH, MR. DRESDEN, GOOD—

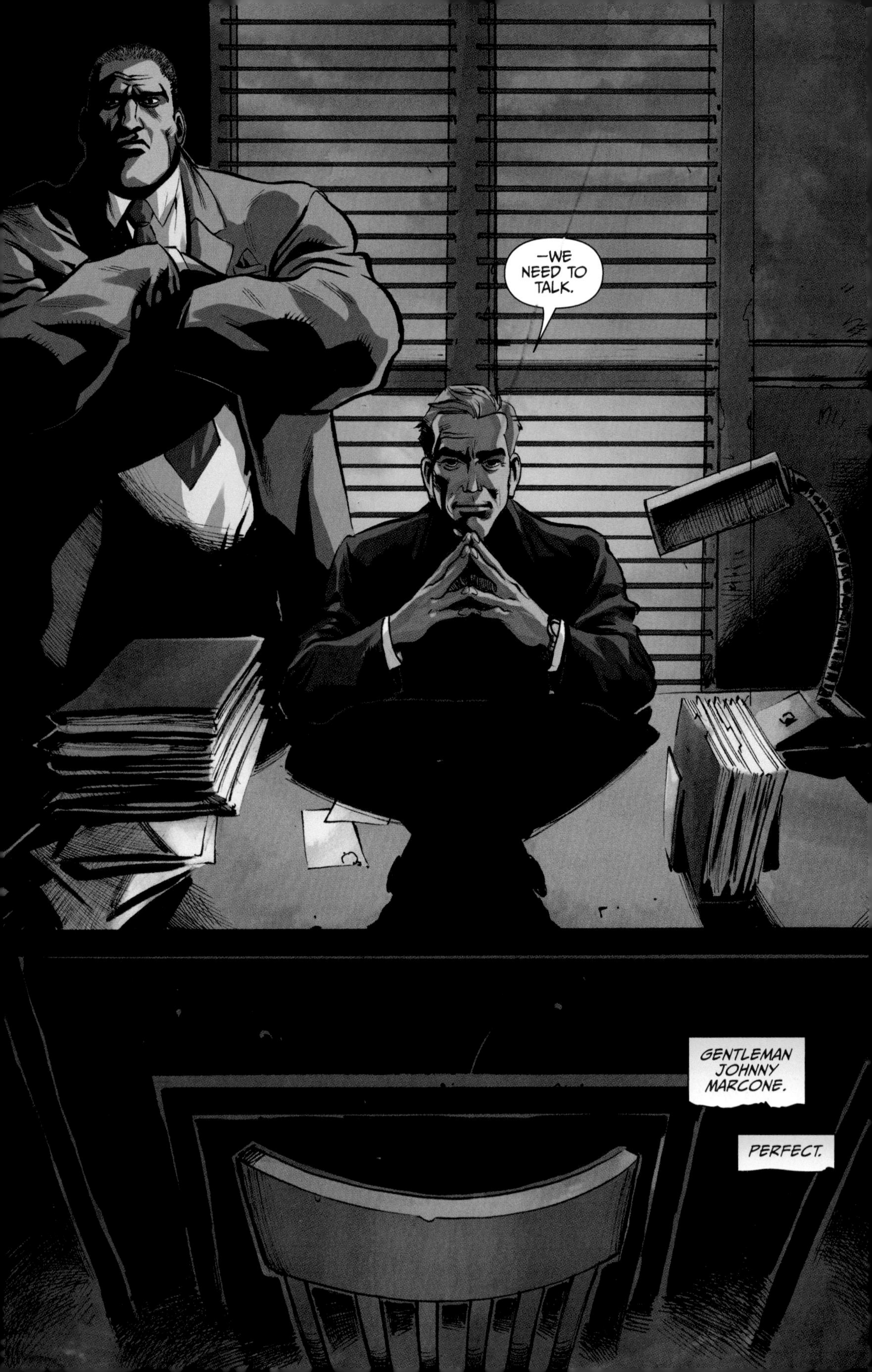
—WE NEED TO TALK.
GENTLEMAN JOHNNY MARCONE.
PERFECT.

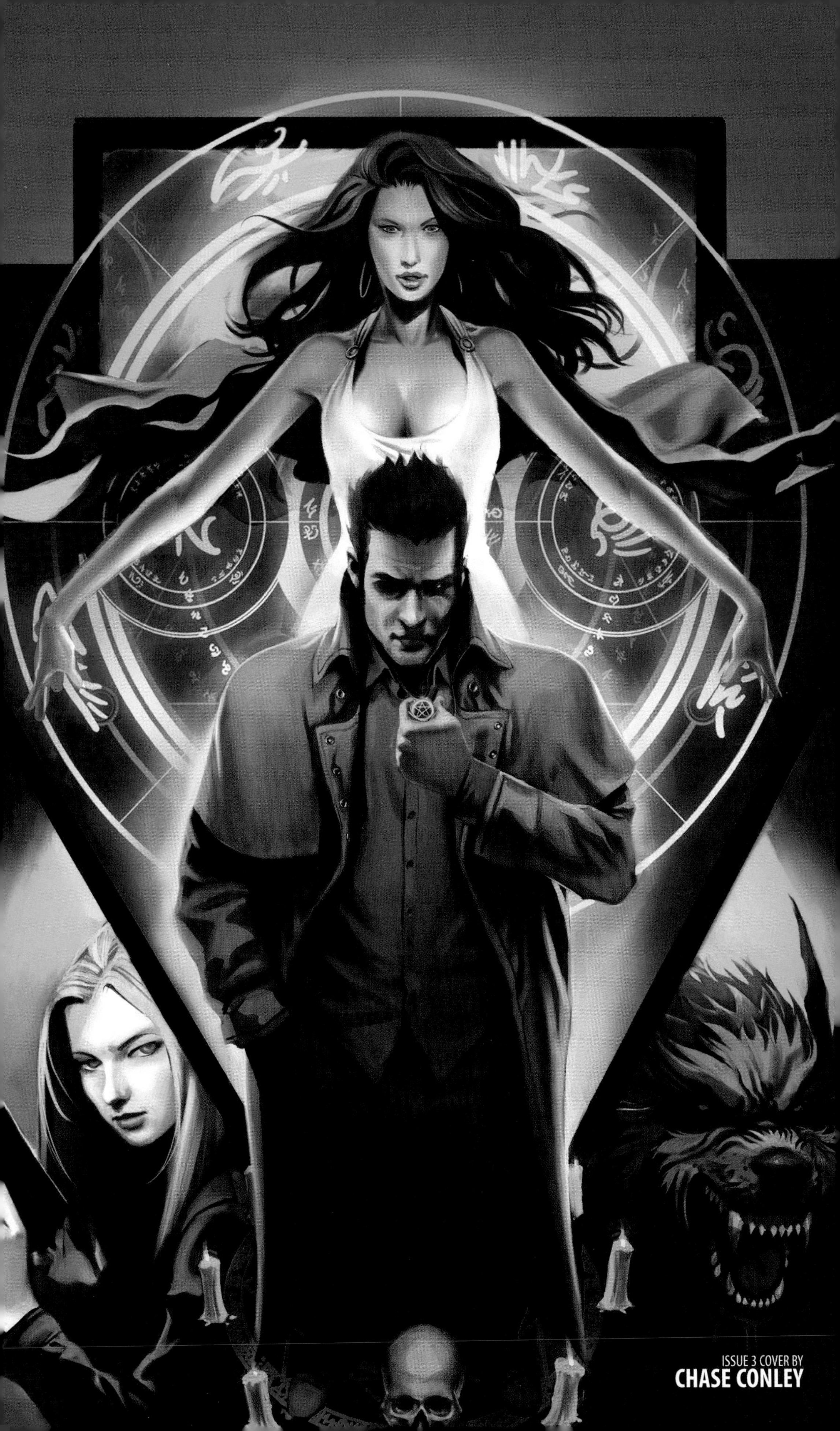

ISSUE 3 COVER BY
CHASE CONLEY

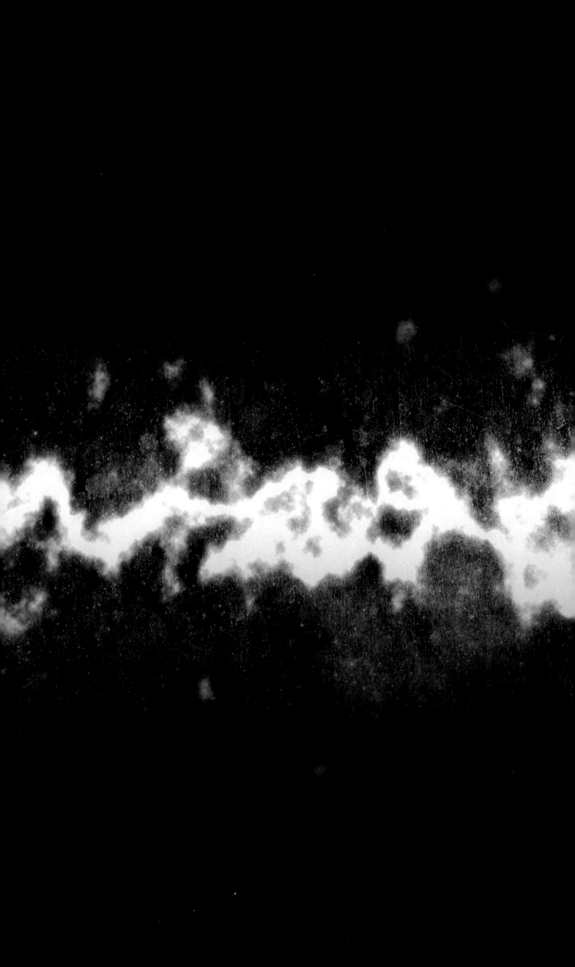

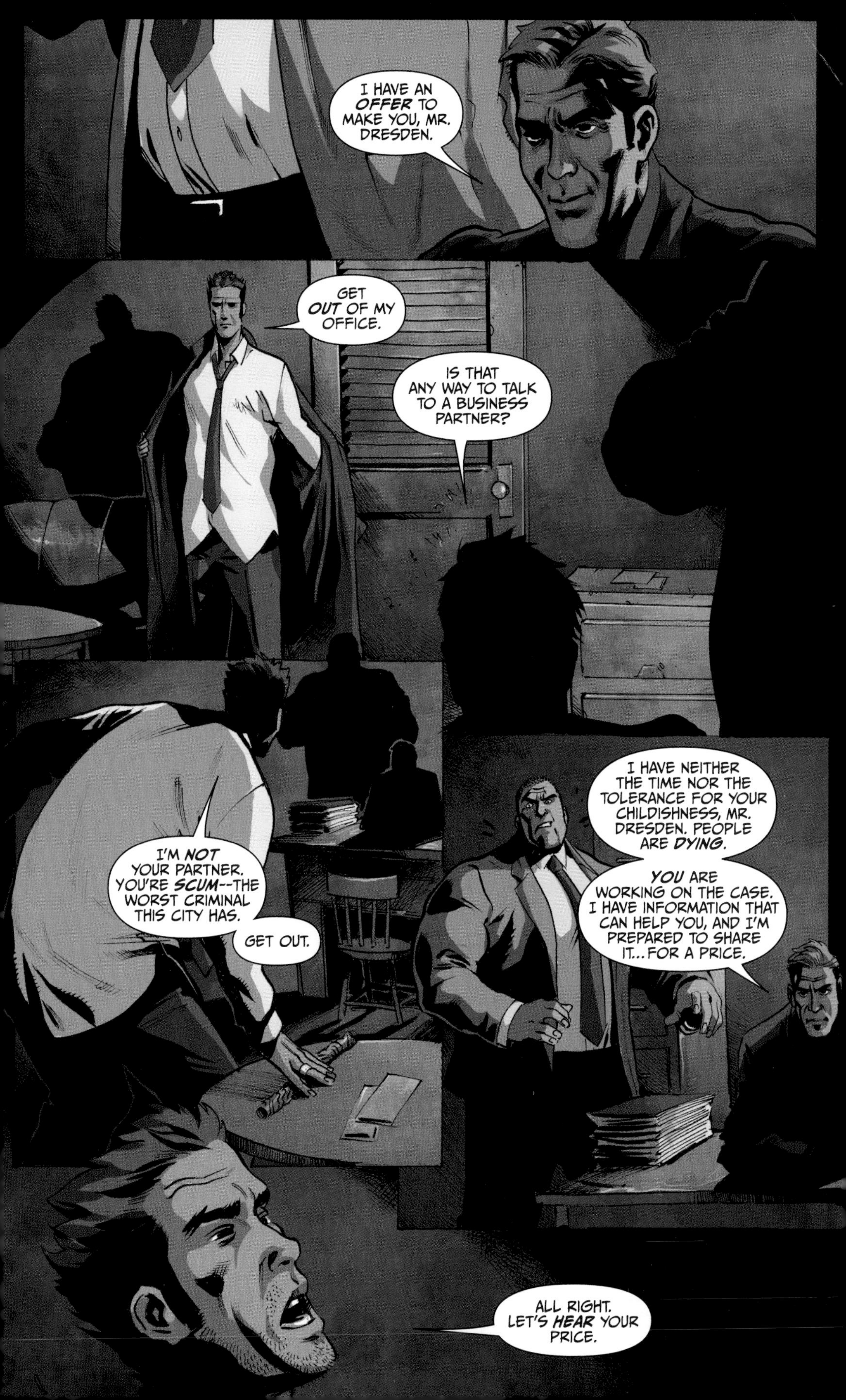
I HAVE AN *OFFER* TO MAKE YOU, MR. DRESDEN.
GET *OUT* OF MY OFFICE.
IS THAT ANY WAY TO TALK TO A BUSINESS PARTNER?
I'M *NOT* YOUR PARTNER. YOU'RE *SCUM*--THE WORST CRIMINAL THIS CITY HAS.
GET OUT.
I HAVE NEITHER THE TIME NOR THE TOLERANCE FOR YOUR CHILDISHNESS, MR. DRESDEN. PEOPLE ARE *DYING*.
YOU ARE WORKING ON THE CASE. I HAVE INFORMATION THAT CAN HELP YOU, AND I'M PREPARED TO SHARE IT...FOR A PRICE.
ALL RIGHT. LET'S *HEAR* YOUR PRICE.

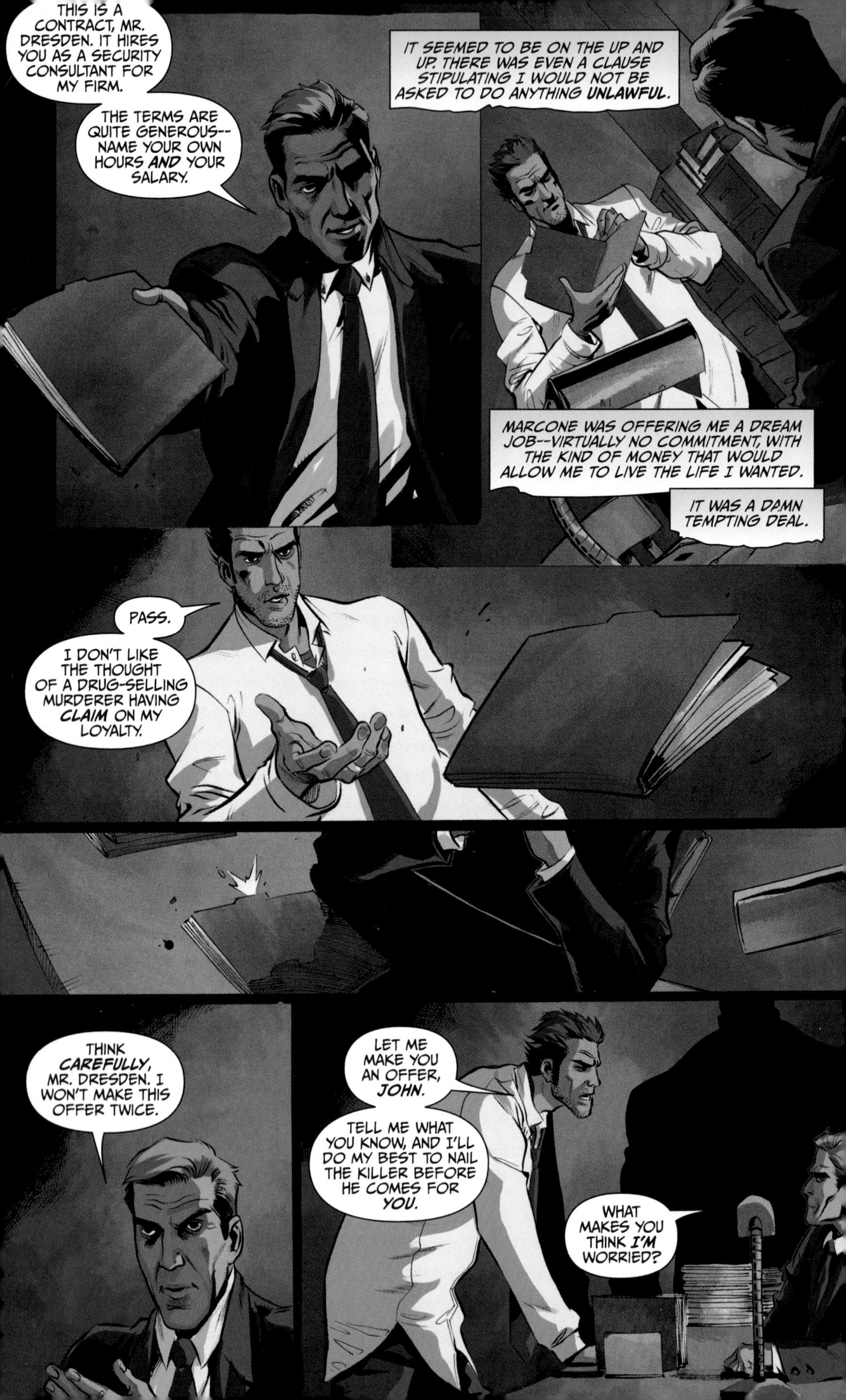
THIS IS A CONTRACT, MR. DRESDEN. IT HIRES YOU AS A SECURITY CONSULTANT FOR MY FIRM.
THE TERMS ARE QUITE GENEROUS-- NAME YOUR OWN HOURS AND YOUR SALARY.
IT SEEMED TO BE ON THE UP AND UP. THERE WAS EVEN A CLAUSE STIPULATING I WOULD NOT BE ASKED TO DO ANYTHING UNLAWFUL.
MARCONE WAS OFFERING ME A DREAM JOB--VIRTUALLY NO COMMITMENT, WITH THE KIND OF MONEY THAT WOULD ALLOW ME TO LIVE THE LIFE I WANTED.
IT WAS A DAMN TEMPTING DEAL.
PASS.
I DON'T LIKE THE THOUGHT OF A DRUG-SELLING MURDERER HAVING CLAIM ON MY LOYALTY.
THINK CAREFULLY, MR. DRESDEN. I WON'T MAKE THIS OFFER TWICE.
LET ME MAKE YOU AN OFFER, JOHN.
TELL ME WHAT YOU KNOW, AND I'LL DO MY BEST TO NAIL THE KILLER BEFORE HE COMES FOR YOU.
WHAT MAKES YOU THINK I'M WORRIED?

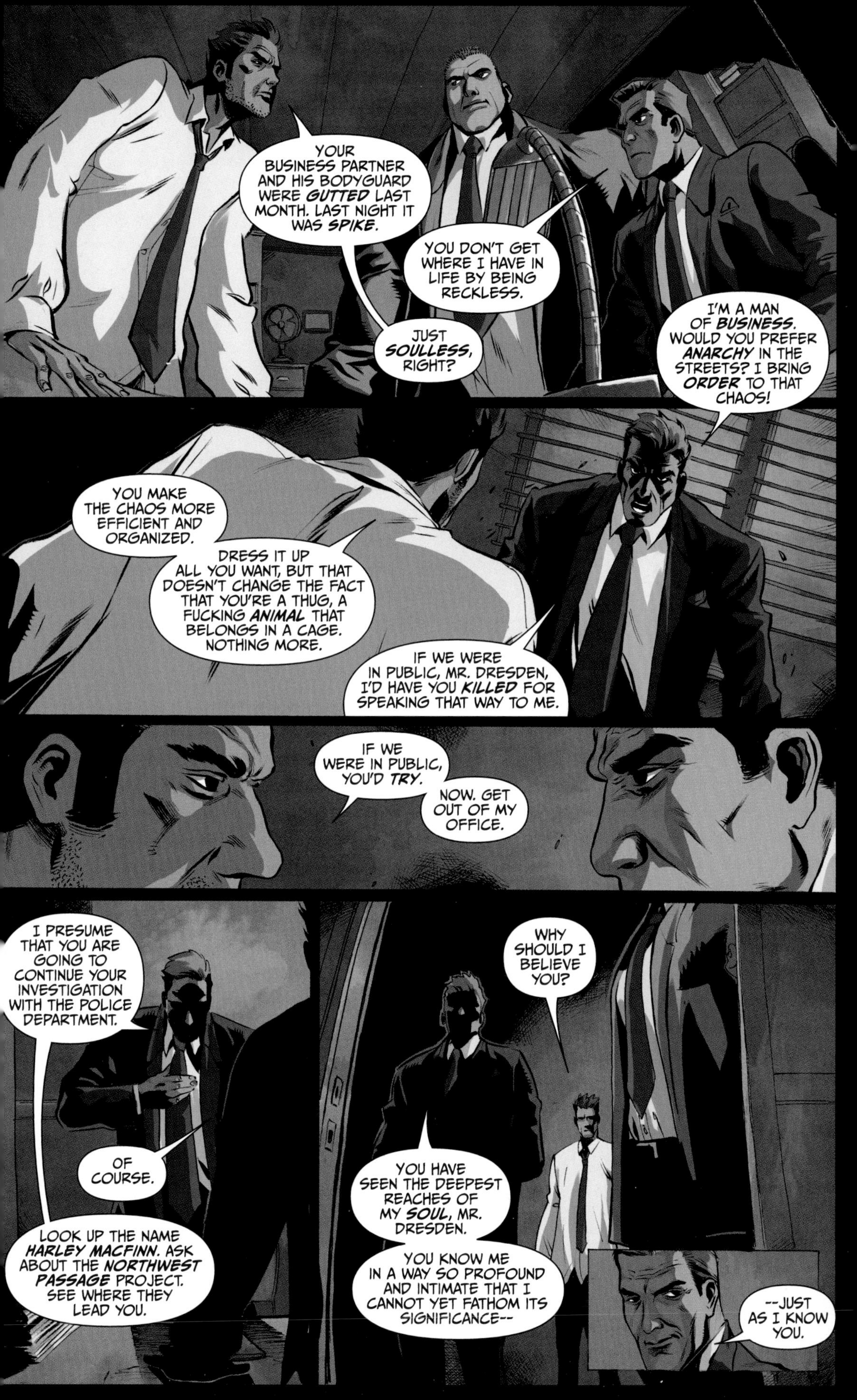
YOUR BUSINESS PARTNER AND HIS BODYGUARD WERE GUTTED LAST MONTH. LAST NIGHT IT WAS SPIKE.
YOU DON'T GET WHERE I HAVE IN LIFE BY BEING RECKLESS.
JUST SOULLESS, RIGHT?
I'M A MAN OF BUSINESS. WOULD YOU PREFER ANARCHY IN THE STREETS? I BRING ORDER TO THAT CHAOS!
YOU MAKE THE CHAOS MORE EFFICIENT AND ORGANIZED.
DRESS IT UP ALL YOU WANT, BUT THAT DOESN'T CHANGE THE FACT THAT YOU'RE A THUG, A FUCKING ANIMAL THAT BELONGS IN A CAGE. NOTHING MORE.
IF WE WERE IN PUBLIC, MR. DRESDEN, I'D HAVE YOU KILLED FOR SPEAKING THAT WAY TO ME.
IF WE WERE IN PUBLIC, YOU'D TRY.
NOW. GET OUT OF MY OFFICE.
I PRESUME THAT YOU ARE GOING TO CONTINUE YOUR INVESTIGATION WITH THE POLICE DEPARTMENT.
OF COURSE.
LOOK UP THE NAME HARLEY MACFINN. ASK ABOUT THE NORTHWEST PASSAGE PROJECT. SEE WHERE THEY LEAD YOU.
WHY SHOULD I BELIEVE YOU?
YOU HAVE SEEN THE DEEPEST REACHES OF MY SOUL, MR. DRESDEN.
YOU KNOW ME IN A WAY SO PROFOUND AND INTIMATE THAT I CANNOT YET FATHOM ITS SIGNIFICANCE--
--JUST AS I KNOW YOU.

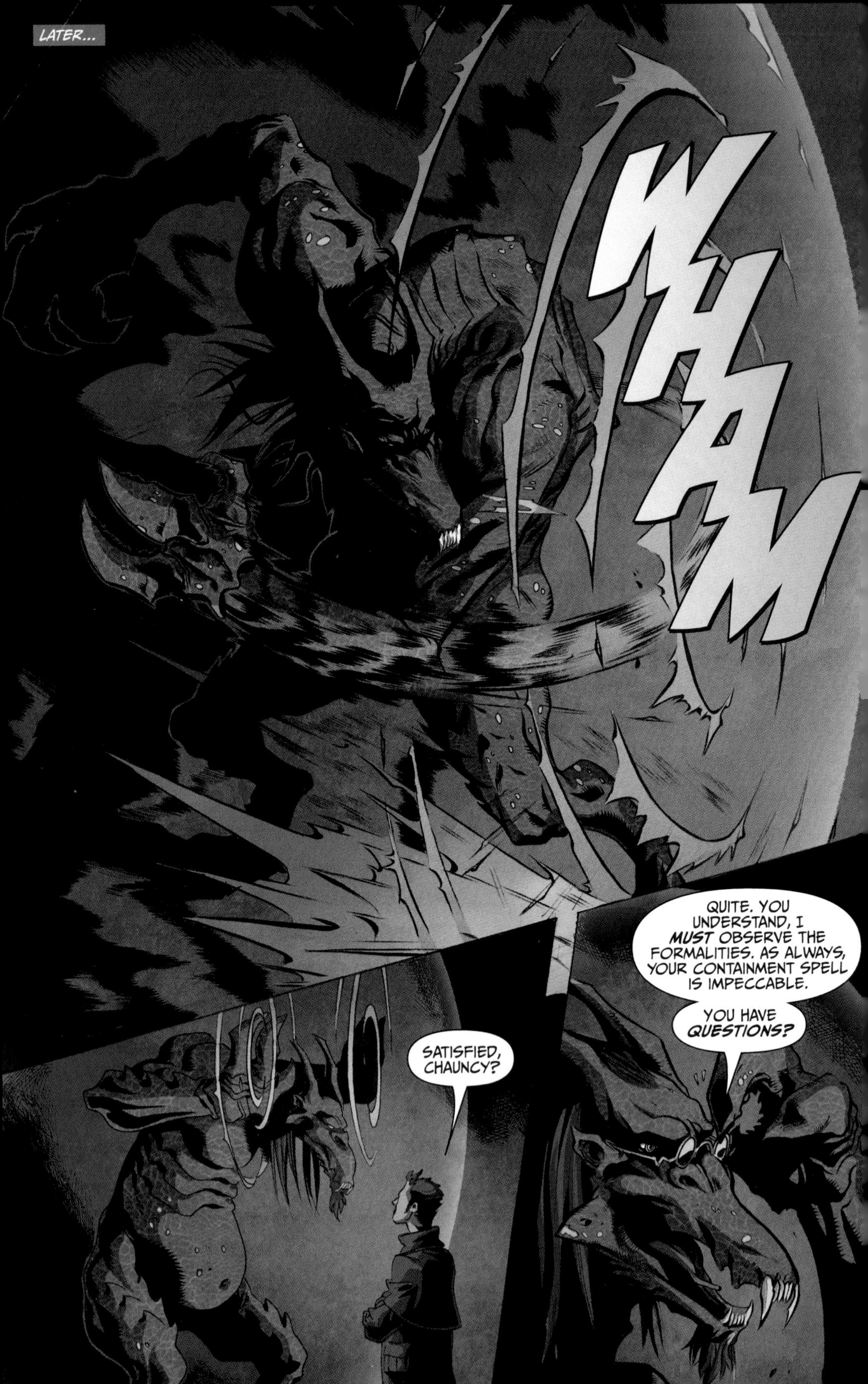
LATER...
WHAM
SATISFIED, CHAUNCY?
QUITE. YOU UNDERSTAND, I **MUST** OBSERVE THE FORMALITIES. AS ALWAYS, YOUR CONTAINMENT SPELL IS IMPECCABLE.
YOU HAVE **QUESTIONS?**

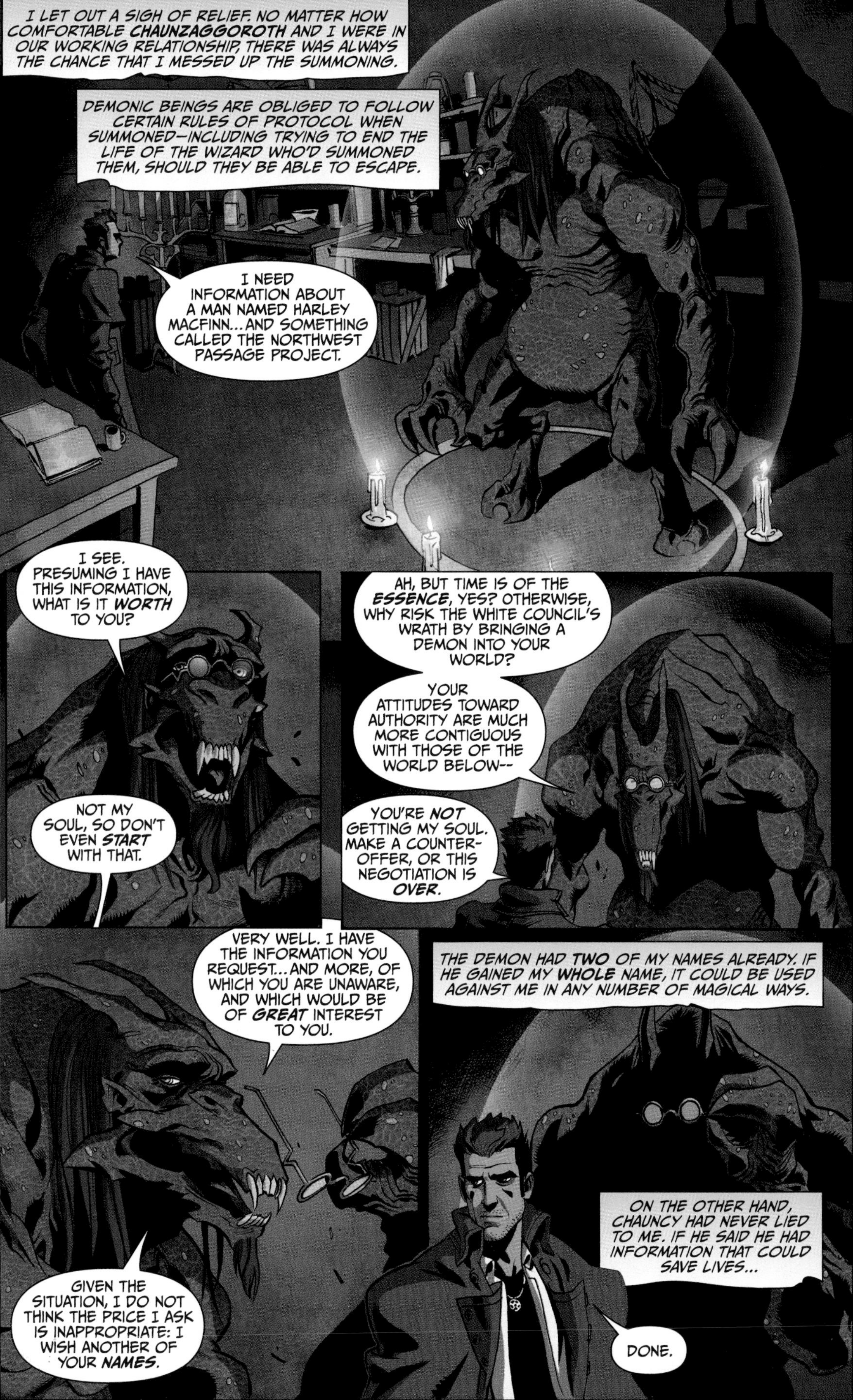
I LET OUT A SIGH OF RELIEF. NO MATTER HOW COMFORTABLE CHAUNZAGGOROTH AND I WERE IN OUR WORKING RELATIONSHIP, THERE WAS ALWAYS THE CHANCE THAT I MESSED UP THE SUMMONING.
DEMONIC BEINGS ARE OBLIGED TO FOLLOW CERTAIN RULES OF PROTOCOL WHEN SUMMONED—INCLUDING TRYING TO END THE LIFE OF THE WIZARD WHO'D SUMMONED THEM, SHOULD THEY BE ABLE TO ESCAPE.
I NEED INFORMATION ABOUT A MAN NAMED HARLEY MACFINN...AND SOMETHING CALLED THE NORTHWEST PASSAGE PROJECT.
I SEE. PRESUMING I HAVE THIS INFORMATION, WHAT IS IT WORTH TO YOU?
NOT MY SOUL, SO DON'T EVEN START WITH THAT.
AH, BUT TIME IS OF THE ESSENCE, YES? OTHERWISE, WHY RISK THE WHITE COUNCIL'S WRATH BY BRINGING A DEMON INTO YOUR WORLD?
YOUR ATTITUDES TOWARD AUTHORITY ARE MUCH MORE CONTIGUOUS WITH THOSE OF THE WORLD BELOW--
YOU'RE NOT GETTING MY SOUL. MAKE A COUNTER-OFFER, OR THIS NEGOTIATION IS OVER.
VERY WELL. I HAVE THE INFORMATION YOU REQUEST...AND MORE, OF WHICH YOU ARE UNAWARE, AND WHICH WOULD BE OF GREAT INTEREST TO YOU.
GIVEN THE SITUATION, I DO NOT THINK THE PRICE I ASK IS INAPPROPRIATE: I WISH ANOTHER OF YOUR NAMES.
THE DEMON HAD TWO OF MY NAMES ALREADY. IF HE GAINED MY WHOLE NAME, IT COULD BE USED AGAINST ME IN ANY NUMBER OF MAGICAL WAYS.
ON THE OTHER HAND, CHAUNCY HAD NEVER LIED TO ME. IF HE SAID HE HAD INFORMATION THAT COULD SAVE LIVES...
DONE.

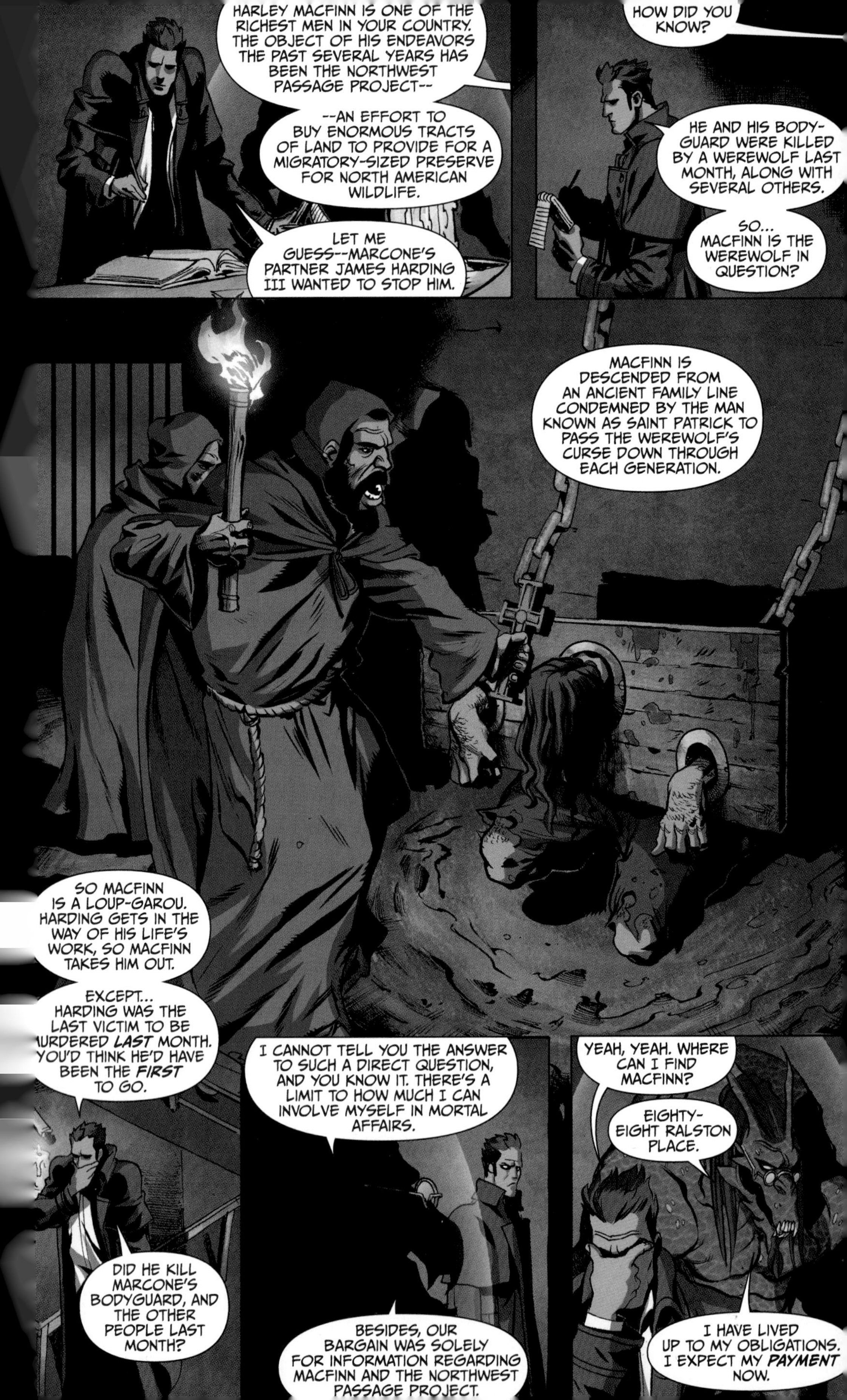
HARLEY MACFINN IS ONE OF THE RICHEST MEN IN YOUR COUNTRY. THE OBJECT OF HIS ENDEAVORS THE PAST SEVERAL YEARS HAS BEEN THE NORTHWEST PASSAGE PROJECT--
--AN EFFORT TO BUY ENORMOUS TRACTS OF LAND TO PROVIDE FOR A MIGRATORY-SIZED PRESERVE FOR NORTH AMERICAN WILDLIFE.
LET ME GUESS--MARCONE'S PARTNER JAMES HARDING III WANTED TO STOP HIM.
HOW DID YOU KNOW?
HE AND HIS BODY-GUARD WERE KILLED BY A WEREWOLF LAST MONTH, ALONG WITH SEVERAL OTHERS.
SO... MACFINN IS THE WEREWOLF IN QUESTION?
MACFINN IS DESCENDED FROM AN ANCIENT FAMILY LINE CONDEMNED BY THE MAN KNOWN AS SAINT PATRICK TO PASS THE WEREWOLF'S CURSE DOWN THROUGH EACH GENERATION.
SO MACFINN IS A LOUP-GAROU. HARDING GETS IN THE WAY OF HIS LIFE'S WORK, SO MACFINN TAKES HIM OUT.
EXCEPT... HARDING WAS THE LAST VICTIM TO BE URDERED *LAST* MONTH. YOU'D THINK HE'D HAVE BEEN THE *FIRST* TO GO.
DID HE KILL MARCONE'S BODYGUARD, AND THE OTHER PEOPLE LAST MONTH?
I CANNOT TELL YOU THE ANSWER TO SUCH A DIRECT QUESTION, AND YOU KNOW IT. THERE'S A LIMIT TO HOW MUCH I CAN INVOLVE MYSELF IN MORTAL AFFAIRS.
BESIDES, OUR BARGAIN WAS SOLELY FOR INFORMATION REGARDING MACFINN AND THE NORTHWEST PASSAGE PROJECT.
YEAH, YEAH. WHERE CAN I FIND MACFINN?
EIGHTY-EIGHT RALSTON PLACE.
I HAVE LIVED UP TO MY OBLIGATIONS. I EXPECT MY *PAYMENT* NOW.

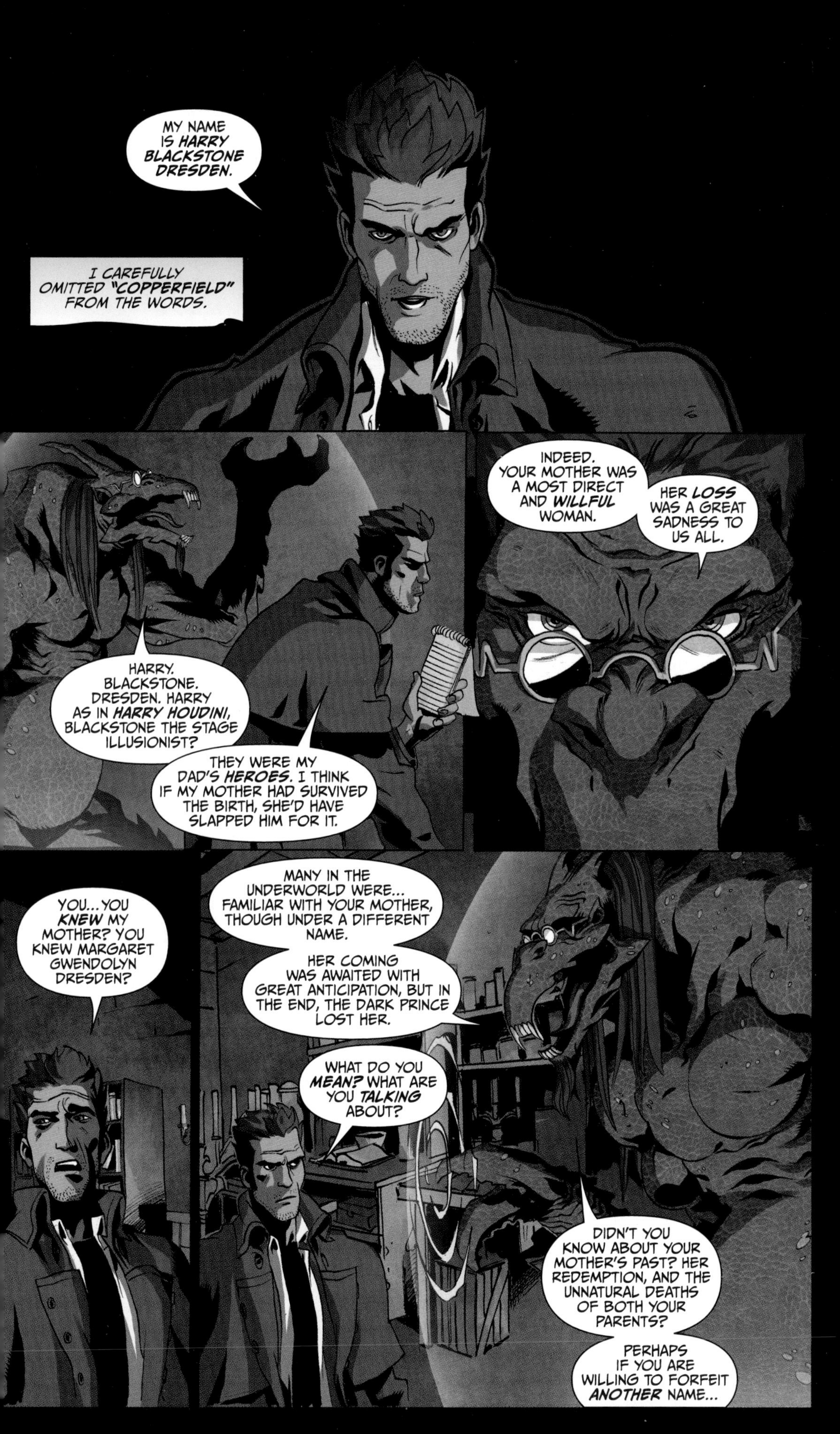
MY NAME IS HARRY BLACKSTONE DRESDEN.
I CAREFULLY OMITTED "COPPERFIELD" FROM THE WORDS.
HARRY. BLACKSTONE. DRESDEN. HARRY AS IN HARRY HOUDINI, BLACKSTONE THE STAGE ILLUSIONIST?
THEY WERE MY DAD'S HEROES. I THINK IF MY MOTHER HAD SURVIVED THE BIRTH, SHE'D HAVE SLAPPED HIM FOR IT.
INDEED. YOUR MOTHER WAS A MOST DIRECT AND WILLFUL WOMAN.
HER LOSS WAS A GREAT SADNESS TO US ALL.
YOU...YOU KNEW MY MOTHER? YOU KNEW MARGARET GWENDOLYN DRESDEN?
MANY IN THE UNDERWORLD WERE... FAMILIAR WITH YOUR MOTHER, THOUGH UNDER A DIFFERENT NAME.
HER COMING WAS AWAITED WITH GREAT ANTICIPATION, BUT IN THE END, THE DARK PRINCE LOST HER.
WHAT DO YOU MEAN? WHAT ARE YOU TALKING ABOUT?
DIDN'T YOU KNOW ABOUT YOUR MOTHER'S PAST? HER REDEMPTION, AND THE UNNATURAL DEATHS OF BOTH YOUR PARENTS?
PERHAPS IF YOU ARE WILLING TO FORFEIT ANOTHER NAME...

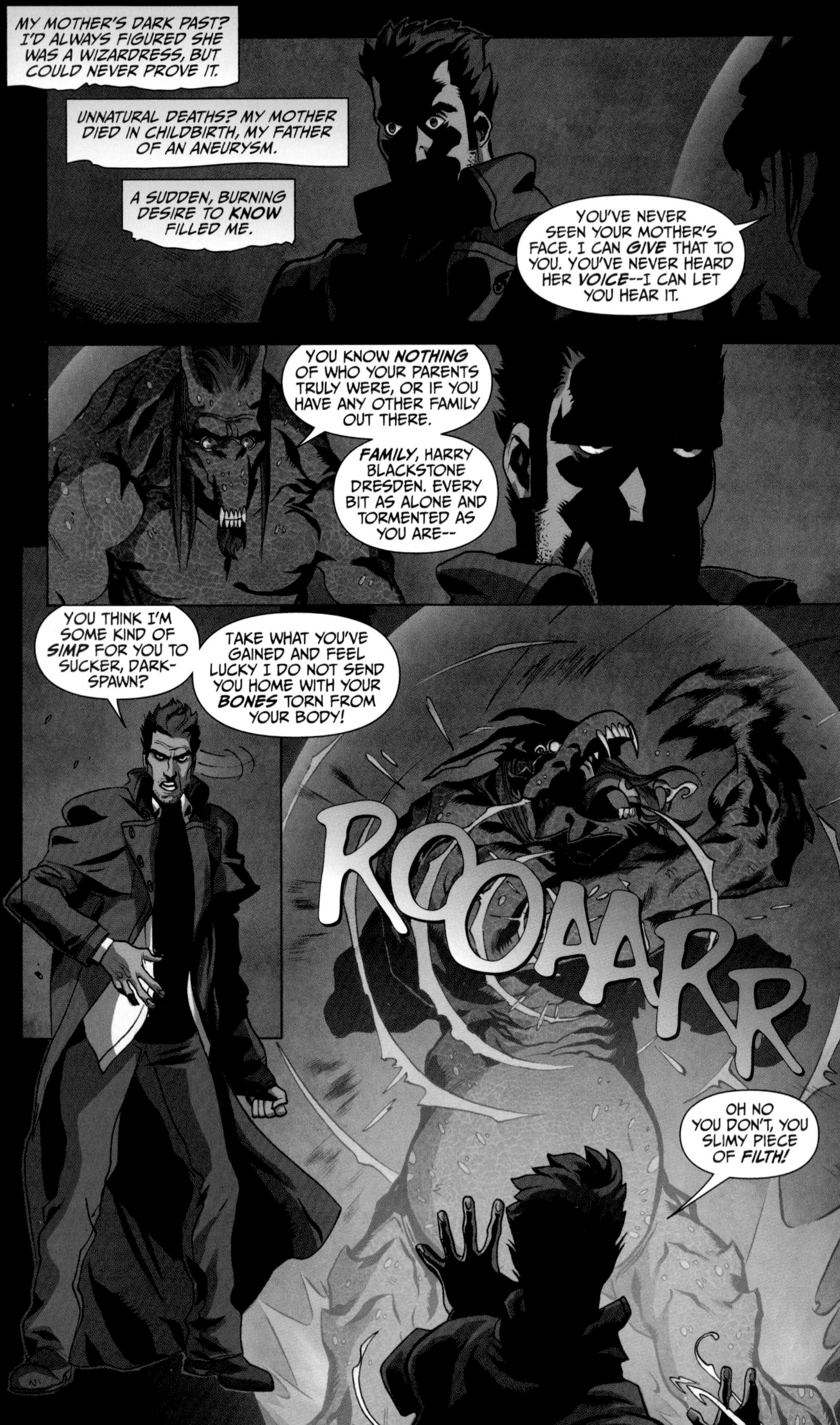
MY MOTHER'S DARK PAST? I'D ALWAYS FIGURED SHE WAS A WIZARDRESS, BUT COULD NEVER PROVE IT.
UNNATURAL DEATHS? MY MOTHER DIED IN CHILDBIRTH, MY FATHER OF AN ANEURYSM.
A SUDDEN, BURNING DESIRE TO KNOW FILLED ME.
YOU'VE NEVER SEEN YOUR MOTHER'S FACE. I CAN GIVE THAT TO YOU. YOU'VE NEVER HEARD HER VOICE--I CAN LET YOU HEAR IT.
YOU KNOW NOTHING OF WHO YOUR PARENTS TRULY WERE, OR IF YOU HAVE ANY OTHER FAMILY OUT THERE.
FAMILY, HARRY BLACKSTONE DRESDEN. EVERY BIT AS ALONE AND TORMENTED AS YOU ARE--
YOU THINK I'M SOME KIND OF SIMP FOR YOU TO SUCKER, DARK-SPAWN?
TAKE WHAT YOU'VE GAINED AND FEEL LUCKY I DO NOT SEND YOU HOME WITH YOUR BONES TORN FROM YOUR BODY!
ROOOAARR
OH NO YOU DON'T, YOU SLIMY PIECE OF FILTH!

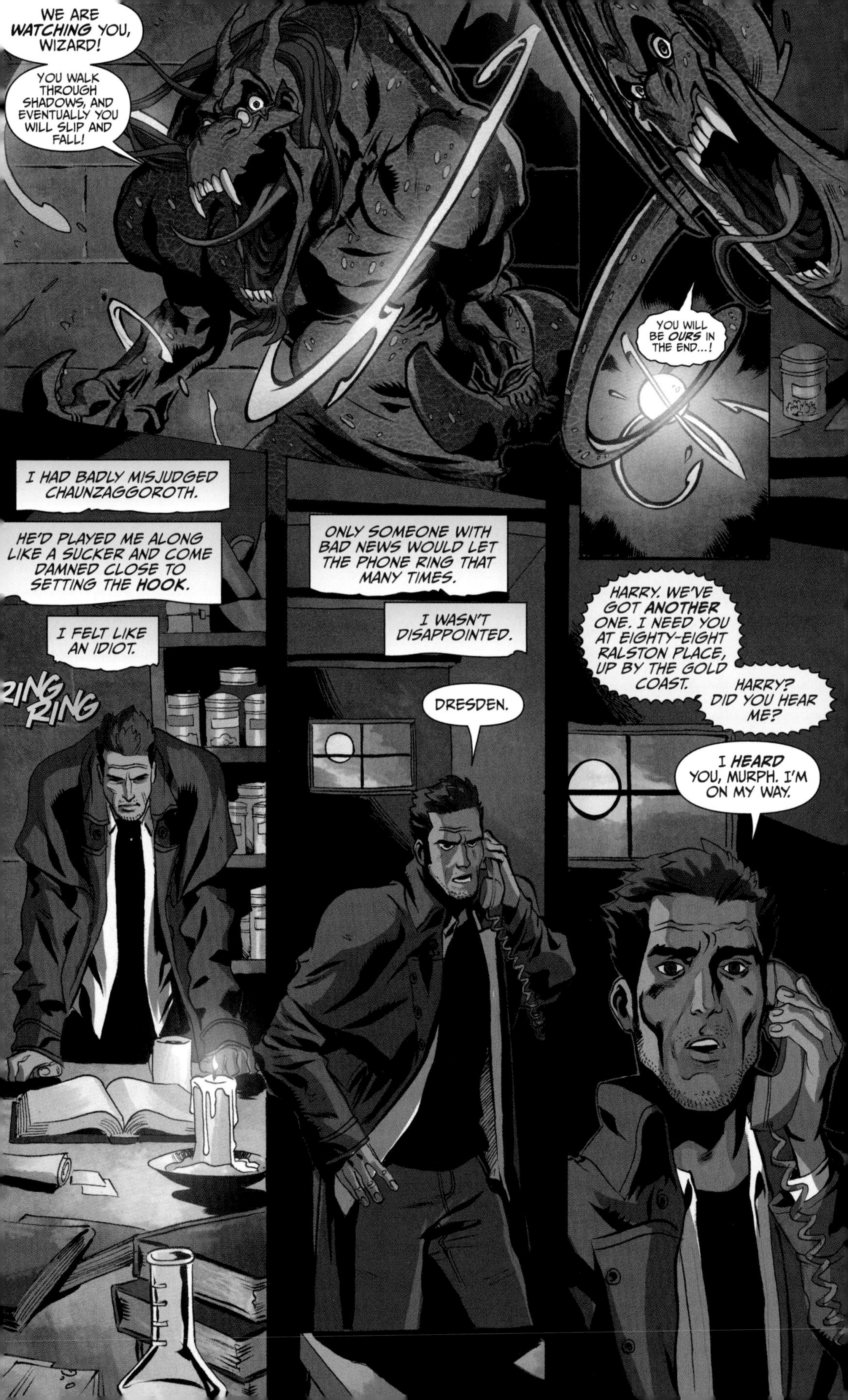
WE ARE WATCHING YOU, WIZARD!
YOU WALK THROUGH SHADOWS, AND EVENTUALLY YOU WILL SLIP AND FALL!
YOU WILL BE OURS IN THE END...!
I HAD BADLY MISJUDGED CHAUNZAGGOROTH.
HE'D PLAYED ME ALONG LIKE A SUCKER AND COME DAMNED CLOSE TO SETTING THE HOOK.
I FELT LIKE AN IDIOT.
RING RING
ONLY SOMEONE WITH BAD NEWS WOULD LET THE PHONE RING THAT MANY TIMES.
I WASN'T DISAPPOINTED.
DRESDEN.
HARRY. WE'VE GOT ANOTHER ONE. I NEED YOU AT EIGHTY-EIGHT RALSTON PLACE, UP BY THE GOLD COAST.
HARRY? DID YOU HEAR ME?
I HEARD YOU, MURPH. I'M ON MY WAY.

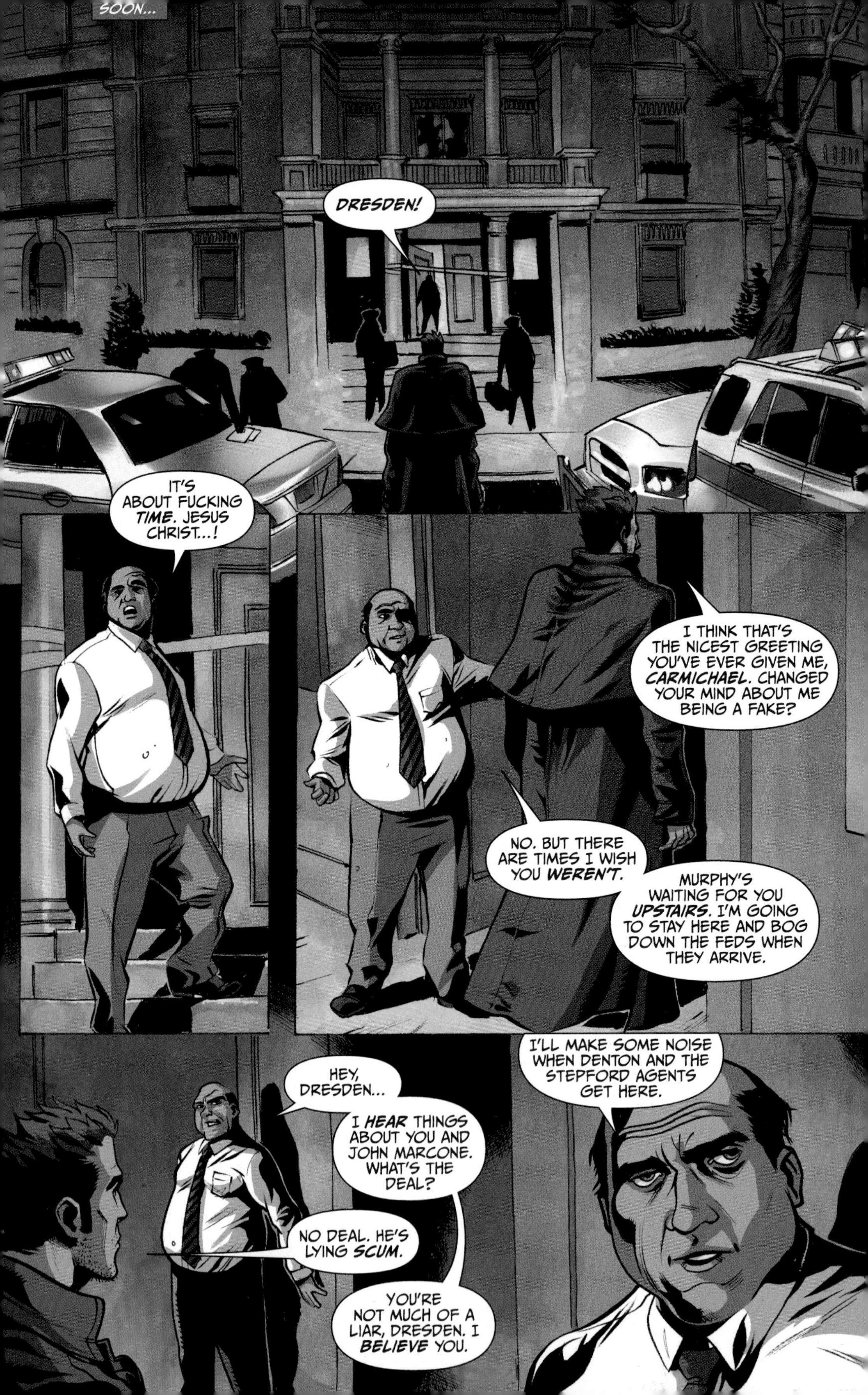
SOON...
DRESDEN!
IT'S ABOUT FUCKING TIME. JESUS CHRIST...!
I THINK THAT'S THE NICEST GREETING YOU'VE EVER GIVEN ME, CARMICHAEL. CHANGED YOUR MIND ABOUT ME BEING A FAKE?
NO. BUT THERE ARE TIMES I WISH YOU WEREN'T.
MURPHY'S WAITING FOR YOU UPSTAIRS. I'M GOING TO STAY HERE AND BOG DOWN THE FEDS WHEN THEY ARRIVE.
HEY, DRESDEN...
I HEAR THINGS ABOUT YOU AND JOHN MARCONE. WHAT'S THE DEAL?
NO DEAL. HE'S LYING SCUM.
YOU'RE NOT MUCH OF A LIAR, DRESDEN. I BELIEVE YOU.
I'LL MAKE SOME NOISE WHEN DENTON AND THE STEPFORD AGENTS GET HERE.

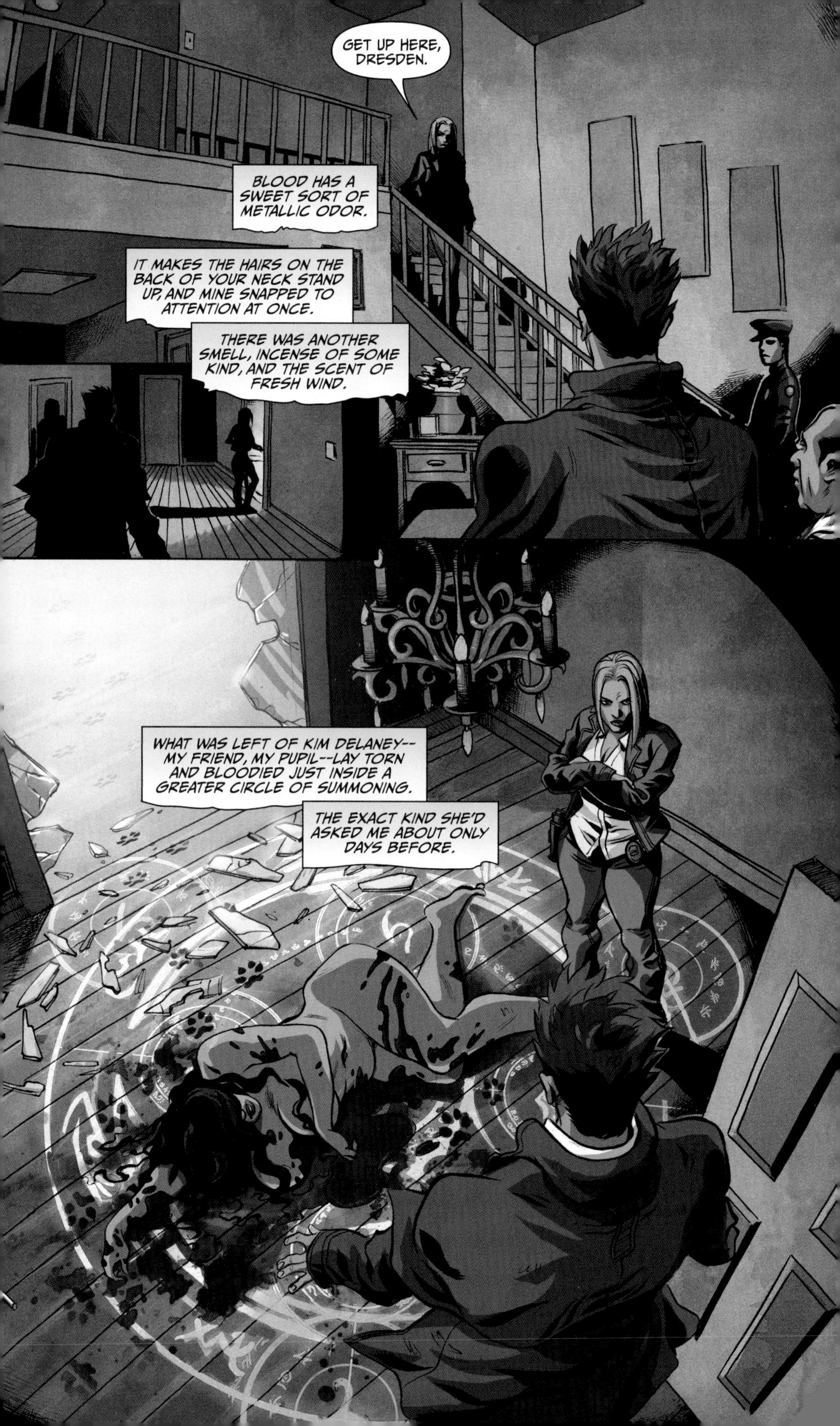
GET UP HERE, DRESDEN.
BLOOD HAS A SWEET SORT OF METALLIC ODOR.
IT MAKES THE HAIRS ON THE BACK OF YOUR NECK STAND UP, AND MINE SNAPPED TO ATTENTION AT ONCE.
THERE WAS ANOTHER SMELL, INCENSE OF SOME KIND, AND THE SCENT OF FRESH WIND.
WHAT WAS LEFT OF KIM DELANEY--MY FRIEND, MY PUPIL--LAY TORN AND BLOODIED JUST INSIDE A GREATER CIRCLE OF SUMMONING.
THE EXACT KIND SHE'D ASKED ME ABOUT ONLY DAYS BEFORE.

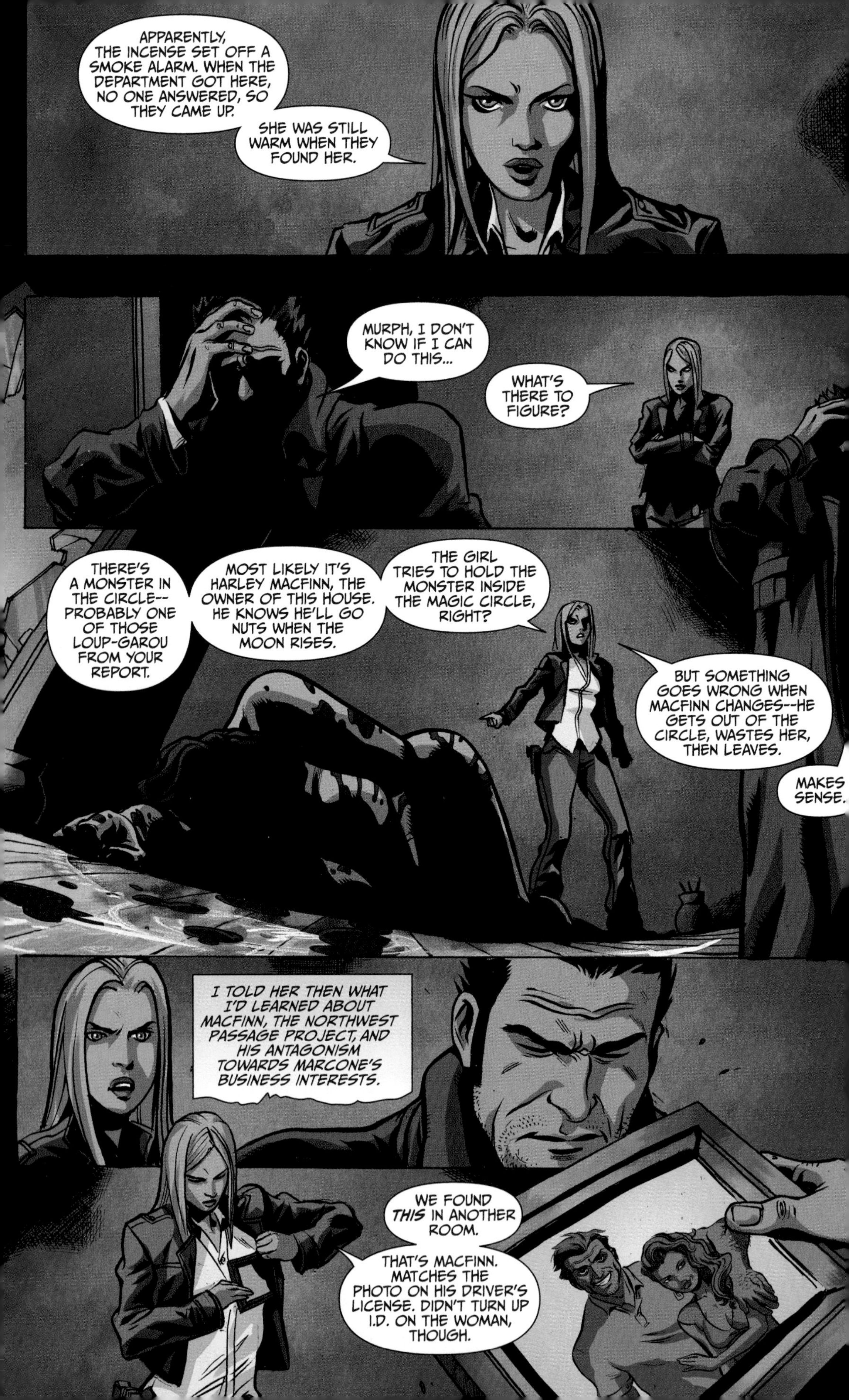
APPARENTLY, THE INCENSE SET OFF A SMOKE ALARM. WHEN THE DEPARTMENT GOT HERE, NO ONE ANSWERED, SO THEY CAME UP.
SHE WAS STILL WARM WHEN THEY FOUND HER.
MURPH, I DON'T KNOW IF I CAN DO THIS...
WHAT'S THERE TO FIGURE?
THERE'S A MONSTER IN THE CIRCLE-- PROBABLY ONE OF THOSE LOUP-GAROU FROM YOUR REPORT.
MOST LIKELY IT'S HARLEY MACFINN, THE OWNER OF THIS HOUSE. HE KNOWS HE'LL GO NUTS WHEN THE MOON RISES.
THE GIRL TRIES TO HOLD THE MONSTER INSIDE THE MAGIC CIRCLE, RIGHT?
BUT SOMETHING GOES WRONG WHEN MACFINN CHANGES--HE GETS OUT OF THE CIRCLE, WASTES HER, THEN LEAVES.
MAKES SENSE.
I TOLD HER THEN WHAT I'D LEARNED ABOUT MACFINN, THE NORTHWEST PASSAGE PROJECT, AND HIS ANTAGONISM TOWARDS MARCONE'S BUSINESS INTERESTS.
WE FOUND THIS IN ANOTHER ROOM.
THAT'S MACFINN. MATCHES THE PHOTO ON HIS DRIVER'S LICENSE. DIDN'T TURN UP I.D. ON THE WOMAN, THOUGH.

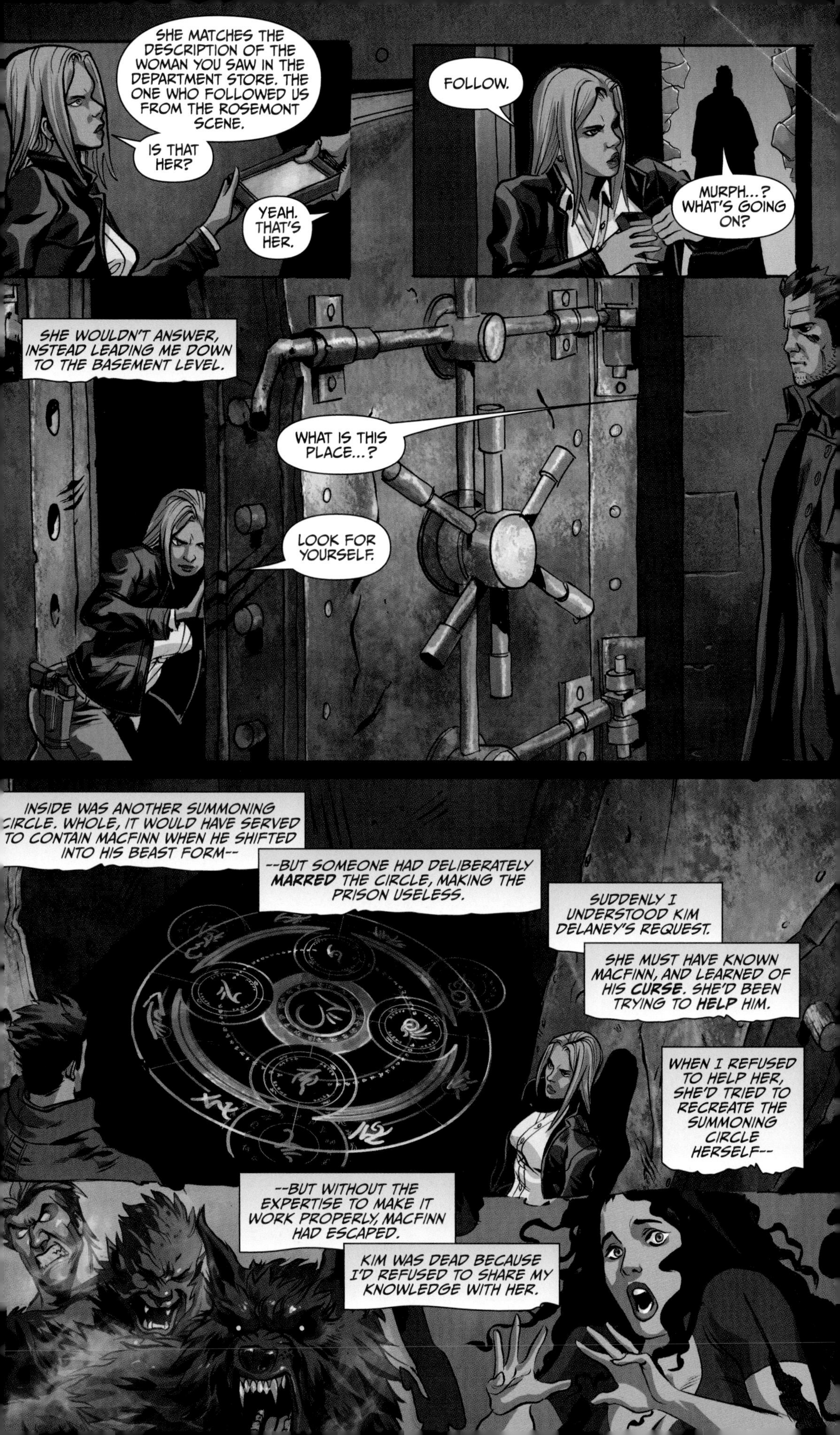
SHE MATCHES THE DESCRIPTION OF THE WOMAN YOU SAW IN THE DEPARTMENT STORE. THE ONE WHO FOLLOWED US FROM THE ROSEMONT SCENE.
IS THAT HER?
YEAH. THAT'S HER.
FOLLOW.
MURPH...? WHAT'S GOING ON?
SHE WOULDN'T ANSWER, INSTEAD LEADING ME DOWN TO THE BASEMENT LEVEL.
WHAT IS THIS PLACE...?
LOOK FOR YOURSELF.
INSIDE WAS ANOTHER SUMMONING CIRCLE. WHOLE, IT WOULD HAVE SERVED TO CONTAIN MACFINN WHEN HE SHIFTED INTO HIS BEAST FORM--
--BUT SOMEONE HAD DELIBERATELY MARRED THE CIRCLE, MAKING THE PRISON USELESS.
SUDDENLY I UNDERSTOOD KIM DELANEY'S REQUEST.
SHE MUST HAVE KNOWN MACFINN, AND LEARNED OF HIS CURSE. SHE'D BEEN TRYING TO HELP HIM.
WHEN I REFUSED TO HELP HER, SHE'D TRIED TO RECREATE THE SUMMONING CIRCLE HERSELF--
--BUT WITHOUT THE EXPERTISE TO MAKE IT WORK PROPERLY, MACFINN HAD ESCAPED.
KIM WAS DEAD BECAUSE I'D REFUSED TO SHARE MY KNOWLEDGE WITH HER.

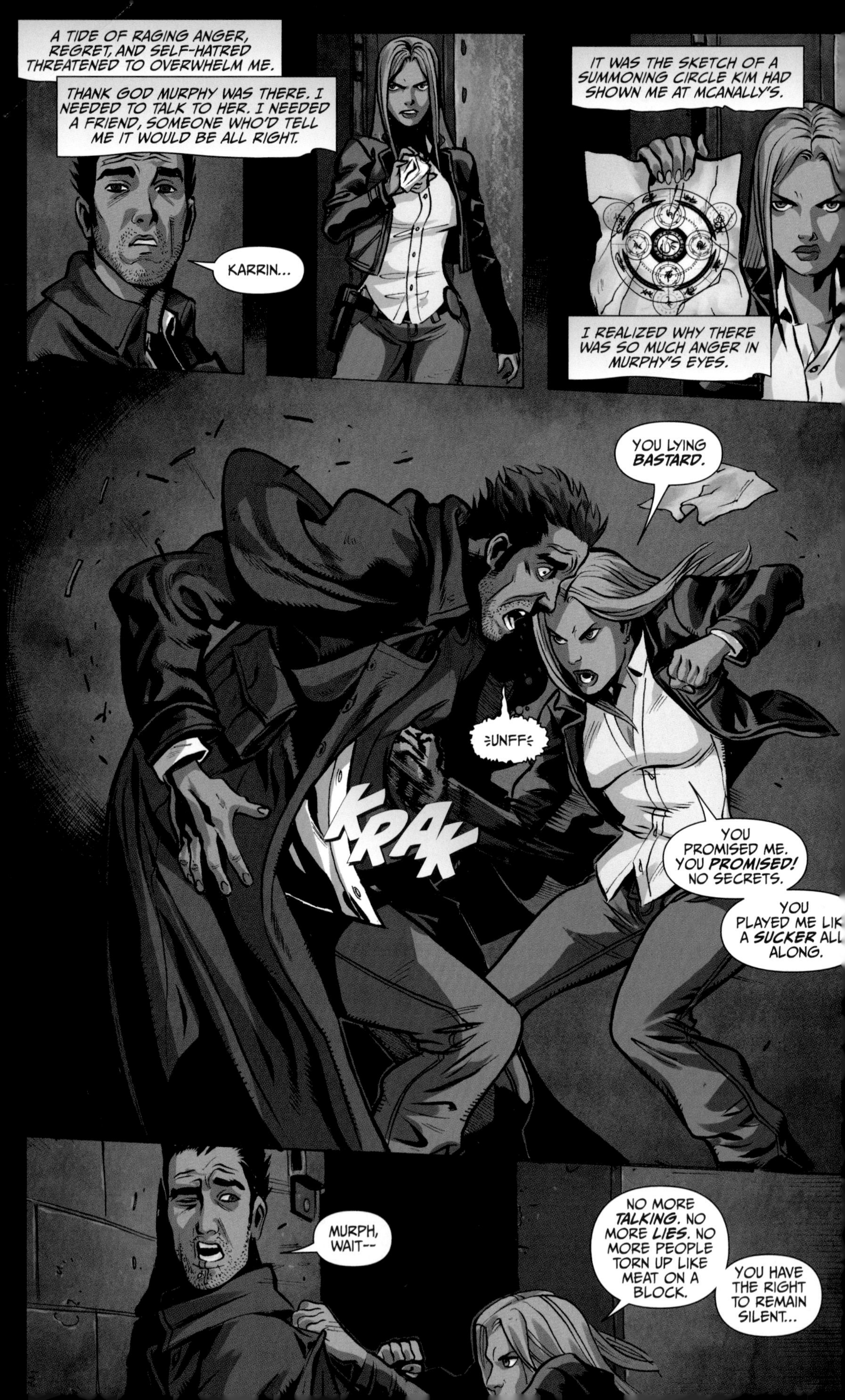
A TIDE OF RAGING ANGER, REGRET, AND SELF-HATRED THREATENED TO OVERWHELM ME.
THANK GOD MURPHY WAS THERE. I NEEDED TO TALK TO HER. I NEEDED A FRIEND, SOMEONE WHO'D TELL ME IT WOULD BE ALL RIGHT.
KARRIN...
IT WAS THE SKETCH OF A SUMMONING CIRCLE KIM HAD SHOWN ME AT MCANALLY'S.
I REALIZED WHY THERE WAS SO MUCH ANGER IN MURPHY'S EYES.
YOU LYING BASTARD.
UNFF
KRAK
YOU PROMISED ME. YOU PROMISED! NO SECRETS.
YOU PLAYED ME LIK A SUCKER ALL ALONG.
MURPH, WAIT--
NO MORE TALKING. NO MORE LIES. NO MORE PEOPLE TORN UP LIKE MEAT ON A BLOCK.
YOU HAVE THE RIGHT TO REMAIN SILENT...

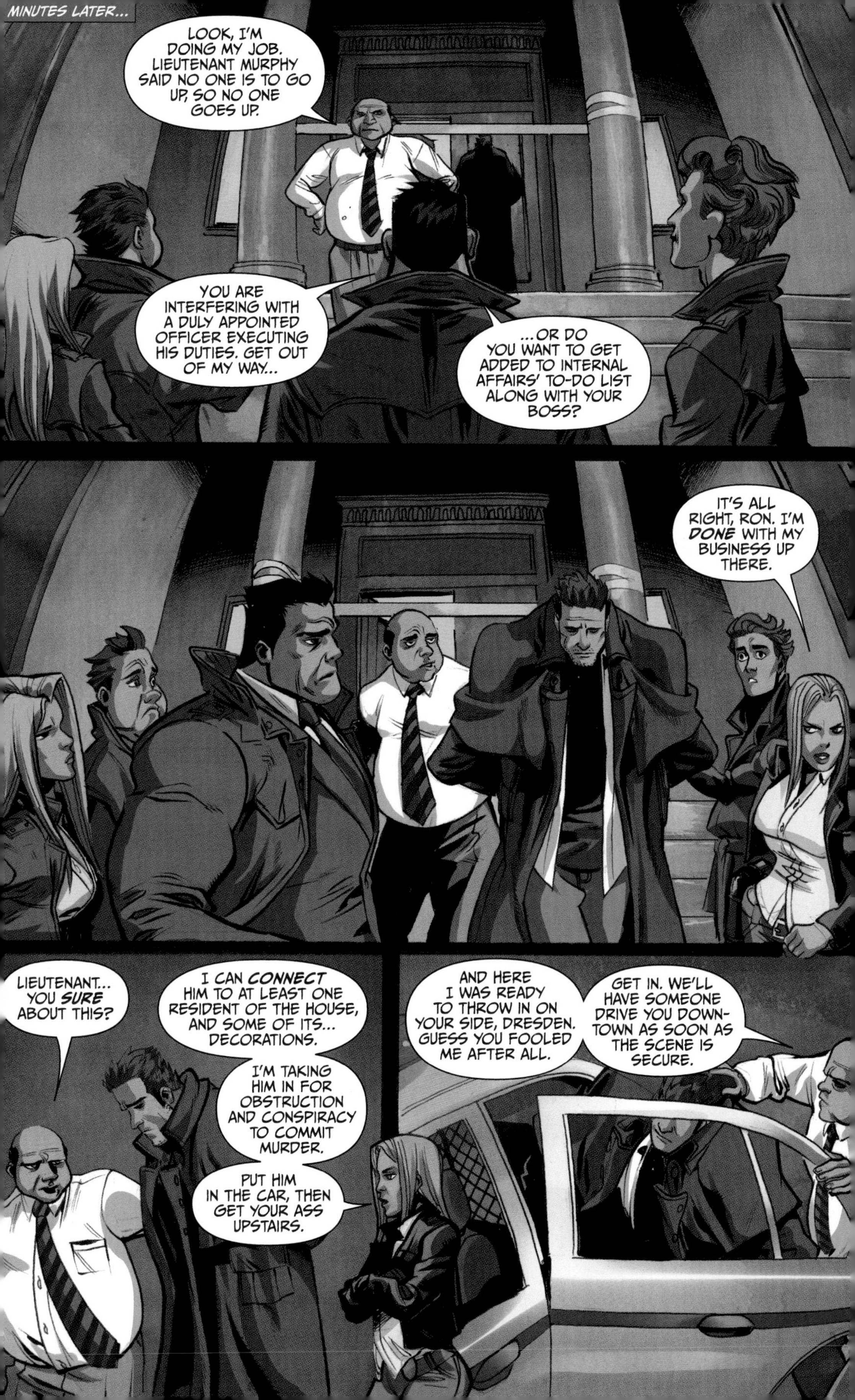
MINUTES LATER...
LOOK, I'M DOING MY JOB. LIEUTENANT MURPHY SAID NO ONE IS TO GO UP, SO NO ONE GOES UP.
YOU ARE INTERFERING WITH A DULY APPOINTED OFFICER EXECUTING HIS DUTIES. GET OUT OF MY WAY...
...OR DO YOU WANT TO GET ADDED TO INTERNAL AFFAIRS' TO-DO LIST ALONG WITH YOUR BOSS?
IT'S ALL RIGHT, RON. I'M *DONE* WITH MY BUSINESS UP THERE.
LIEUTENANT... YOU *SURE* ABOUT THIS?
I CAN *CONNECT* HIM TO AT LEAST ONE RESIDENT OF THE HOUSE, AND SOME OF ITS... DECORATIONS.
I'M TAKING HIM IN FOR OBSTRUCTION AND CONSPIRACY TO COMMIT MURDER.
PUT HIM IN THE CAR, THEN GET YOUR ASS UPSTAIRS.
AND HERE I WAS READY TO THROW IN ON YOUR SIDE, DRESDEN. GUESS YOU FOOLED ME AFTER ALL.
GET IN. WE'LL HAVE SOMEONE DRIVE YOU DOWNTOWN AS SOON AS THE SCENE IS SECURE.

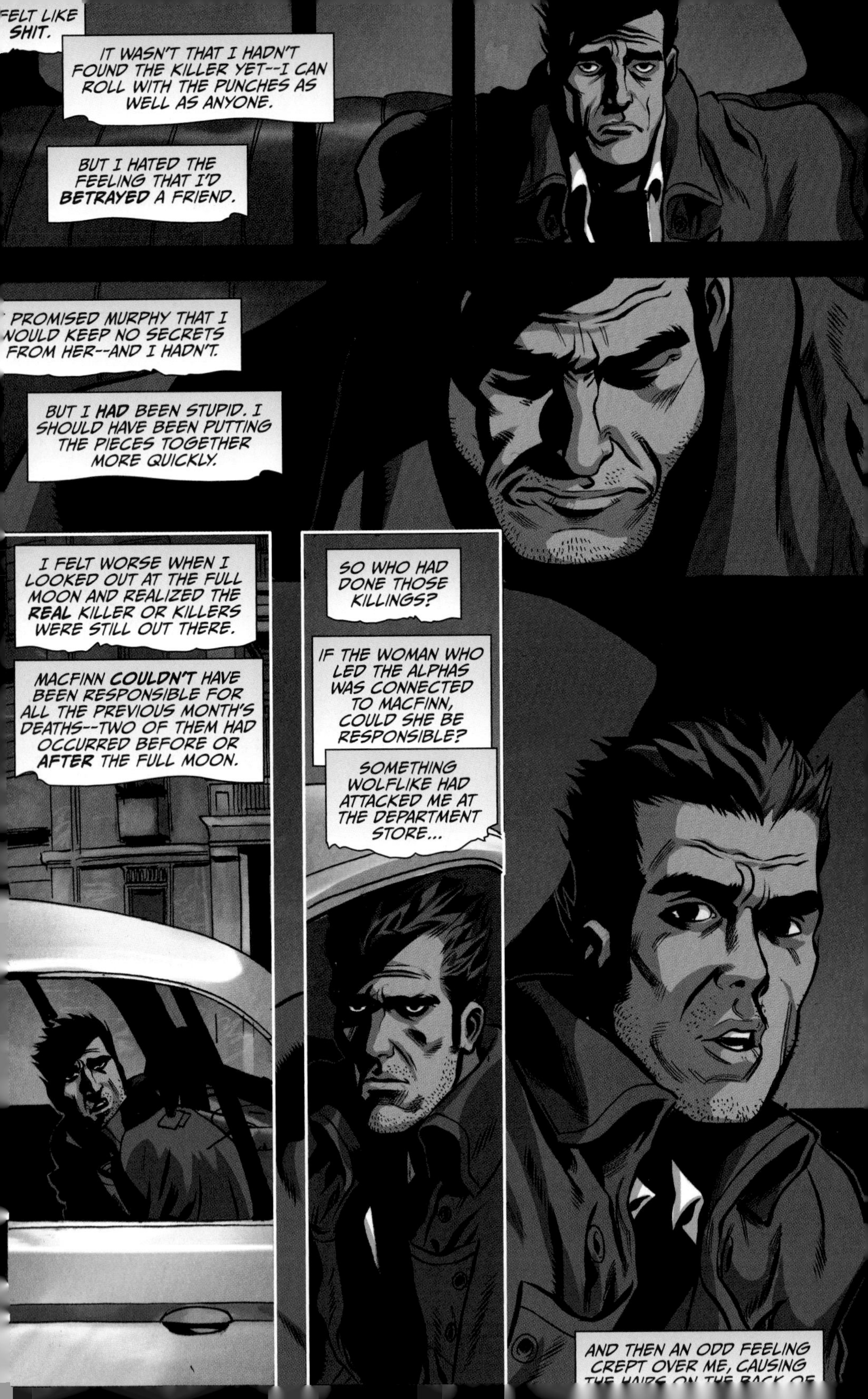
FELT LIKE SHIT.
IT WASN'T THAT I HADN'T FOUND THE KILLER YET--I CAN ROLL WITH THE PUNCHES AS WELL AS ANYONE.
BUT I HATED THE FEELING THAT I'D BETRAYED A FRIEND.
PROMISED MURPHY THAT I WOULD KEEP NO SECRETS FROM HER--AND I HADN'T.
BUT I HAD BEEN STUPID. I SHOULD HAVE BEEN PUTTING THE PIECES TOGETHER MORE QUICKLY.
I FELT WORSE WHEN I LOOKED OUT AT THE FULL MOON AND REALIZED THE REAL KILLER OR KILLERS WERE STILL OUT THERE.
MACFINN COULDN'T HAVE BEEN RESPONSIBLE FOR ALL THE PREVIOUS MONTH'S DEATHS--TWO OF THEM HAD OCCURRED BEFORE OR AFTER THE FULL MOON.
SO WHO HAD DONE THOSE KILLINGS?
IF THE WOMAN WHO LED THE ALPHAS WAS CONNECTED TO MACFINN, COULD SHE BE RESPONSIBLE?
SOMETHING WOLFLIKE HAD ATTACKED ME AT THE DEPARTMENT STORE...
AND THEN AN ODD FEELING CREPT OVER ME, CAUSING

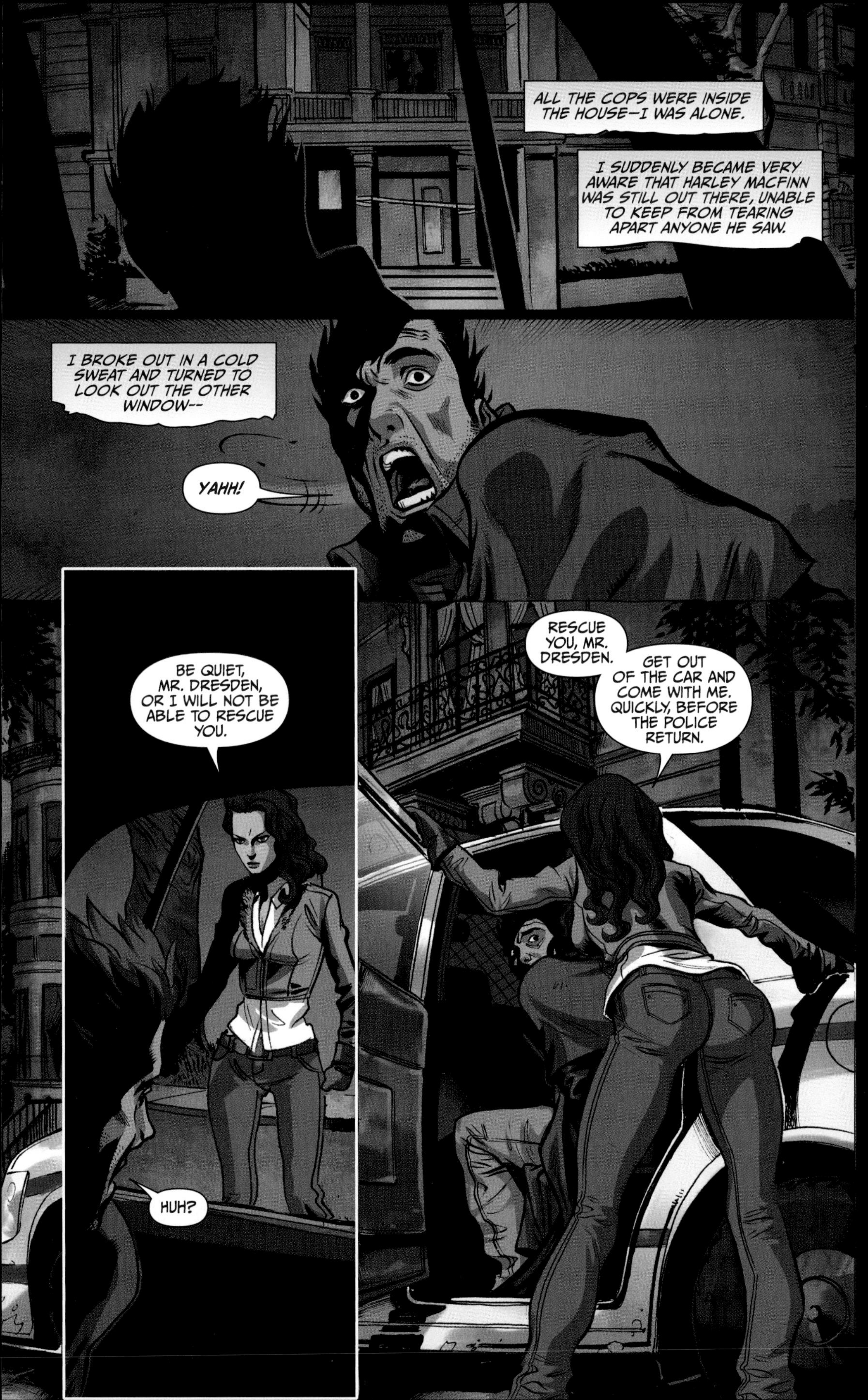
ALL THE COPS WERE INSIDE THE HOUSE—I WAS ALONE.
I SUDDENLY BECAME VERY AWARE THAT HARLEY MACFINN WAS STILL OUT THERE, UNABLE TO KEEP FROM TEARING APART ANYONE HE SAW.
I BROKE OUT IN A COLD SWEAT AND TURNED TO LOOK OUT THE OTHER WINDOW--
YAHH!
BE QUIET, MR. DRESDEN, OR I WILL NOT BE ABLE TO RESCUE YOU.
HUH?
RESCUE YOU, MR. DRESDEN.
GET OUT OF THE CAR AND COME WITH ME. QUICKLY, BEFORE THE POLICE RETURN.

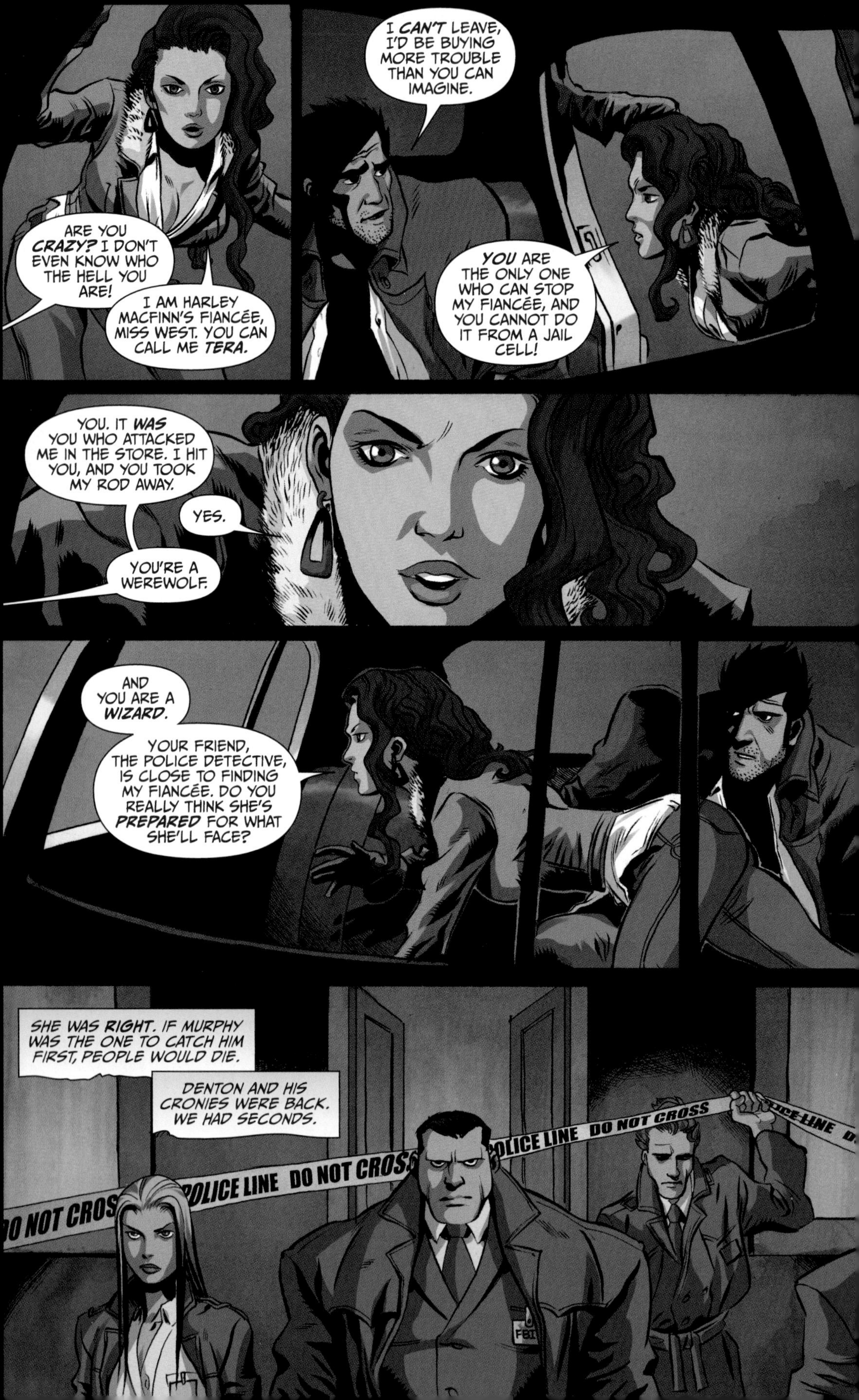
ARE YOU CRAZY? I DON'T EVEN KNOW WHO THE HELL YOU ARE!
I AM HARLEY MACFINN'S FIANCÉE, MISS WEST. YOU CAN CALL ME TERA.
I CAN'T LEAVE, I'D BE BUYING MORE TROUBLE THAN YOU CAN IMAGINE.
YOU ARE THE ONLY ONE WHO CAN STOP MY FIANCÉE, AND YOU CANNOT DO IT FROM A JAIL CELL!
YOU. IT WAS YOU WHO ATTACKED ME IN THE STORE. I HIT YOU, AND YOU TOOK MY ROD AWAY.
YES.
YOU'RE A WEREWOLF.
AND YOU ARE A WIZARD.
YOUR FRIEND, THE POLICE DETECTIVE, IS CLOSE TO FINDING MY FIANCÉE. DO YOU REALLY THINK SHE'S PREPARED FOR WHAT SHE'LL FACE?
SHE WAS RIGHT. IF MURPHY WAS THE ONE TO CATCH HIM FIRST, PEOPLE WOULD DIE.
DENTON AND HIS CRONIES WERE BACK. WE HAD SECONDS.
POLICE LINE DO NOT CROSS
DO NOT CROSS POLICE LINE DO NOT CROSS
FBI

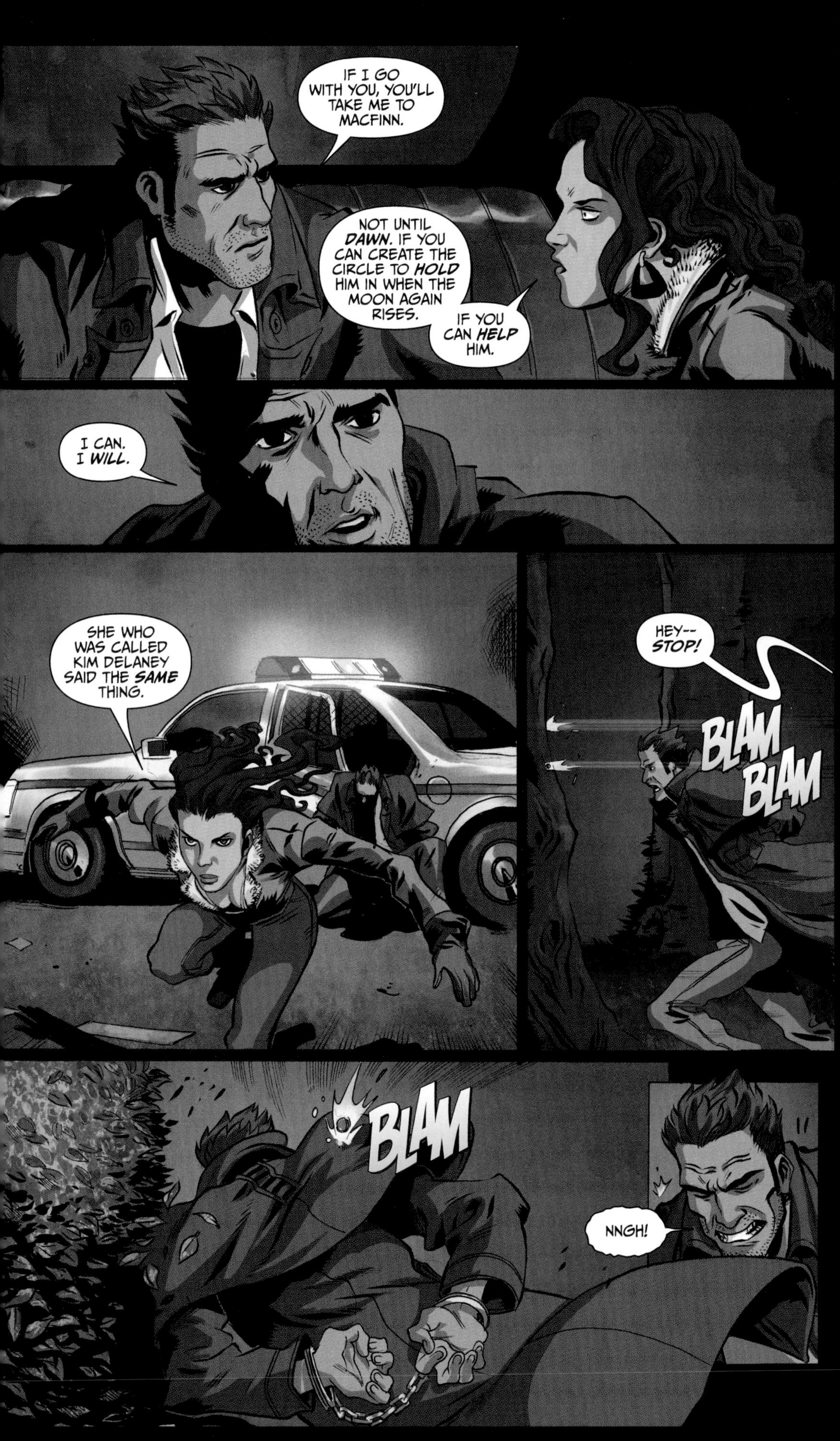
IF I GO WITH YOU, YOU'LL TAKE ME TO MACFINN.
NOT UNTIL ***DAWN.*** IF YOU CAN CREATE THE CIRCLE TO ***HOLD*** HIM IN WHEN THE MOON AGAIN RISES.
IF YOU CAN ***HELP*** HIM.
I CAN. I ***WILL.***
SHE WHO WAS CALLED KIM DELANEY SAID THE ***SAME*** THING.
HEY-- ***STOP!***
BLAM
BLAM
BLAM
NNGH!

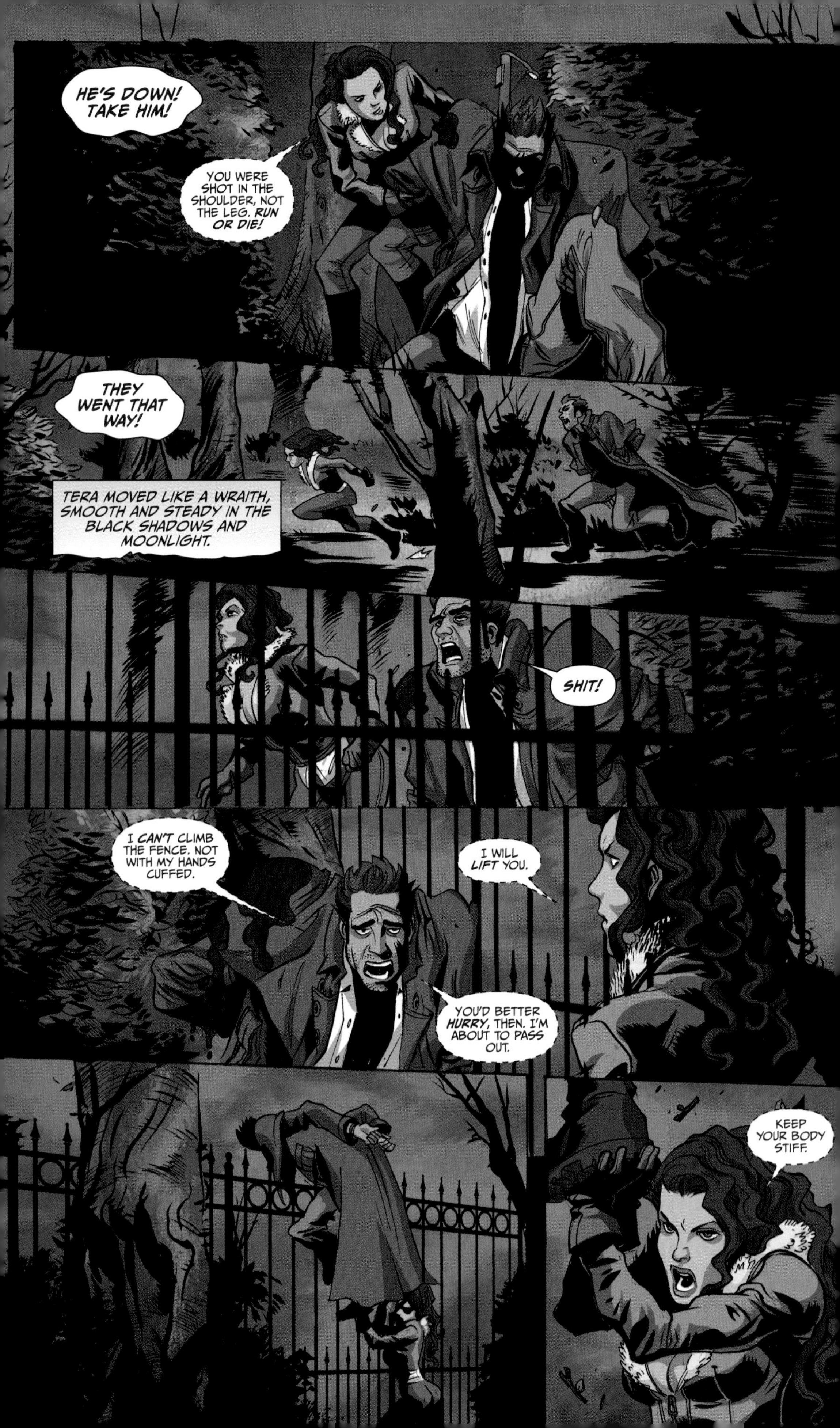

HE'S DOWN! TAKE HIM!
YOU WERE SHOT IN THE SHOULDER, NOT THE LEG. RUN OR DIE!
THEY WENT THAT WAY!
TERA MOVED LIKE A WRAITH, SMOOTH AND STEADY IN THE BLACK SHADOWS AND MOONLIGHT.
SHIT!
I CAN'T CLIMB THE FENCE. NOT WITH MY HANDS CUFFED.
I WILL LIFT YOU.
YOU'D BETTER HURRY, THEN. I'M ABOUT TO PASS OUT.
KEEP YOUR BODY STIFF.

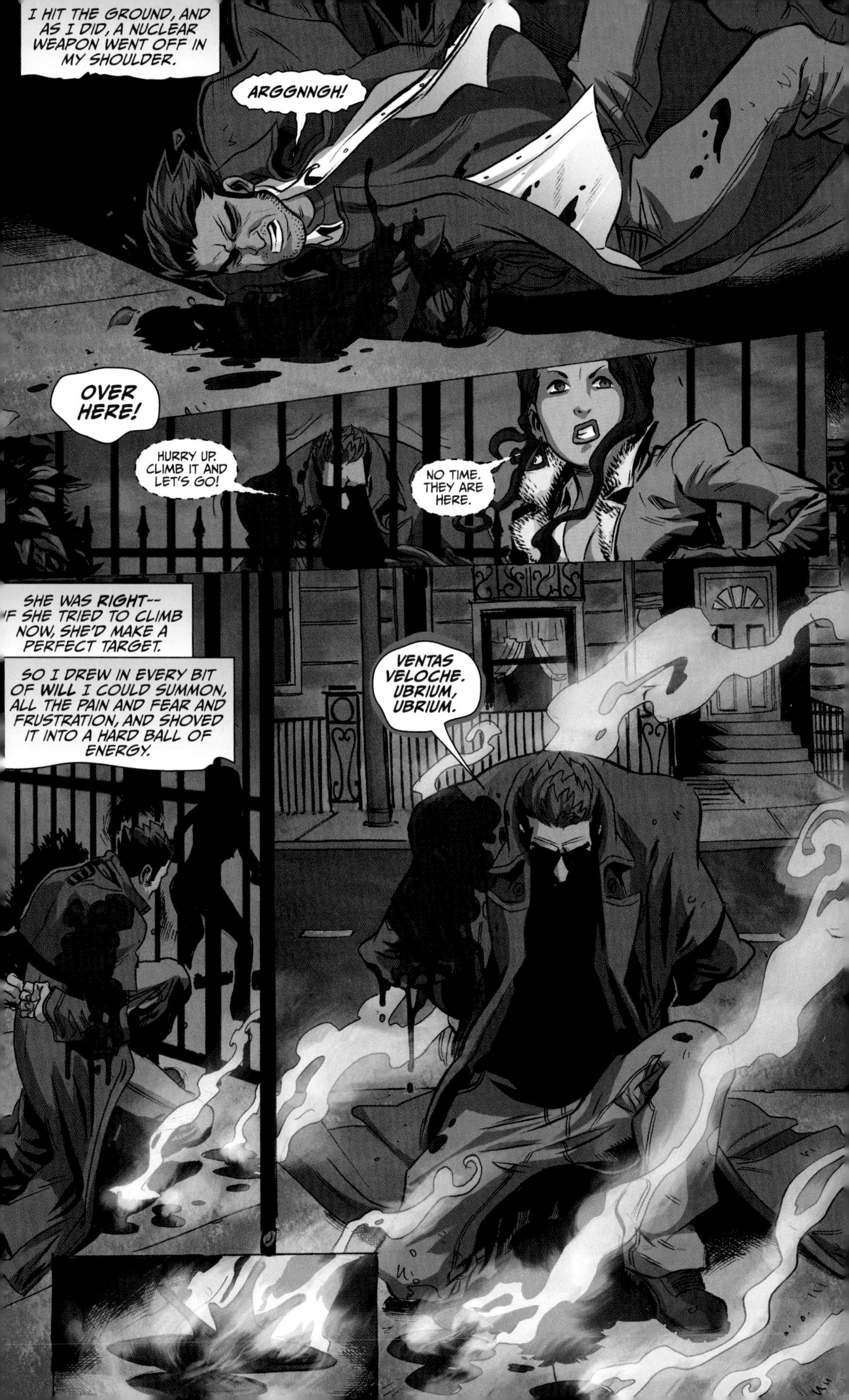
I HIT THE GROUND, AND AS I DID, A NUCLEAR WEAPON WENT OFF IN MY SHOULDER.
ARGGNNGH!
OVER HERE!
HURRY UP. CLIMB IT AND LET'S GO!
NO TIME. THEY ARE HERE.
SHE WAS RIGHT-- IF SHE TRIED TO CLIMB NOW, SHE'D MAKE A PERFECT TARGET.
SO I DREW IN EVERY BIT OF WILL I COULD SUMMON, ALL THE PAIN AND FEAR AND FRUSTRATION, AND SHOVED IT INTO A HARD BALL OF ENERGY.
VENTAS VELOCHE. UBRIUM, UBRIUM.

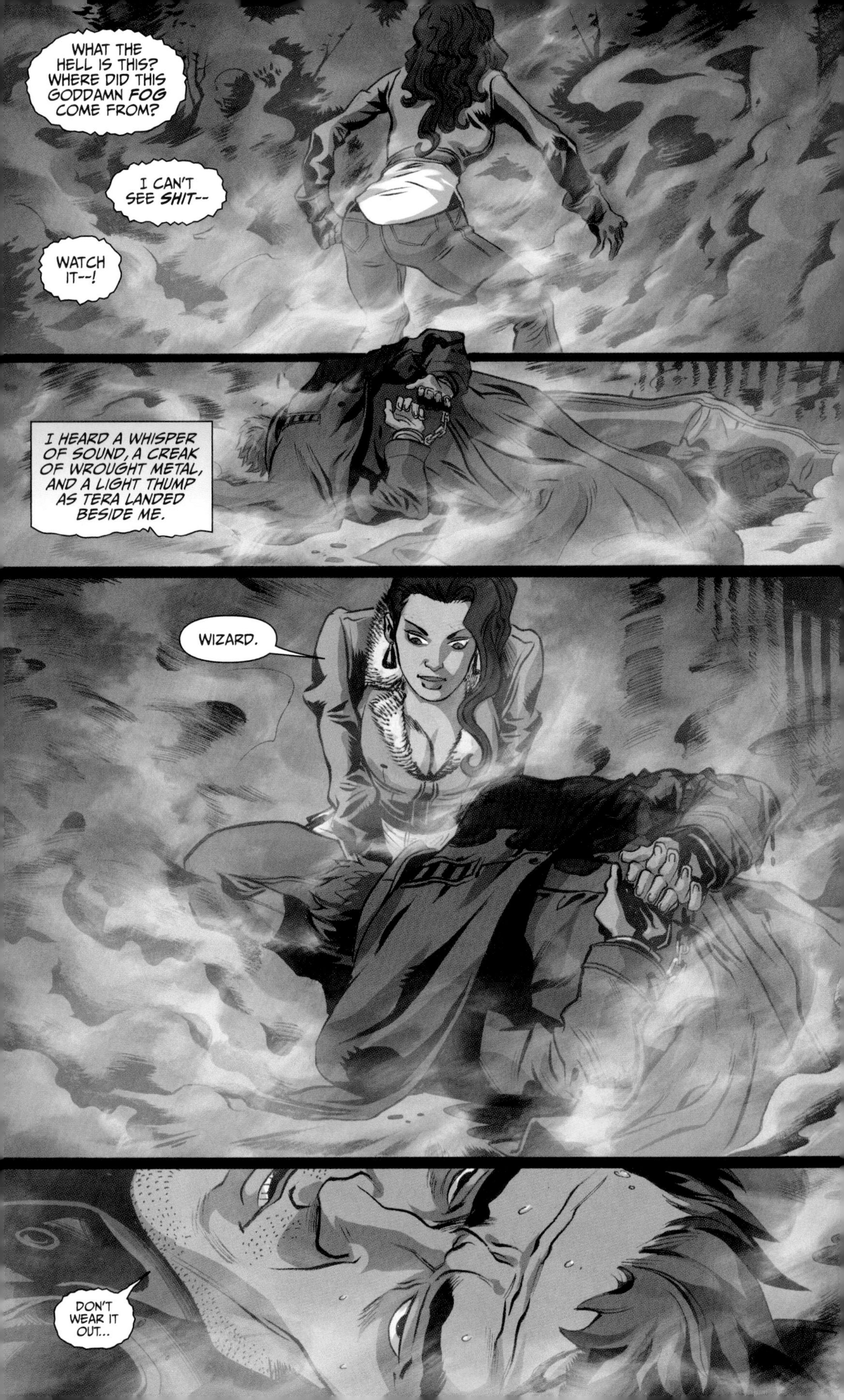
WHAT THE HELL IS THIS? WHERE DID THIS GODDAMN *FOG* COME FROM?
I CAN'T SEE *SHIT*--
WATCH IT--!
I HEARD A WHISPER OF SOUND, A CREAK OF WROUGHT METAL, AND A LIGHT THUMP AS TERA LANDED BESIDE ME.
WIZARD.
DON'T WEAR IT OUT...

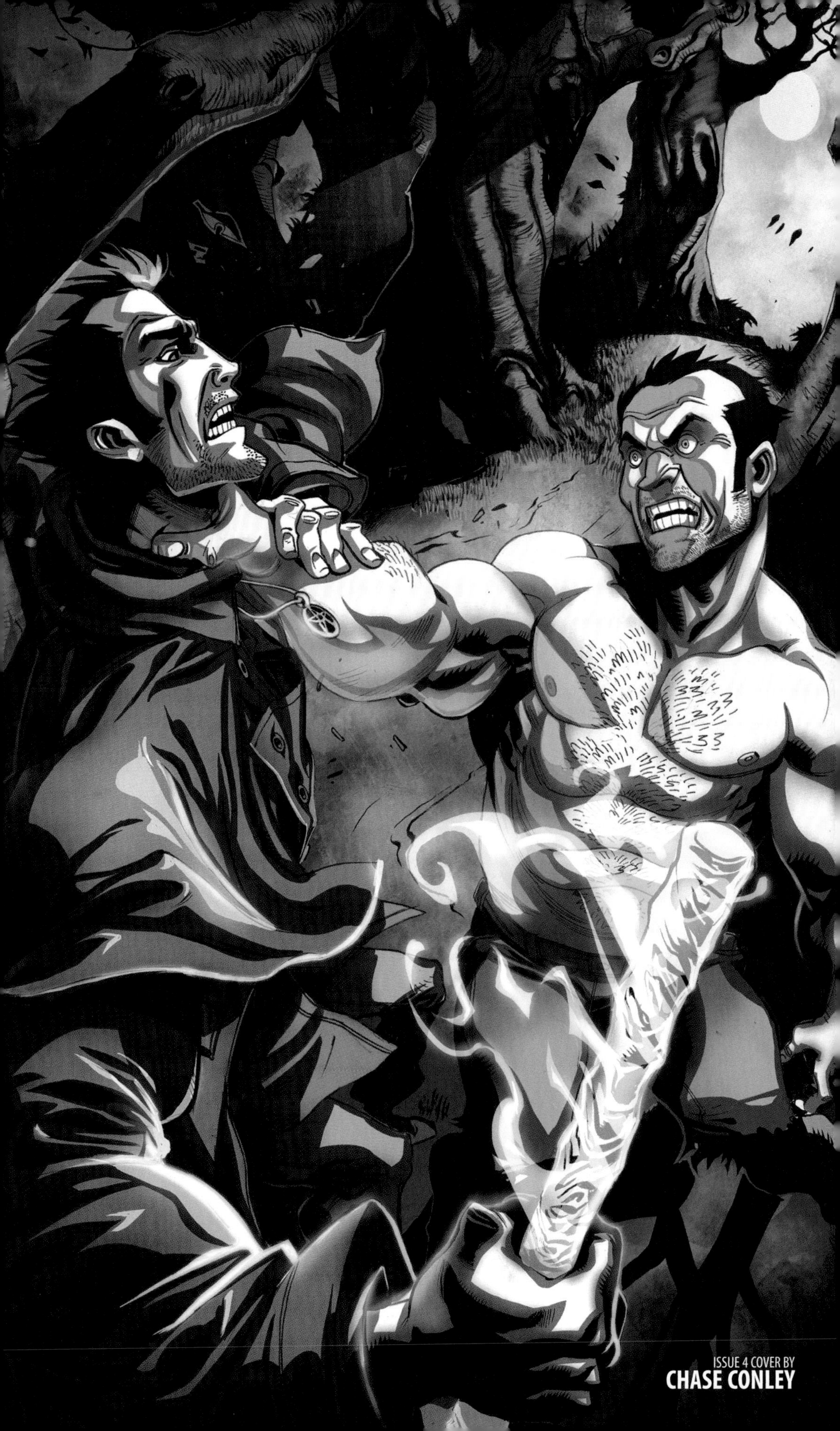

ISSUE 4 COVER BY
CHASE CONLEY

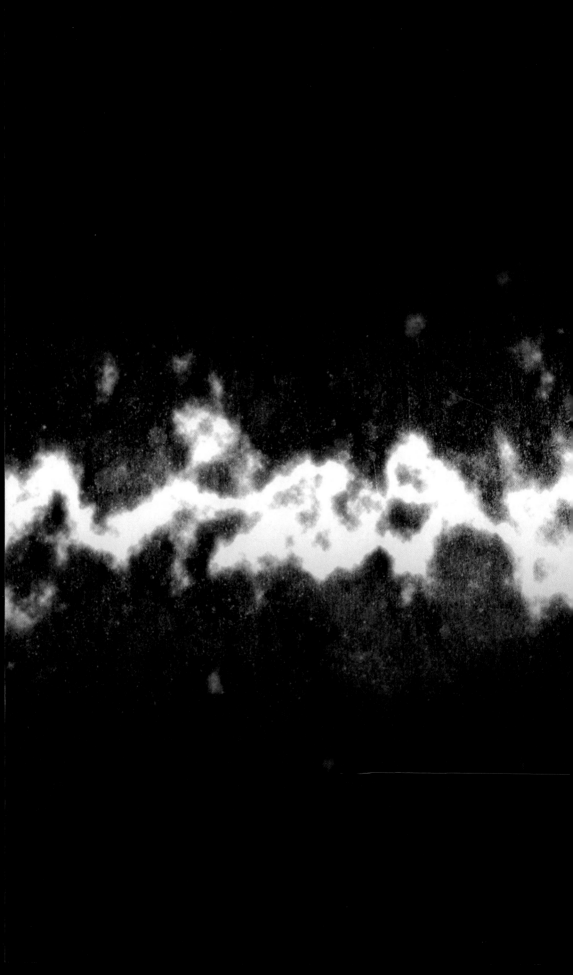

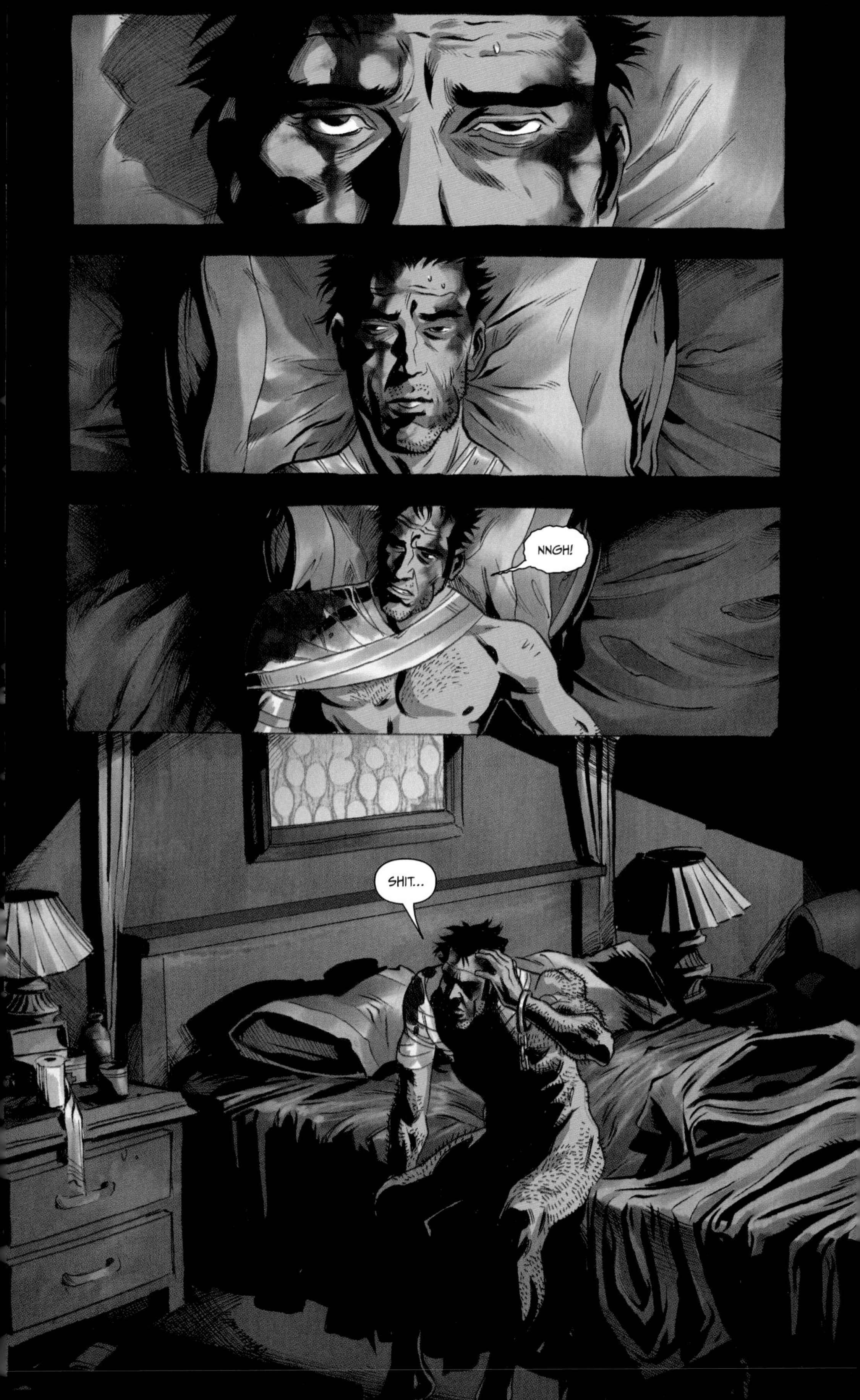
NNGH!
SHIT...

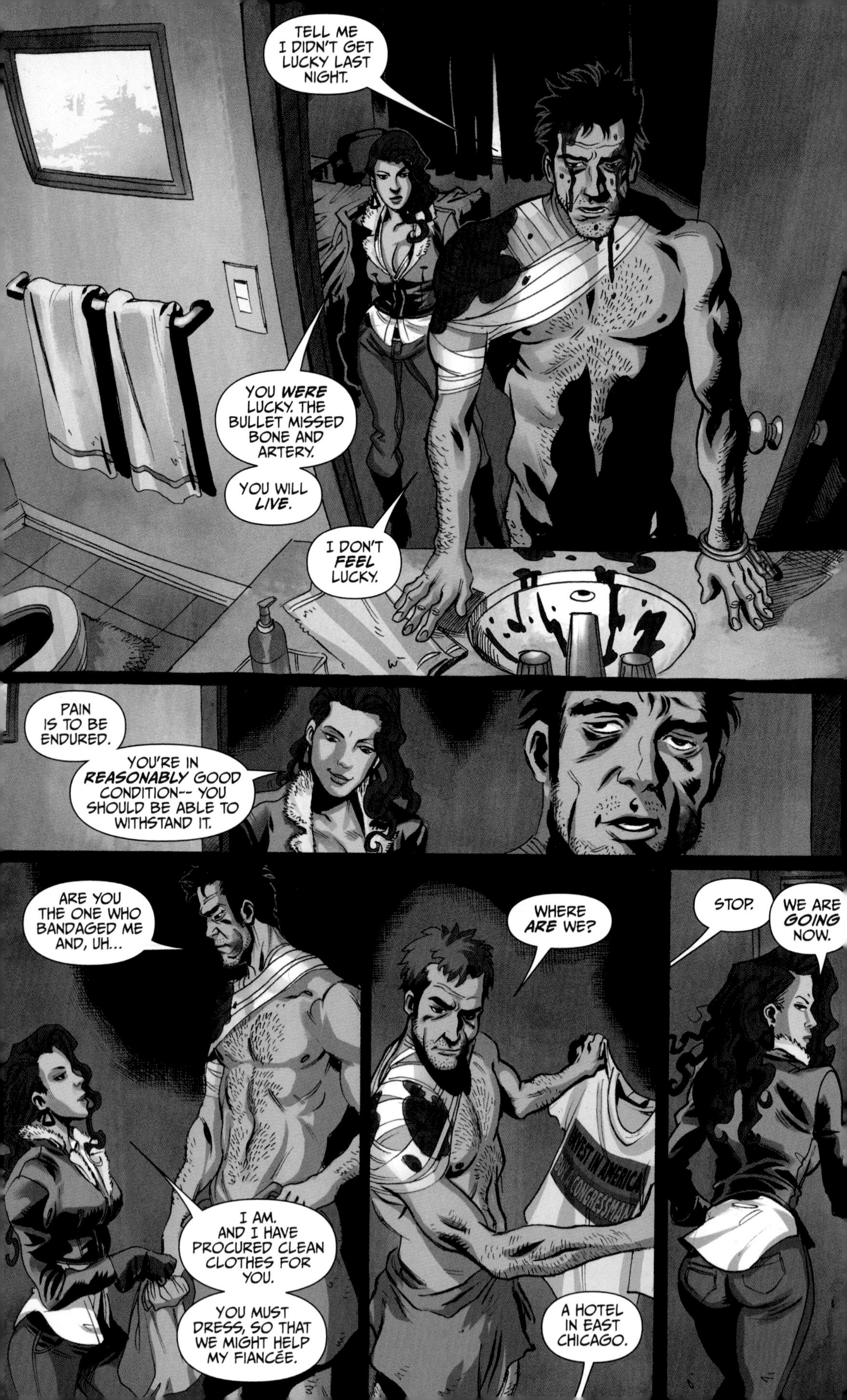
TELL ME I DIDN'T GET LUCKY LAST NIGHT.
YOU *WERE* LUCKY. THE BULLET MISSED BONE AND ARTERY.
YOU WILL *LIVE.*
I DON'T *FEEL* LUCKY.
PAIN IS TO BE ENDURED.
YOU'RE IN *REASONABLY* GOOD CONDITION-- YOU SHOULD BE ABLE TO WITHSTAND IT.
ARE YOU THE ONE WHO BANDAGED ME AND, UH...
I AM. AND I HAVE PROCURED CLEAN CLOTHES FOR YOU.
YOU MUST DRESS, SO THAT WE MIGHT HELP MY FIANCÉE.
WHERE *ARE* WE?
A HOTEL IN EAST CHICAGO.
STOP.
WE ARE *GOING* NOW.

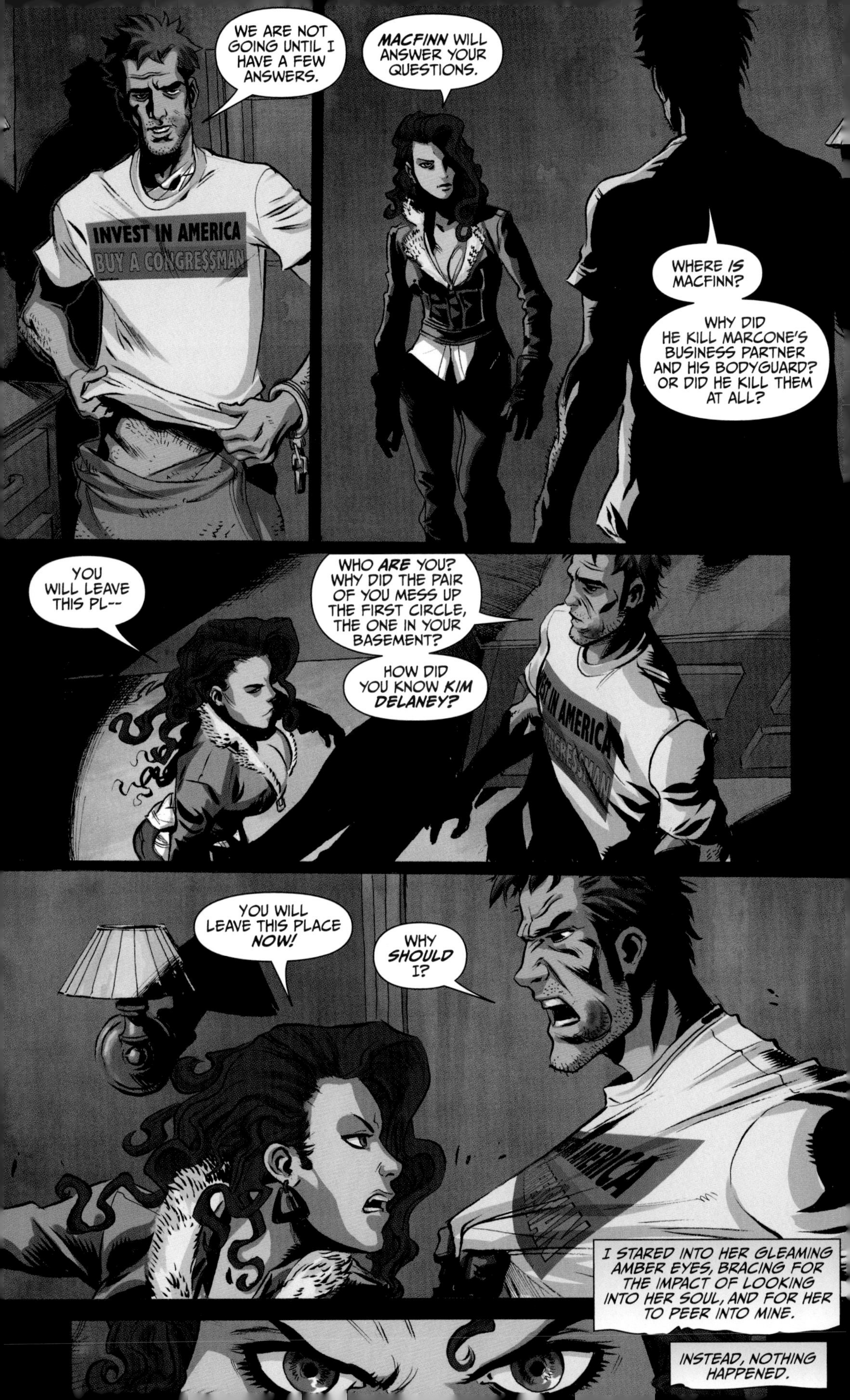

WE ARE NOT GOING UNTIL I HAVE A FEW ANSWERS.
INVEST IN AMERICA
BUY A CONGRE$$MAN
MACFINN WILL ANSWER YOUR QUESTIONS.
WHERE *IS* MACFINN?
WHY DID HE KILL MARCONE'S BUSINESS PARTNER AND HIS BODYGUARD? OR DID HE KILL THEM AT ALL?
YOU WILL LEAVE THIS PL--
WHO *ARE* YOU? WHY DID THE PAIR OF YOU MESS UP THE FIRST CIRCLE, THE ONE IN YOUR BASEMENT?
HOW DID YOU KNOW *KIM DELANEY?*
YOU WILL LEAVE THIS PLACE *NOW!*
WHY *SHOULD* I?
I STARED INTO HER GLEAMING AMBER EYES, BRACING FOR THE IMPACT OF LOOKING INTO HER SOUL, AND FOR HER TO PEER INTO MINE.
INSTEAD, NOTHING HAPPENED.

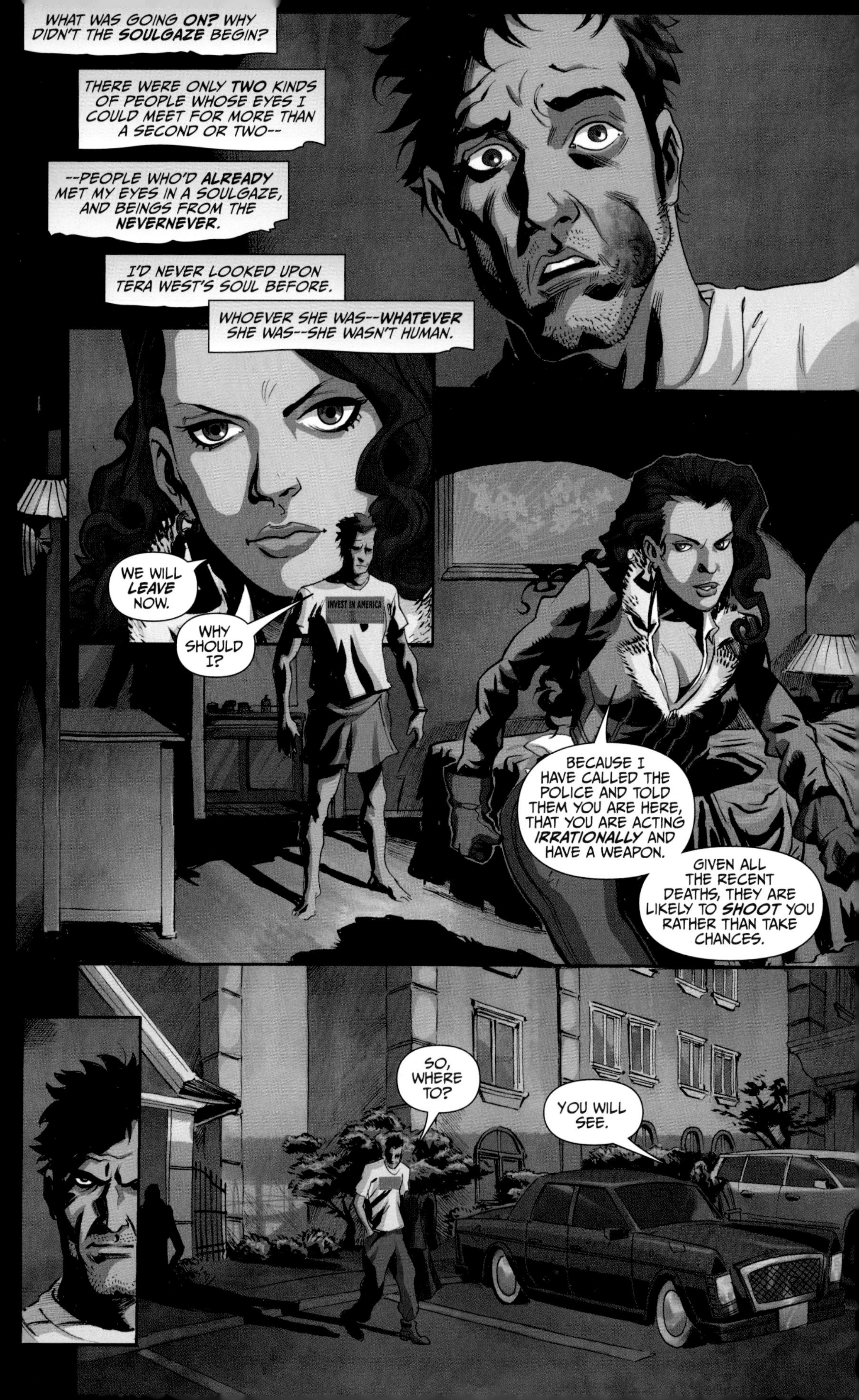
WHAT WAS GOING ON? WHY DIDN'T THE SOULGAZE BEGIN?
THERE WERE ONLY TWO KINDS OF PEOPLE WHOSE EYES I COULD MEET FOR MORE THAN A SECOND OR TWO--
--PEOPLE WHO'D ALREADY MET MY EYES IN A SOULGAZE, AND BEINGS FROM THE NEVERNEVER.
I'D NEVER LOOKED UPON TERA WEST'S SOUL BEFORE.
WHOEVER SHE WAS--WHATEVER SHE WAS--SHE WASN'T HUMAN.
WE WILL LEAVE NOW.
INVEST IN AMERICA
WHY SHOULD I?
BECAUSE I HAVE CALLED THE POLICE AND TOLD THEM YOU ARE HERE, THAT YOU ARE ACTING IRRATIONALLY AND HAVE A WEAPON.
GIVEN ALL THE RECENT DEATHS, THEY ARE LIKELY TO SHOOT YOU RATHER THAN TAKE CHANCES.
SO, WHERE TO?
YOU WILL SEE.

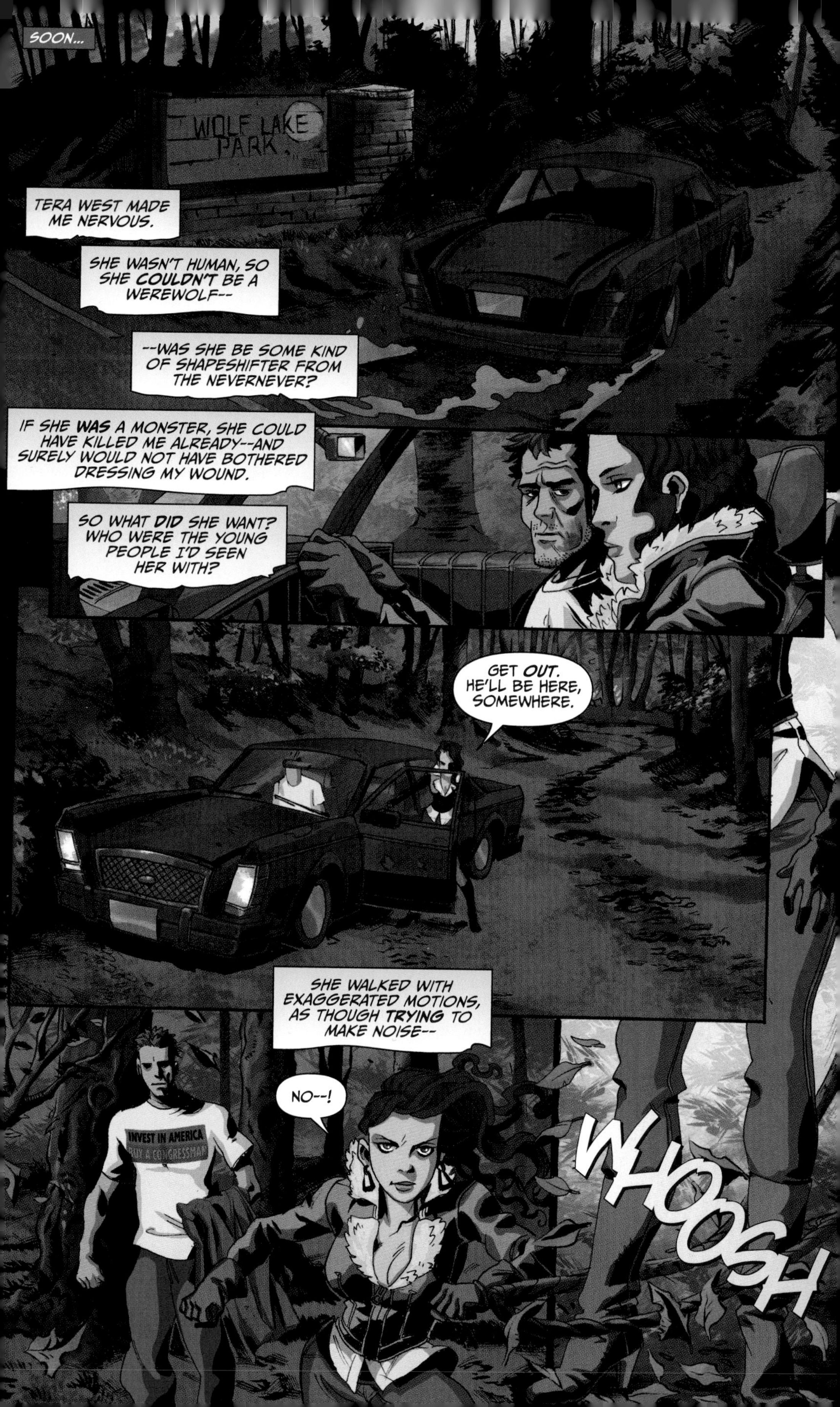
SOON...
WOLF LAKE PARK
TERA WEST MADE ME NERVOUS.
SHE WASN'T HUMAN, SO SHE COULDN'T BE A WEREWOLF--
--WAS SHE BE SOME KIND OF SHAPESHIFTER FROM THE NEVERNEVER?
IF SHE WAS A MONSTER, SHE COULD HAVE KILLED ME ALREADY--AND SURELY WOULD NOT HAVE BOTHERED DRESSING MY WOUND.
SO WHAT DID SHE WANT? WHO WERE THE YOUNG PEOPLE I'D SEEN HER WITH?
GET OUT. HE'LL BE HERE, SOMEWHERE.
SHE WALKED WITH EXAGGERATED MOTIONS, AS THOUGH TRYING TO MAKE NOISE--
NO--!
INVEST IN AMERICA
BUY A CONGRESSMAN
WHOOSH

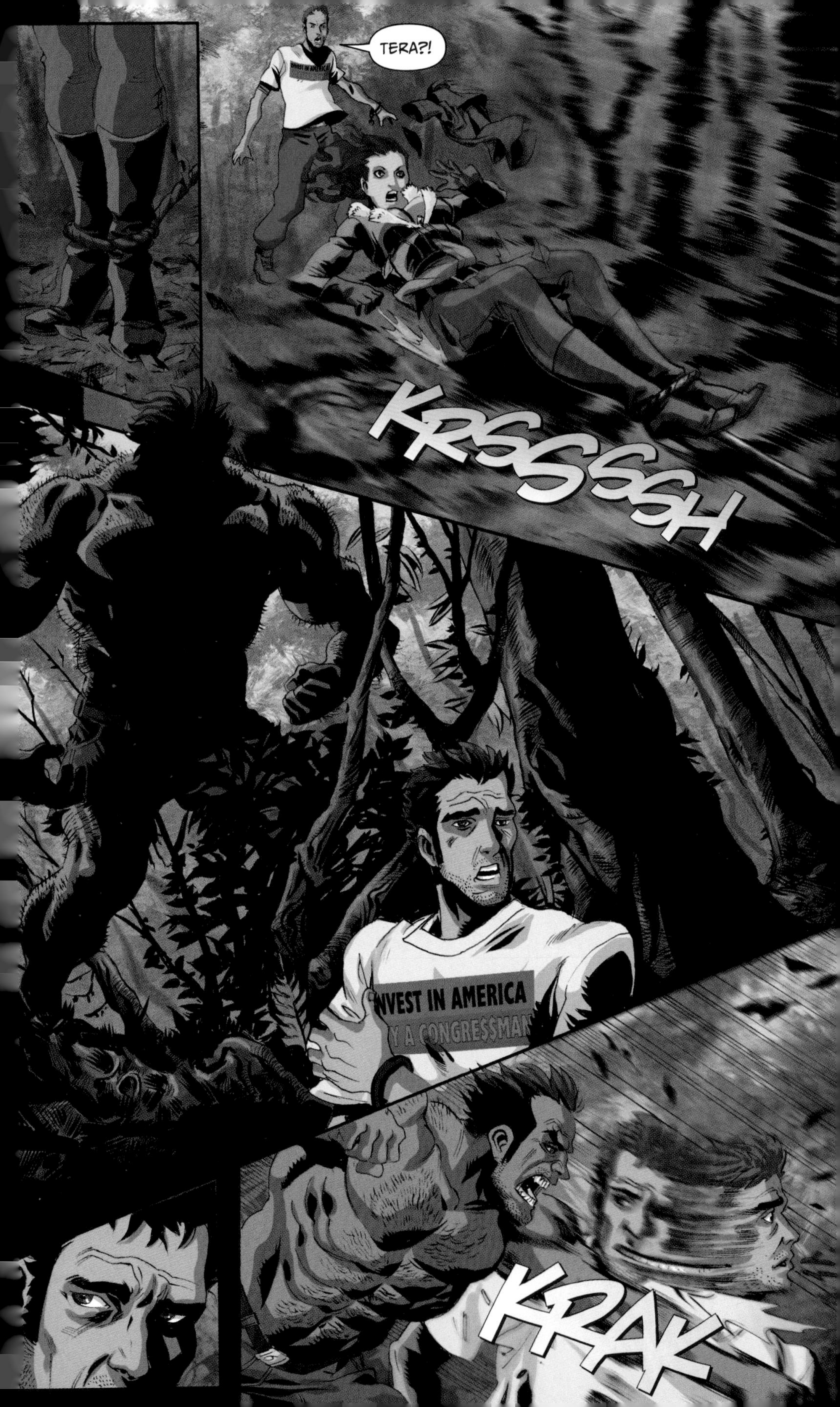
TERA?!
INVEST IN AMERICA
KRSSSSH
NVEST IN AMERICA
Y A CONGRE$$MAN
KRAK

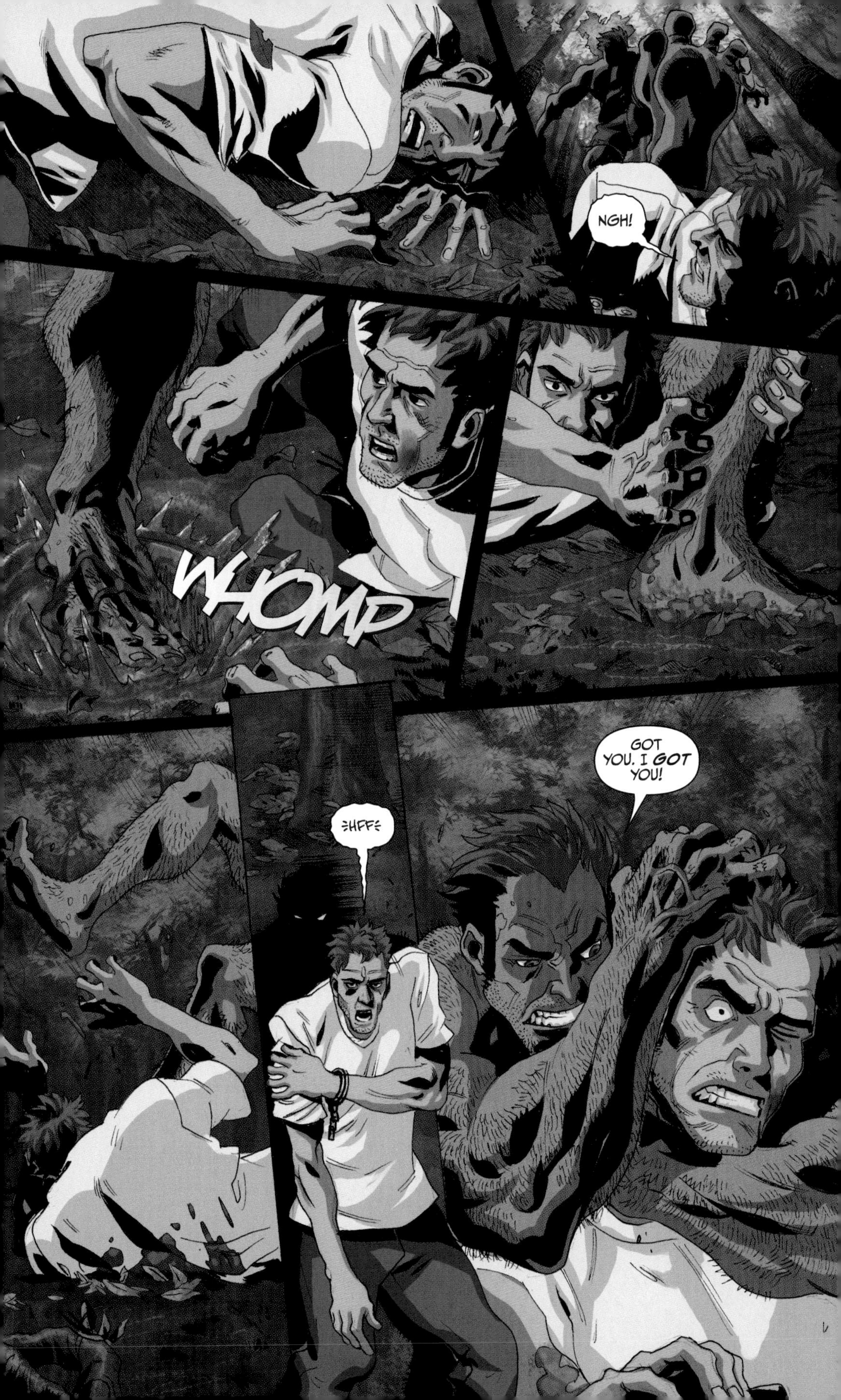
NGH!
WHOMP
HFF
GOT YOU. I GOT YOU!

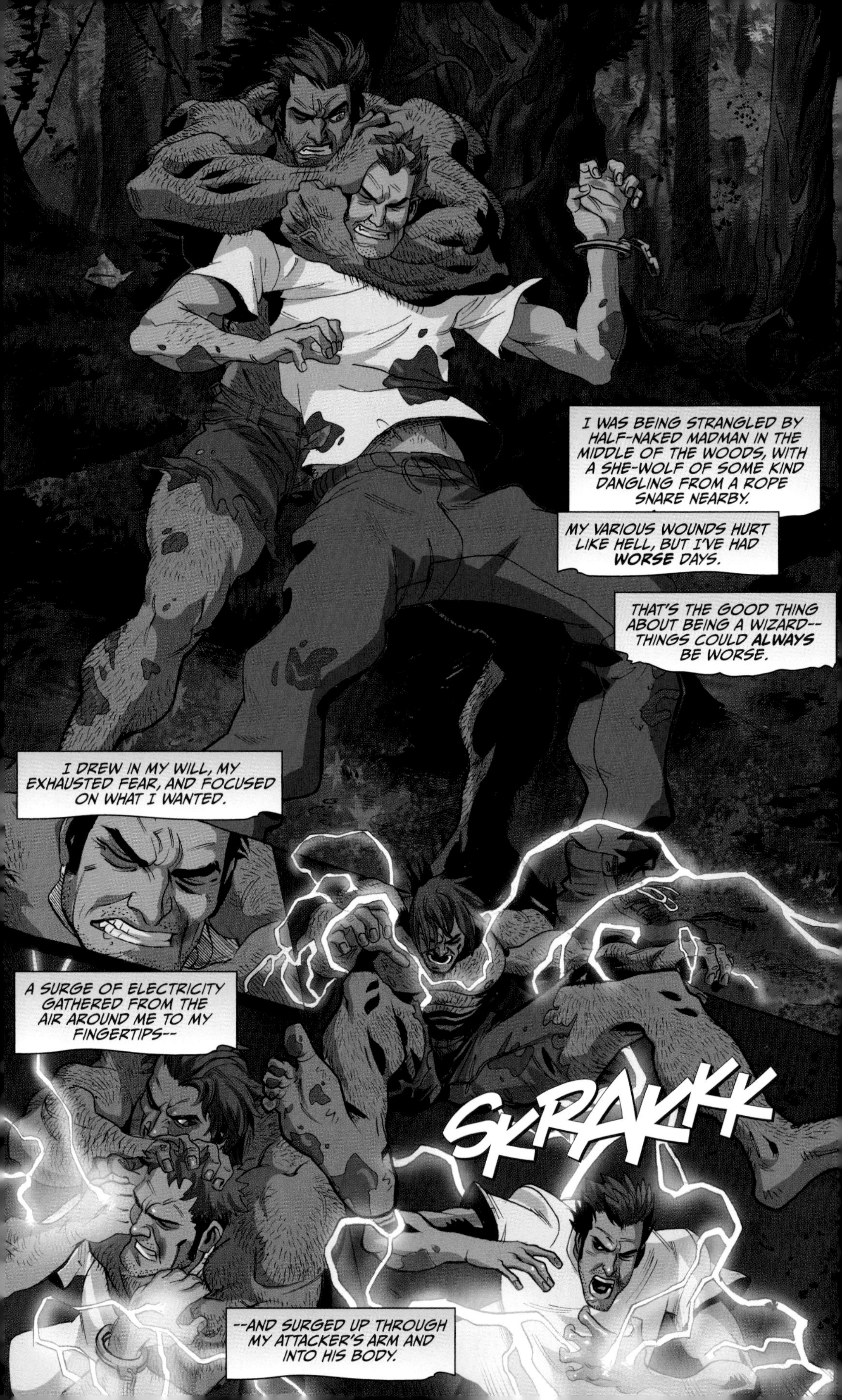
I WAS BEING STRANGLED BY HALF-NAKED MADMAN IN THE MIDDLE OF THE WOODS, WITH A SHE-WOLF OF SOME KIND DANGLING FROM A ROPE SNARE NEARBY.
MY VARIOUS WOUNDS HURT LIKE HELL, BUT I'VE HAD **WORSE** DAYS.
THAT'S THE GOOD THING ABOUT BEING A WIZARD-- THINGS COULD **ALWAYS** BE WORSE.
I DREW IN MY WILL, MY EXHAUSTED FEAR, AND FOCUSED ON WHAT I WANTED.
A SURGE OF ELECTRICITY GATHERED FROM THE AIR AROUND ME TO MY FINGERTIPS--
SKRAKKK
--AND SURGED UP THROUGH MY ATTACKER'S ARM AND INTO HIS BODY.

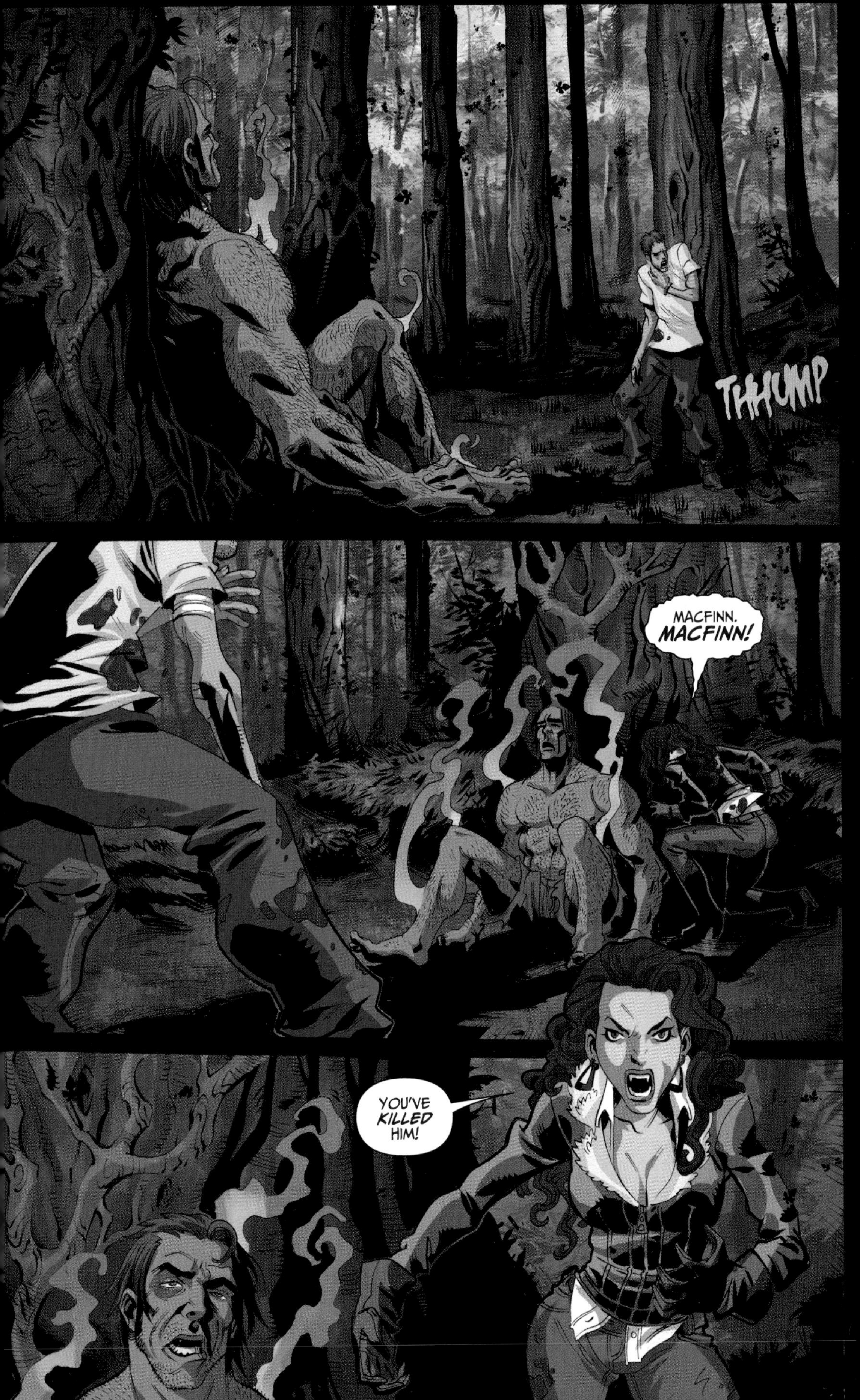
THHUMP
MACFINN. MACFINN!
YOU'VE KILLED HIM!

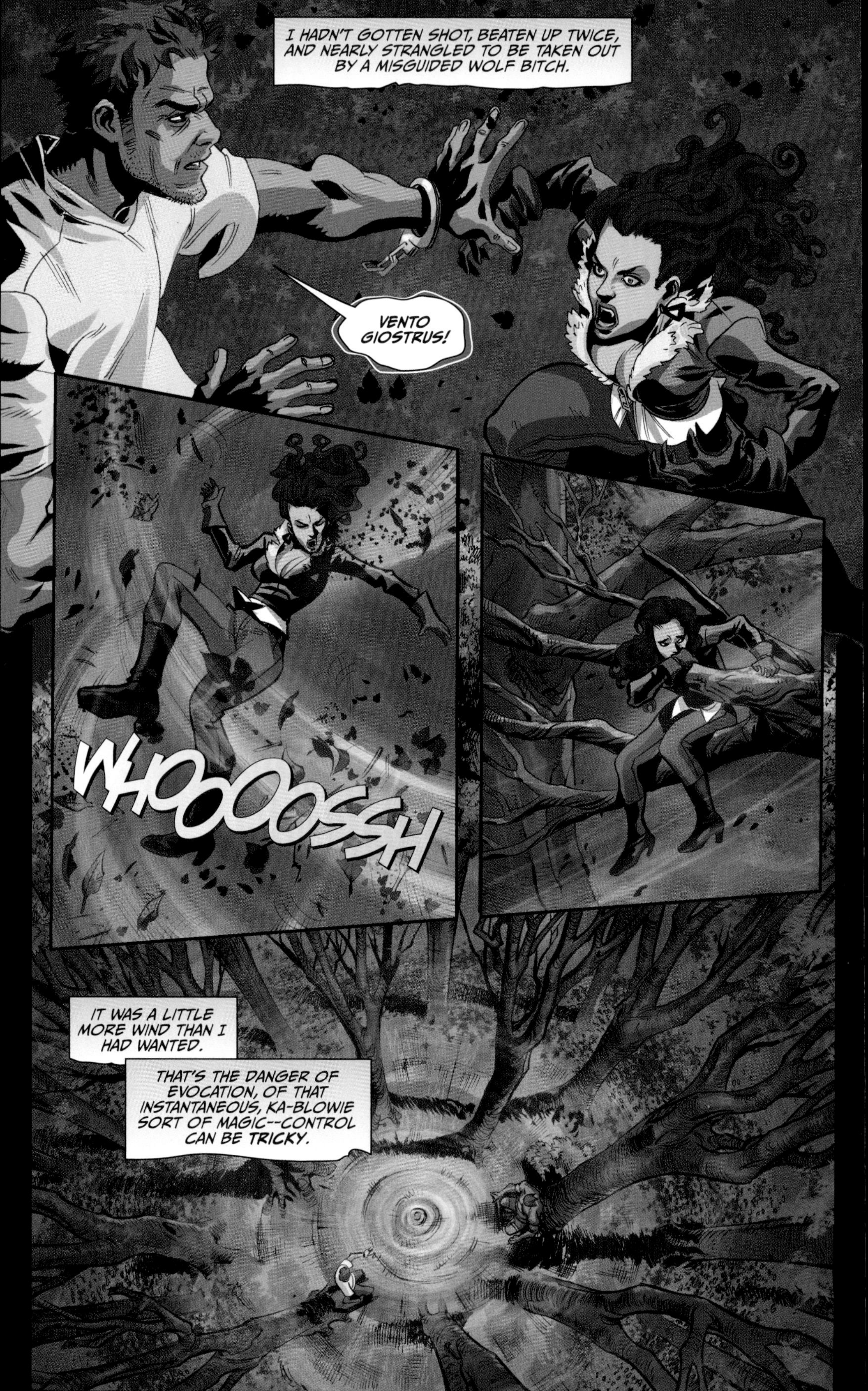
I HADN'T GOTTEN SHOT, BEATEN UP TWICE, AND NEARLY STRANGLED TO BE TAKEN OUT BY A MISGUIDED WOLF BITCH.
VENTO GIOSTRUS!
WHOOOOOSSH
IT WAS A LITTLE MORE WIND THAN I HAD WANTED.
THAT'S THE DANGER OF EVOCATION, OF THAT INSTANTANEOUS, KA-BLOWIE SORT OF MAGIC--CONTROL CAN BE TRICKY.

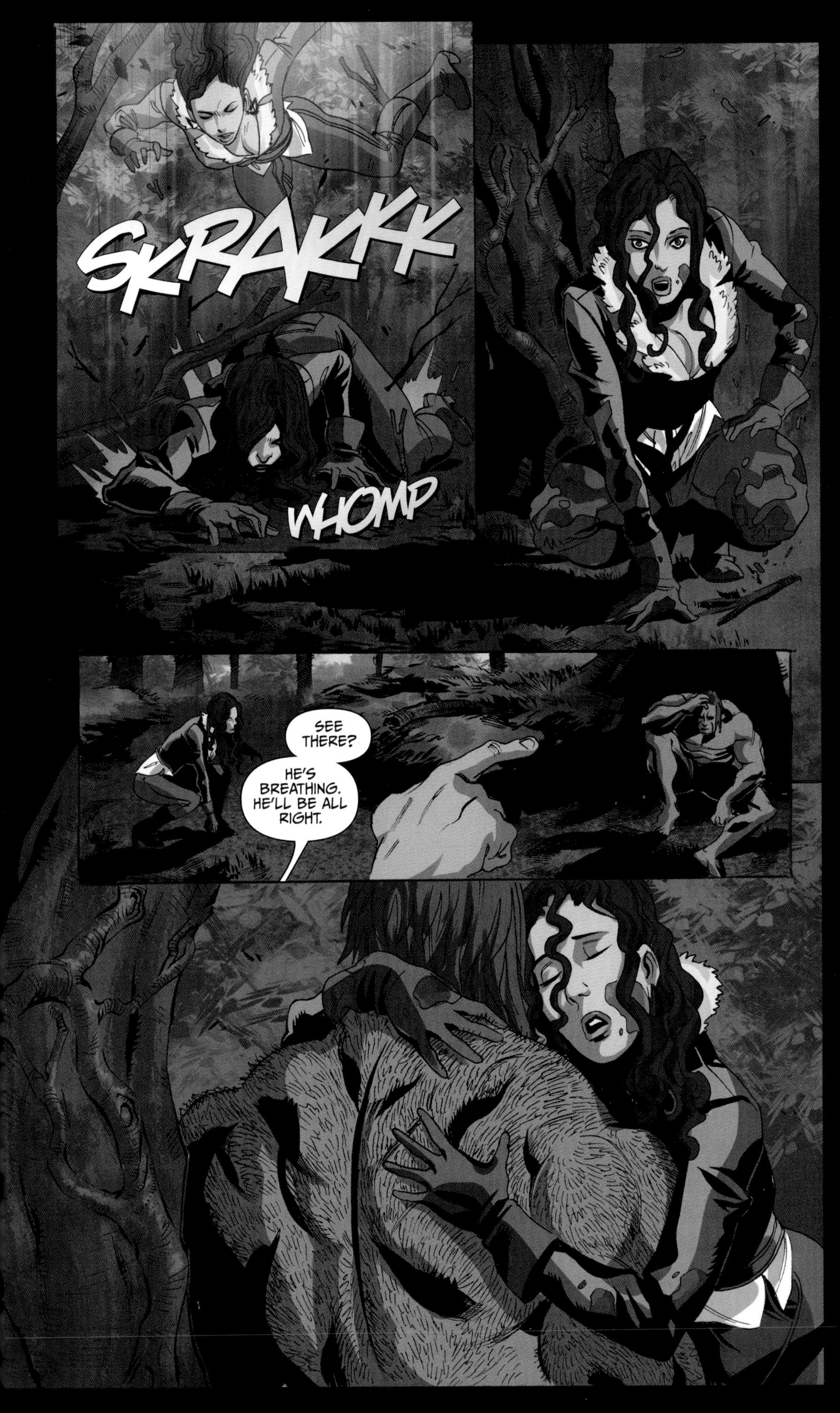
SKRAKK
WHOMP
SEE THERE?
HE'S BREATHING. HE'LL BE ALL RIGHT.

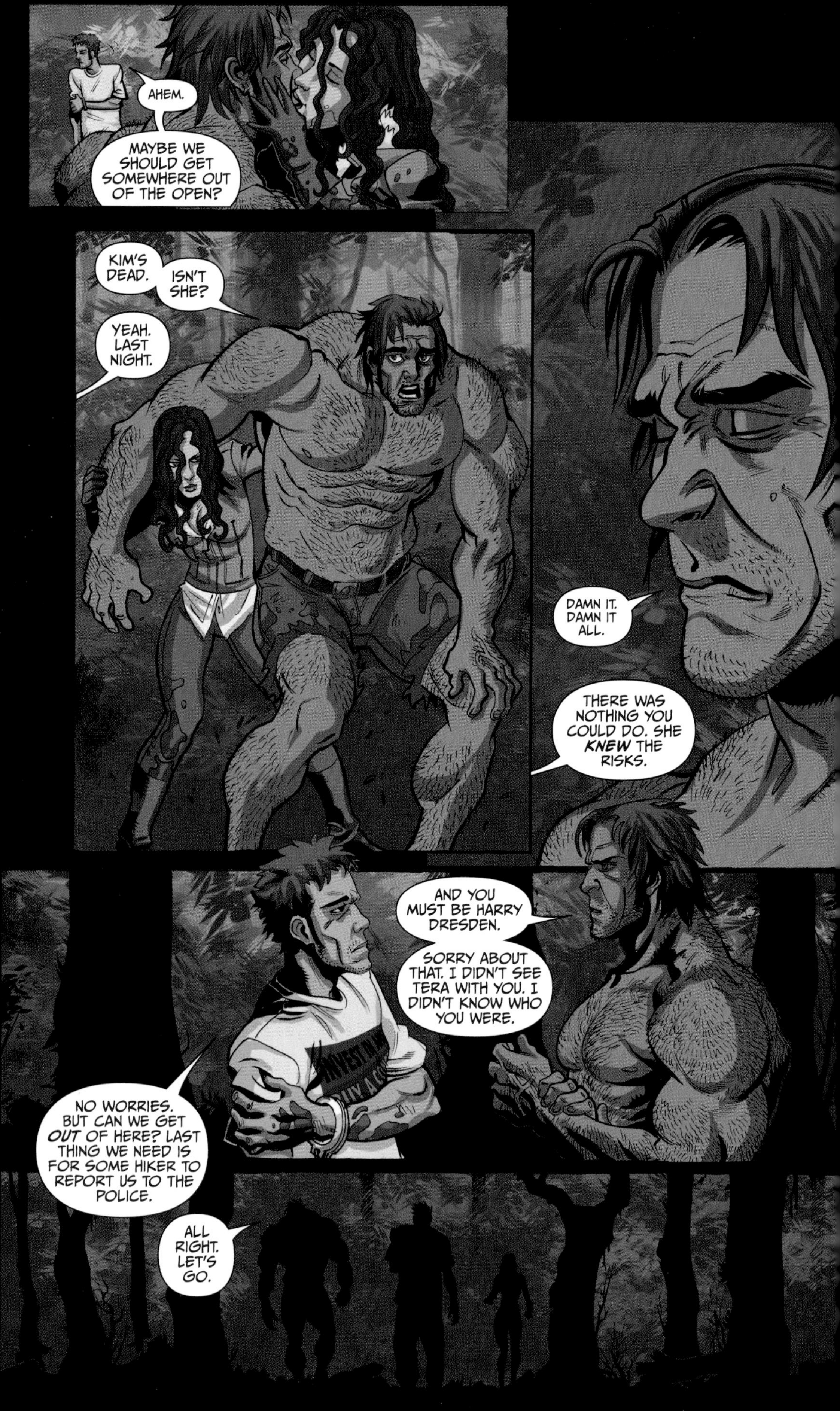
AHEM.
MAYBE WE SHOULD GET SOMEWHERE OUT OF THE OPEN?
KIM'S DEAD.
ISN'T SHE?
YEAH. LAST NIGHT.
DAMN IT. DAMN IT ALL.
THERE WAS NOTHING YOU COULD DO. SHE *KNEW* THE RISKS.
AND YOU MUST BE HARRY DRESDEN.
SORRY ABOUT THAT. I DIDN'T SEE TERA WITH YOU. I DIDN'T KNOW WHO YOU WERE.
NO WORRIES. BUT CAN WE GET *OUT* OF HERE? LAST THING WE NEED IS FOR SOME HIKER TO REPORT US TO THE POLICE.
ALL RIGHT. LET'S GO.

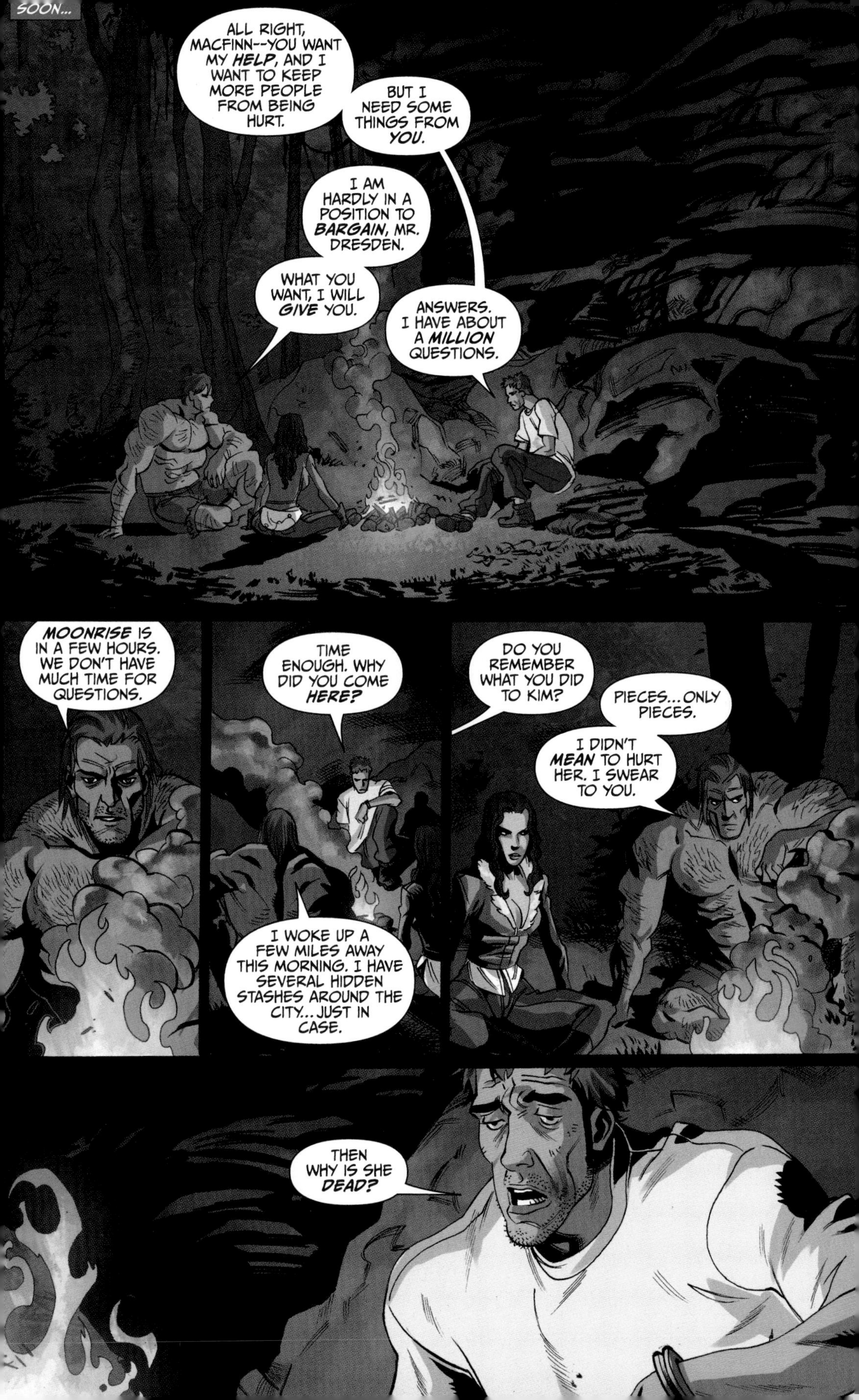
SOON...
ALL RIGHT, MACFINN--YOU WANT MY HELP, AND I WANT TO KEEP MORE PEOPLE FROM BEING HURT.
BUT I NEED SOME THINGS FROM YOU.
I AM HARDLY IN A POSITION TO BARGAIN, MR. DRESDEN.
WHAT YOU WANT, I WILL GIVE YOU.
ANSWERS. I HAVE ABOUT A MILLION QUESTIONS.
MOONRISE IS IN A FEW HOURS. WE DON'T HAVE MUCH TIME FOR QUESTIONS.
TIME ENOUGH. WHY DID YOU COME HERE?
I WOKE UP A FEW MILES AWAY THIS MORNING. I HAVE SEVERAL HIDDEN STASHES AROUND THE CITY... JUST IN CASE.
DO YOU REMEMBER WHAT YOU DID TO KIM?
PIECES... ONLY PIECES.
I DIDN'T MEAN TO HURT HER. I SWEAR TO YOU.
THEN WHY IS SHE DEAD?

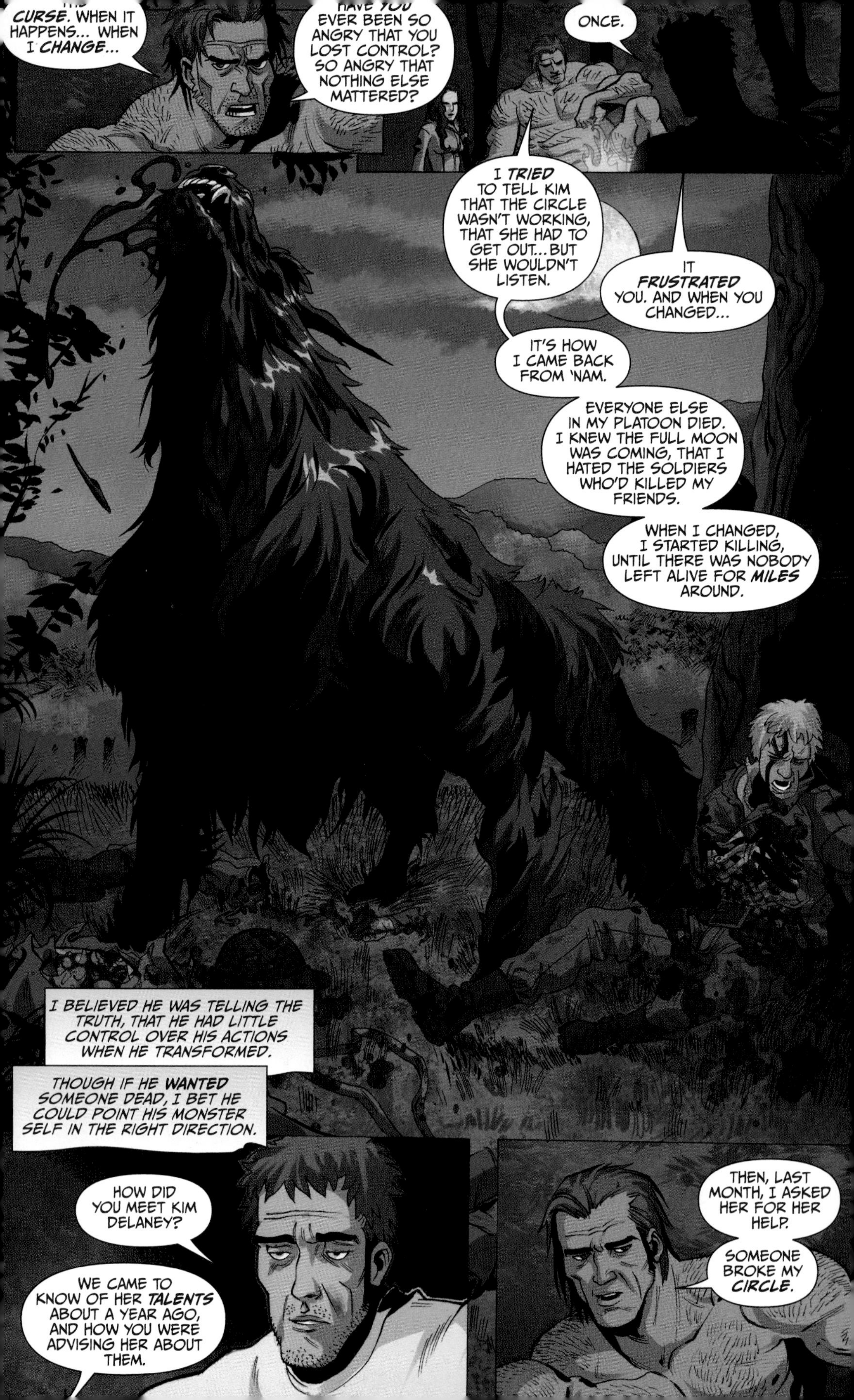
CURSE. WHEN IT HAPPENS... WHEN I CHANGE...
HAVE YOU EVER BEEN SO ANGRY THAT YOU LOST CONTROL? SO ANGRY THAT NOTHING ELSE MATTERED?
ONCE.
I TRIED TO TELL KIM THAT THE CIRCLE WASN'T WORKING, THAT SHE HAD TO GET OUT...BUT SHE WOULDN'T LISTEN.
IT FRUSTRATED YOU. AND WHEN YOU CHANGED...
IT'S HOW I CAME BACK FROM 'NAM.
EVERYONE ELSE IN MY PLATOON DIED. I KNEW THE FULL MOON WAS COMING, THAT I HATED THE SOLDIERS WHO'D KILLED MY FRIENDS.
WHEN I CHANGED, I STARTED KILLING, UNTIL THERE WAS NOBODY LEFT ALIVE FOR MILES AROUND.
I BELIEVED HE WAS TELLING THE TRUTH, THAT HE HAD LITTLE CONTROL OVER HIS ACTIONS WHEN HE TRANSFORMED.
THOUGH IF HE WANTED SOMEONE DEAD, I BET HE COULD POINT HIS MONSTER SELF IN THE RIGHT DIRECTION.
HOW DID YOU MEET KIM DELANEY?
WE CAME TO KNOW OF HER TALENTS ABOUT A YEAR AGO, AND HOW YOU WERE ADVISING HER ABOUT THEM.
THEN, LAST MONTH, I ASKED HER FOR HER HELP.
SOMEONE BROKE MY CIRCLE.

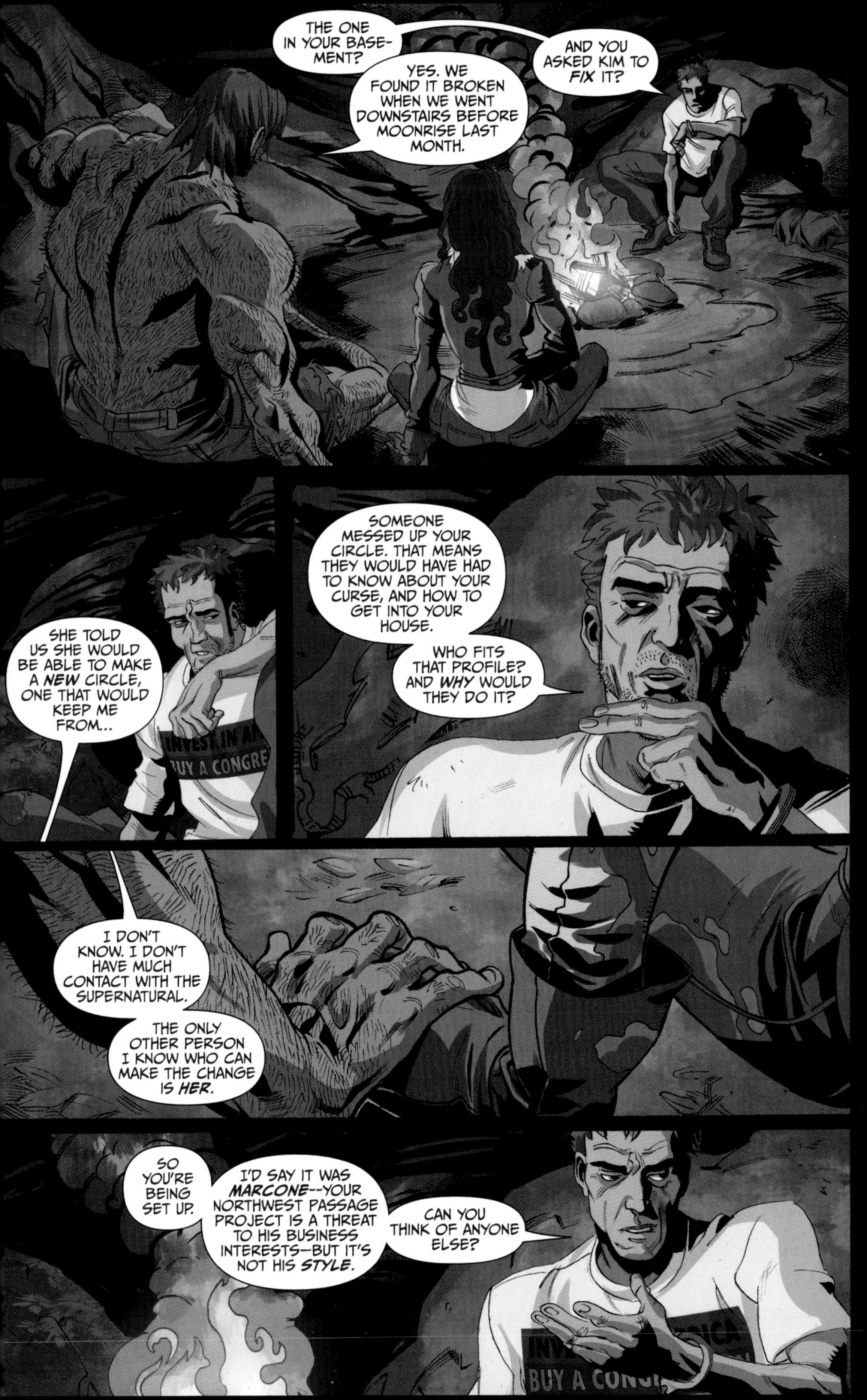

THE ONE IN YOUR BASEMENT?
YES. WE FOUND IT BROKEN WHEN WE WENT DOWNSTAIRS BEFORE MOONRISE LAST MONTH.
AND YOU ASKED KIM TO *FIX* IT?
SHE TOLD US SHE WOULD BE ABLE TO MAKE A *NEW* CIRCLE, ONE THAT WOULD KEEP ME FROM...
INVEST IN AM
BUY A CONGRE
SOMEONE MESSED UP YOUR CIRCLE. THAT MEANS THEY WOULD HAVE HAD TO KNOW ABOUT YOUR CURSE, AND HOW TO GET INTO YOUR HOUSE.
WHO FITS THAT PROFILE? AND *WHY* WOULD THEY DO IT?
I DON'T KNOW. I DON'T HAVE MUCH CONTACT WITH THE SUPERNATURAL.
THE ONLY OTHER PERSON I KNOW WHO CAN MAKE THE CHANGE IS *HER*.
SO YOU'RE BEING SET UP.
I'D SAY IT WAS *MARCONE*--YOUR NORTHWEST PASSAGE PROJECT IS A THREAT TO HIS BUSINESS INTERESTS—BUT IT'S NOT HIS *STYLE*.
CAN YOU THINK OF ANYONE ELSE?
BUY A CONG

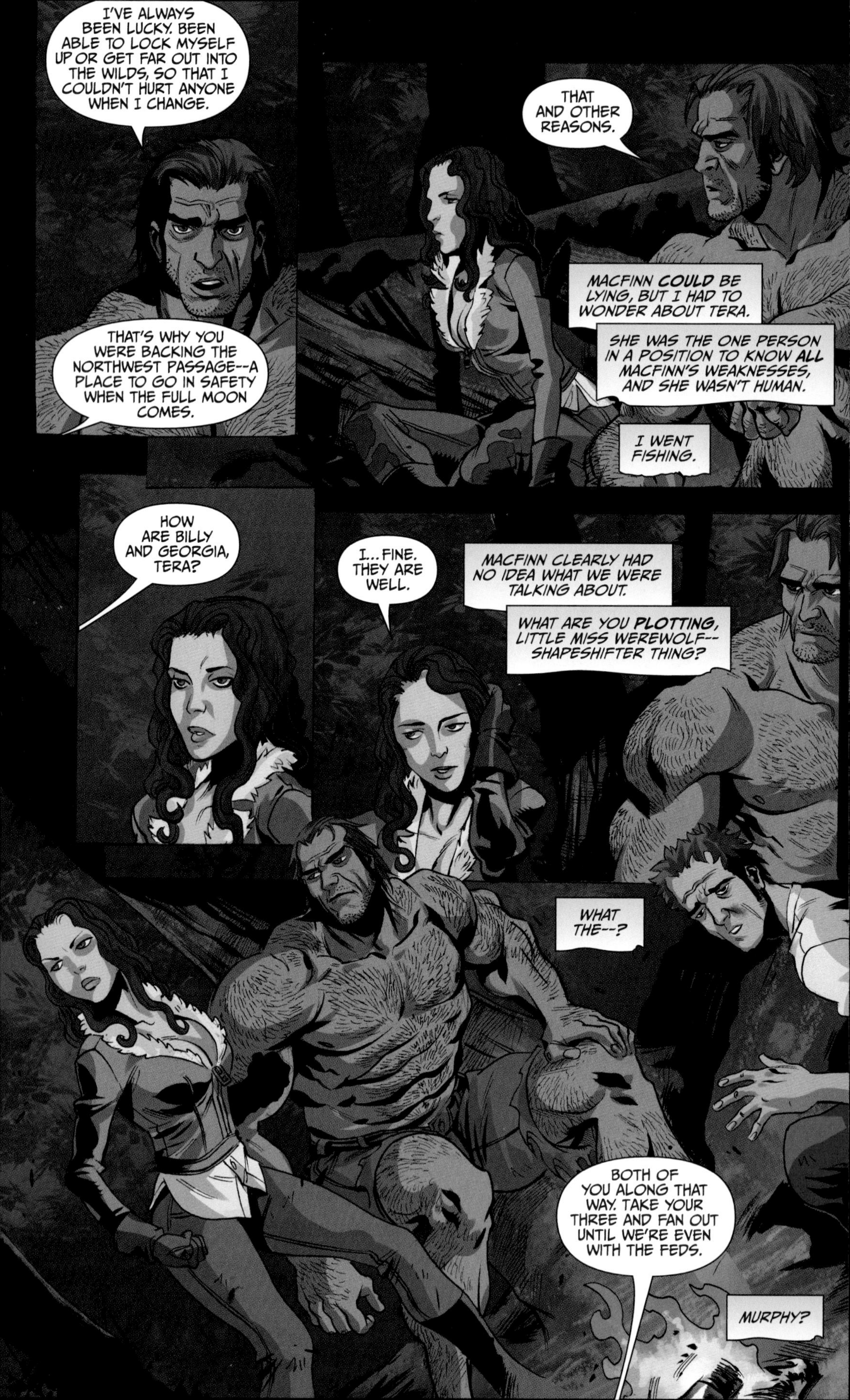
I'VE ALWAYS BEEN LUCKY. BEEN ABLE TO LOCK MYSELF UP OR GET FAR OUT INTO THE WILDS, SO THAT I COULDN'T HURT ANYONE WHEN I CHANGE.
THAT'S WHY YOU WERE BACKING THE NORTHWEST PASSAGE--A PLACE TO GO IN SAFETY WHEN THE FULL MOON COMES.
THAT AND OTHER REASONS.
MACFINN **COULD** BE LYING, BUT I HAD TO WONDER ABOUT TERA.
SHE WAS THE ONE PERSON IN A POSITION TO KNOW **ALL** MACFINN'S WEAKNESSES, AND SHE WASN'T HUMAN.
I WENT FISHING.
HOW ARE BILLY AND GEORGIA, TERA?
I...FINE. THEY ARE WELL.
MACFINN CLEARLY HAD NO IDEA WHAT WE WERE TALKING ABOUT.
WHAT ARE YOU **PLOTTING**, LITTLE MISS WEREWOLF--SHAPESHIFTER THING?
WHAT THE--?
BOTH OF YOU ALONG THAT WAY. TAKE YOUR THREE AND FAN OUT UNTIL WE'RE EVEN WITH THE FEDS.
MURPHY?

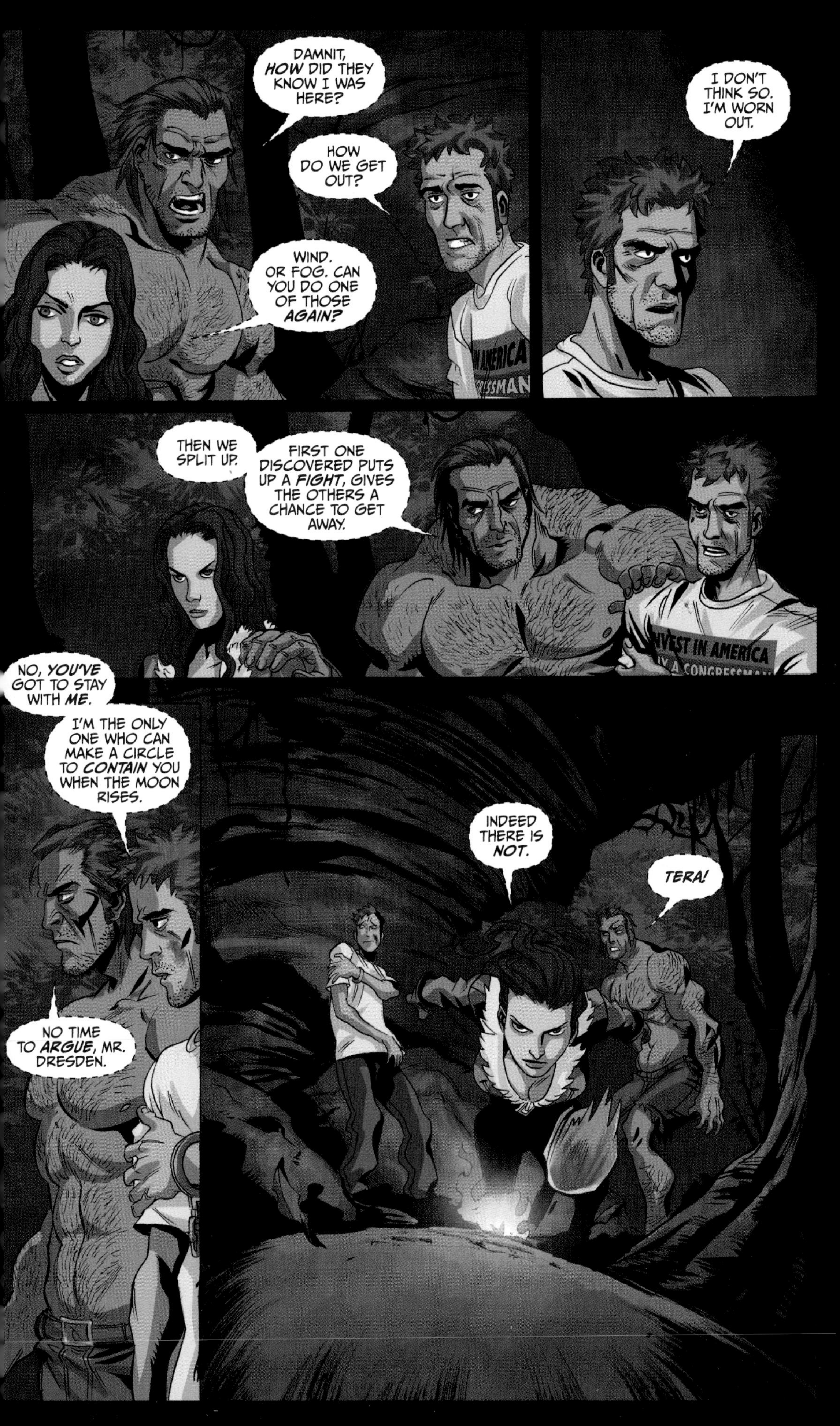
DAMNIT, HOW DID THEY KNOW I WAS HERE?
HOW DO WE GET OUT?
WIND. OR FOG. CAN YOU DO ONE OF THOSE AGAIN?
I DON'T THINK SO. I'M WORN OUT.
THEN WE SPLIT UP.
FIRST ONE DISCOVERED PUTS UP A FIGHT, GIVES THE OTHERS A CHANCE TO GET AWAY.
NO, YOU'VE GOT TO STAY WITH ME.
I'M THE ONLY ONE WHO CAN MAKE A CIRCLE TO CONTAIN YOU WHEN THE MOON RISES.
NO TIME TO ARGUE, MR. DRESDEN.
INDEED THERE IS NOT.
TERA!

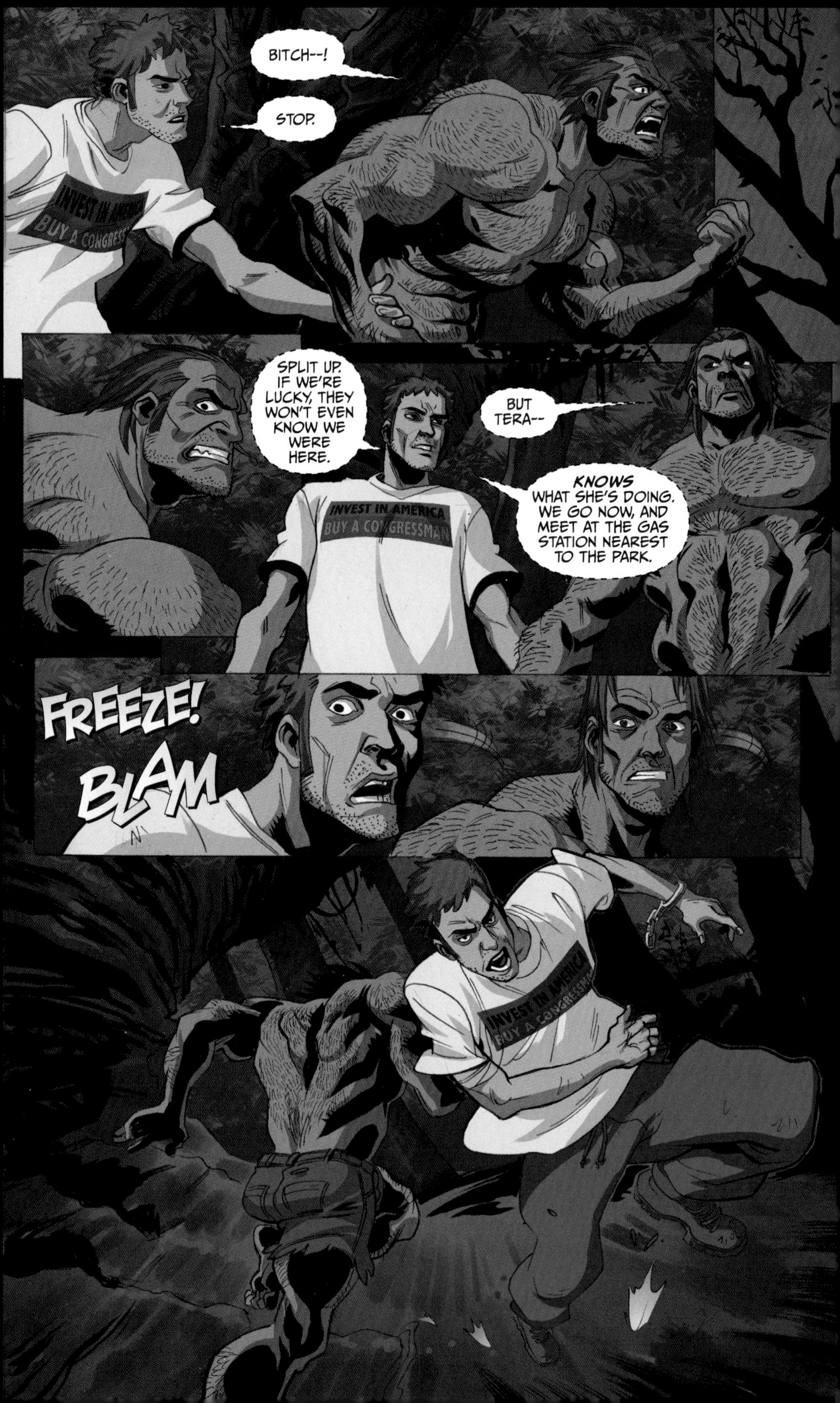
BITCH--!
STOP.
SPLIT UP. IF WE'RE LUCKY, THEY WON'T EVEN KNOW WE WERE HERE.
INVEST IN AMERICA
BUY A CONGRESSMAN
BUT TERA--
KNOWS WHAT SHE'S DOING. WE GO NOW, AND MEET AT THE GAS STATION NEAREST TO THE PARK.
FREEZE!
BLAM

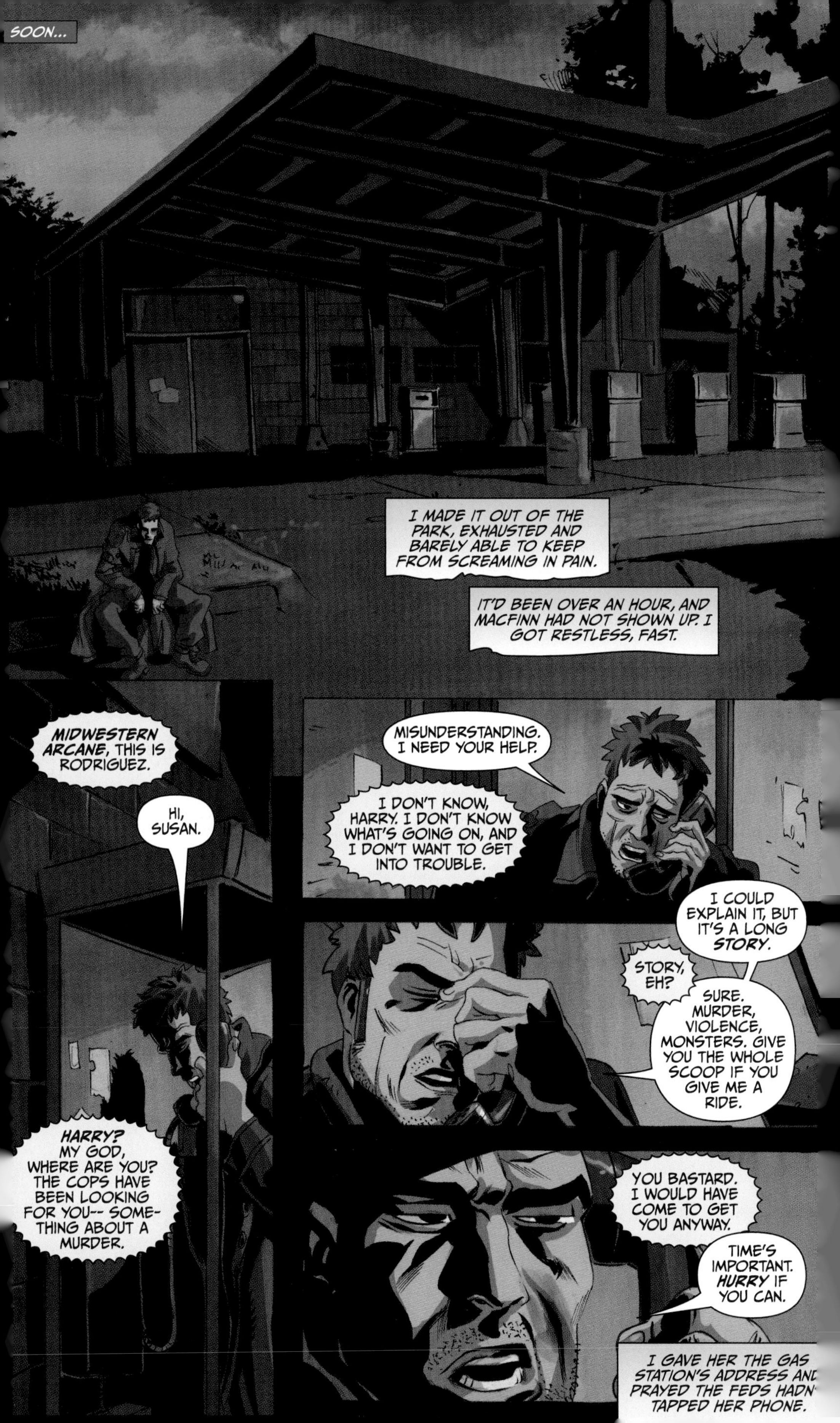

SOON...
I MADE IT OUT OF THE PARK, EXHAUSTED AND BARELY ABLE TO KEEP FROM SCREAMING IN PAIN.
IT'D BEEN OVER AN HOUR, AND MACFINN HAD NOT SHOWN UP. I GOT RESTLESS, FAST.
MIDWESTERN ARCANE, THIS IS RODRIGUEZ.
HI, SUSAN.
HARRY? MY GOD, WHERE ARE YOU? THE COPS HAVE BEEN LOOKING FOR YOU-- SOME-THING ABOUT A MURDER.
MISUNDERSTANDING. I NEED YOUR HELP.
I DON'T KNOW, HARRY. I DON'T KNOW WHAT'S GOING ON, AND I DON'T WANT TO GET INTO TROUBLE.
I COULD EXPLAIN IT, BUT IT'S A LONG STORY.
STORY, EH?
SURE. MURDER, VIOLENCE, MONSTERS. GIVE YOU THE WHOLE SCOOP IF YOU GIVE ME A RIDE.
YOU BASTARD. I WOULD HAVE COME TO GET YOU ANYWAY.
TIME'S IMPORTANT. HURRY IF YOU CAN.
I GAVE HER THE GAS STATION'S ADDRESS AND PRAYED THE FEDS HADN' TAPPED HER PHONE.

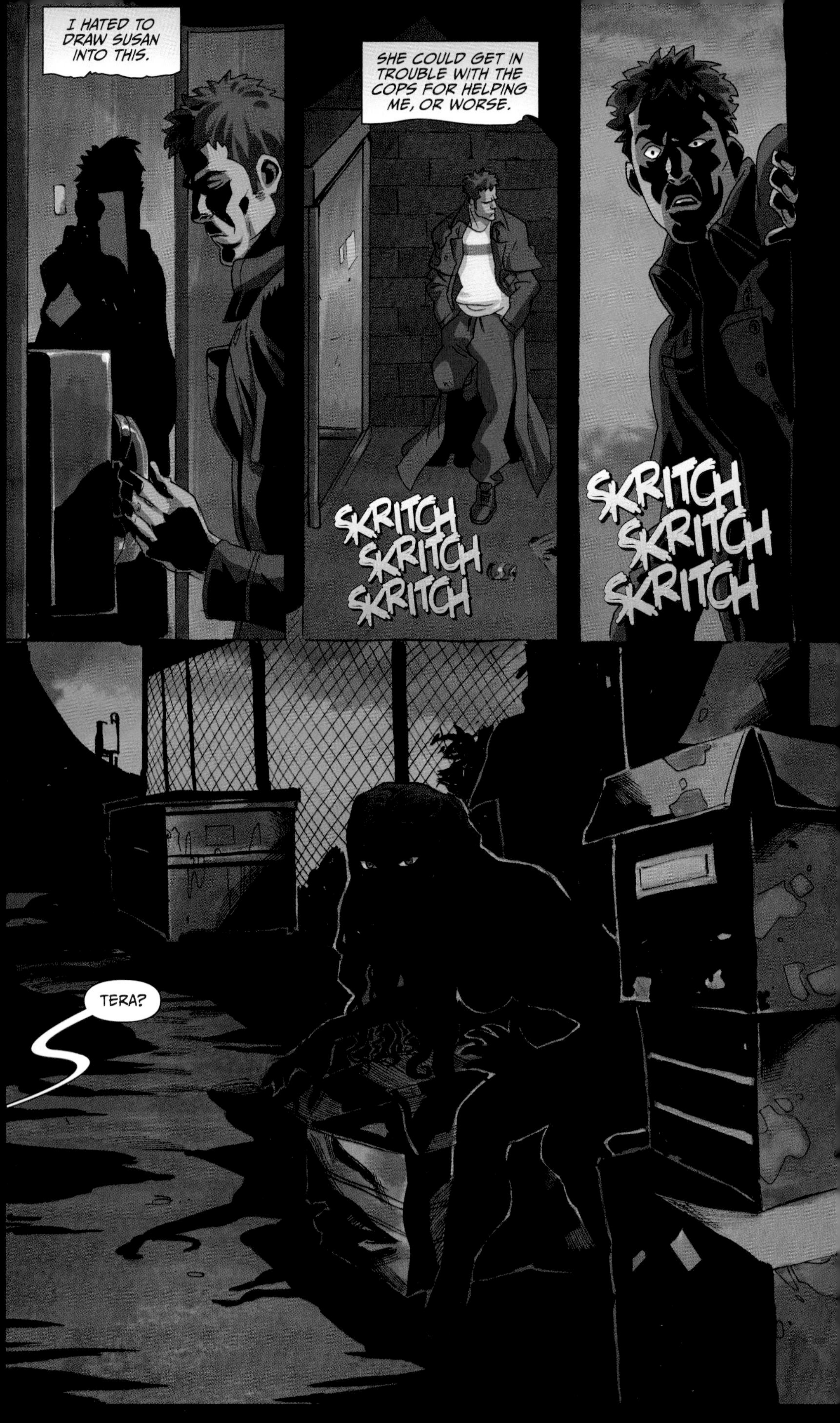
I HATED TO DRAW SUSAN INTO THIS.
SHE COULD GET IN TROUBLE WITH THE COPS FOR HELPING ME, OR WORSE.
SKRITCH SKRITCH SKRITCH
SKRITCH SKRITCH SKRITCH
TERA?

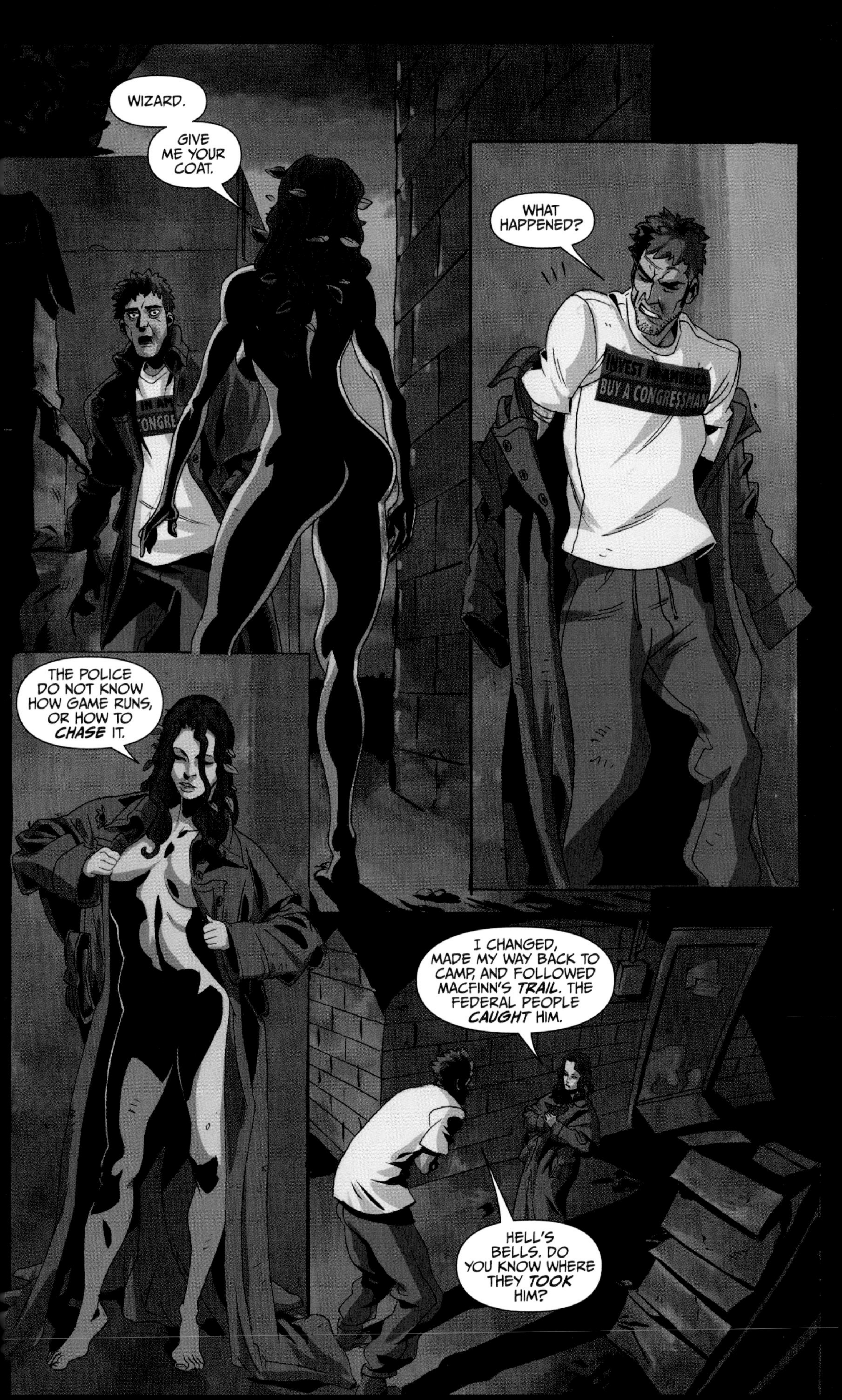
WIZARD.
GIVE ME YOUR COAT.
IN AM CONGRE
WHAT HAPPENED?
INVEST IN AMERICA BUY A CONGRESSMAN
THE POLICE DO NOT KNOW HOW GAME RUNS, OR HOW TO *CHASE* IT.
I CHANGED, MADE MY WAY BACK TO CAMP, AND FOLLOWED MACFINN'S *TRAIL*. THE FEDERAL PEOPLE *CAUGHT* HIM.
HELL'S BELLS. DO YOU KNOW WHERE THEY *TOOK* HIM?

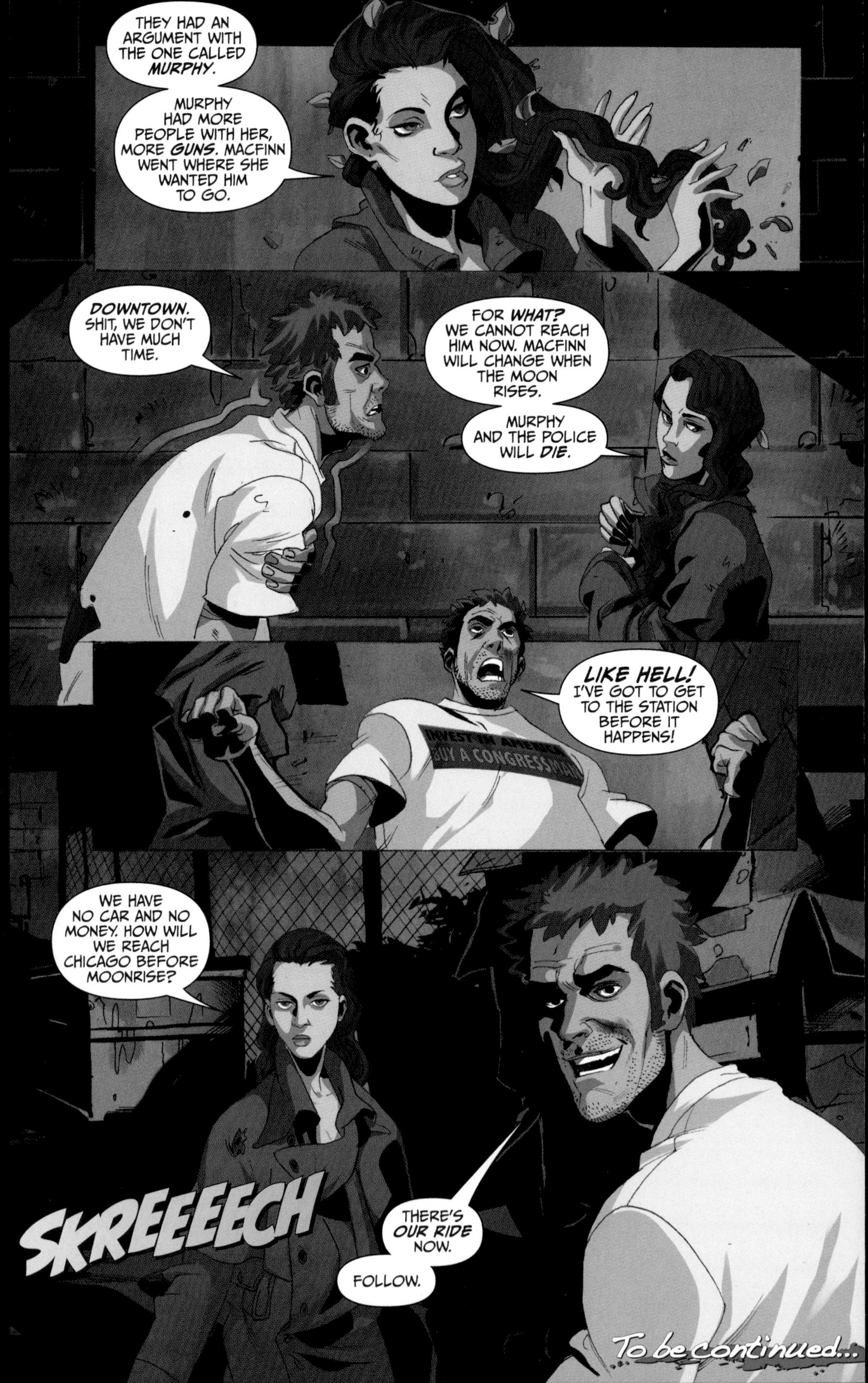
THEY HAD AN ARGUMENT WITH THE ONE CALLED *MURPHY*.
MURPHY HAD MORE PEOPLE WITH HER, MORE *GUNS*. MACFINN WENT WHERE SHE WANTED HIM TO GO.
DOWNTOWN. SHIT, WE DON'T HAVE MUCH TIME.
FOR *WHAT?* WE CANNOT REACH HIM NOW. MACFINN WILL CHANGE WHEN THE MOON RISES.
MURPHY AND THE POLICE WILL *DIE*.
LIKE HELL! I'VE GOT TO GET TO THE STATION BEFORE IT HAPPENS!
BUY A CONGRESSMAN
WE HAVE NO CAR AND NO MONEY. HOW WILL WE REACH CHICAGO BEFORE MOONRISE?
SKREEEEECH
THERE'S *OUR RIDE* NOW.
FOLLOW.
To be continued...

CURRENTLY AVAILABLE AND UPCOMING COLLECTIONS FROM DYNAMITE
For a complete list, visit us online at www.dynamite.net

ARMY OF DARKNESS:
Army of Darkness:
Movie Adaptation
Raimi, Raimi, Bolton

Army of Darkness:
Ashes to Ashes
Hartnell, Bradshaw

Army of Darkness:
Shop 'Till You Drop Dead
Kuhoric, Bradshaw, Greene

Army of Darkness vs.
Re-Animator
Kuhoric, Bradshaw, Greene

Army of Darkness:
Old School & More
Kuhoric, Sharpe

Army of Darkness: Ash vs.
The Classic Monsters
Kuhoric, Sharpe, Blanco

Army of Darkness:
From The Ashes
Kuhoric, Blanco

Army of Darkness:
The Long Road Home
Kuhoric, Raicht, Blanco

Army of Darkness:
Home Sweet Hell
Kuhoric, Raicht, Perez

Army of Darkness:
Hellbillies & Deadnecks
Kuhoric, Raicht, Cohn

Army of Darkness:
League of Light Assemble!
Raicht, Cohn

Army of Darkness
Omnibus Vol. 1
Hartnell, Kuhoric, Kirkman, more

Army of Darkness:
Ash Saves Obama
Serrano, Padilla

Army of Darkness vs. Xena
Vol. 1: Why Not?
Layman, Jerwa, Montenegro

Xena vs. Army of Darkness
Vol. 2: What...Again?!
Jerwa, Serrano, Montenegro

Darkman vs. Army of Darkness
Busiek, Stern, Fry

BATTLESTAR GALACTICA
New Battlestar Galactica Vol. 1
Pak, Raynor

New Battlestar Galactica Vol. 2
Pak, Raynor

New Battlestar Galactica Vol. 3
Pak, Raynor, Lau

New Battlestar Galactica
Complete Omnibus V1
Pak, Raynor, Jerwa, Lau

New Battlestar Galactica: Zarek
Jerwa, Batista

New Battlestar Galactica:
Season Zero Vol. 1
Jerwa, Herbert

New Battlestar Galactica:
Season Zero Vol. 2
Jerwa, Herbert

New Battlestar Galactica
Origins: Baltar
Fahey, Lau

New Battlestar Galactica
Origins: Adama
Napton, Lau

New Battlestar Galactica
Origins: Starbuck & Helo
Fahey, Lau

New Battlestar Galactica:
Ghosts
Jerwa, Lau

New Battlestar Galactica:
Cylon War
Ortega, Nylund, Raynor

New Battlestar Galactica:
The Final Five
Fahey, Reed, Raynor

Classic Battlestar Galactica
Vol. 1
Remender, Rafael

Classic Battlestar Galactica
Vol. 2: Cylon Apocalypse
Grillo-Marxuach, Rafael

GALACTICA 1980
Guggenheim, Razek

THE BOYS
The Boys Vol. 1
The Name of the Game
Ennis, Robertson

The Boys Vol. 2
Get Some
Ennis, Robertson, Snejbjerg

The Boys Vol. 3
Good For The Soul
Ennis, Robertson

The Boys Vol. 4
We Gotta Go Now
Ennis, Robertson

The Boys Vol. 5
Herogasm
Ennis, McCrea

The Boys Vol. 6
The Self-Preservation Society
Ennis, Robertson, Ezquerra

The Boys Vol. 7
The Innocents
Ennis, Robertson, Braun

The Boys Vol. 8
Highland Laddie
Ennis, McCrea

The Boys Vol. 9
The Big Ride
Ennis, Braun

The Boys
Definitive Edition Vol. 1
Ennis, Robertson

The Boys
Definitive Edition Vol. 2
Ennis, Robertson

The Boys
Definitive Edition Vol. 3
Ennis, Robertson, McCrea, more

THE GREEN HORNET
Kevin Smith's Green Hornet
Vol. 1 Sins of the Father
Smith, Hester, Lau

Kevin Smith's Green Hornet
Vol. 2 Wearing 'o the Green
Smith, Hester, Lau

Kevin Smith's Green Hornet
Vol. 3 Idols
Hester, Lau

Kevin Smith's Kato Vol. 1
Not My Father's Daughter
Parks, Garza, Bernard

Kevin Smith's Kato Vol. 2
Living in America
Parks, Bernard

Green Hornet: Blood Ties
Parks, Desjardins

The Green Hornet: Year One
Vol. 1 The Sting of Justice
Wagner, Campbell, Francavilla

The Green Hornet: Year One
Vol. 2 The Biggest of All Game
Wagner, Campbell

Kato Origins Vol. 1
Way of the Ninja
Nitz, Worley

Kato Origins Vol. 2
The Hellfire Club
Nitz, Worley

The Green Hornet: Parallel
Lives
Nitz, Raynor

The Green Hornet Golden Age
Re-Mastered
Various

THE LONE RANGER
The Lone Ranger Vol. 1:
Now & Forever
Matthews, Cariello, Cassaday

The Lone Ranger Vol. 2:
Lines Not Crossed
Matthews, Cariello, Cassaday, Pope

The Lone Ranger Vol. 3:
Scorched Earth
Matthews, Cariello, Cassaday

The Lone Ranger Vol. 4:
Resolve
Matthews, Cariello, Cassaday

The Lone Ranger & Tonto Vol 1
Matthews, Cariello, Guevara, more

The Lone Ranger Definitive
Edition Vol. 1
Matthews, Cariello, Cassaday

PROJECT SUPERPOWERS
Project Superpowers Chapter 1
Ross, Krueger, Paul, Sadowski

Project Superpowers Chapter 2
Vol. 1
Ross, Krueger, Salazar

Project Superpowers Chapter 2
Vol. 2
Ross, Krueger, Salazar

Project Superpowers: Meet The
Bad Guys
Ross, Casey, Lilly, Lau, Paul, Herbert

Black Terror Vol. 1
Ross, Krueger, Lilly

Black Terror Vol. 2
Ross, Hester, Lau

Black Terror Vol. 3
Inhuman Remains
Ross, Hester, Reis, Herbert

Death-Defying 'Devil Vol 1
Ross, Casey, Salazar

Masquerade Vol. 2
Ross, Hester, Laul

RED SONJA
Adventures of Red Sonja Vol. 1
Thomas, Thorne, More

Adventures of Red Sonja Vol. 2
Thomas, Thorne, More

Adventures of Red Sonja Vol. 3
Thomas, Thorne, More

Red Sonja She-Devil With a
Sword Vol. 1
Oeming, Carey, Rubi

Red Sonja She-Devil With a
Sword Vol. 2: Arrowsmiths
Oeming, Rubi, more

Red Sonja She-Devil With a
Sword Vol. 3: The Rise of
Kulan Gath
Oeming, Rubi, more

Red Sonja She-Devil With a
Sword Vol. 4: Animals & More
Oeming, Homs, more

Red Sonja She-Devil With a
Sword Vol. 5: World On Fire
Oeming, Reed, Homs

Red Sonja She-Devil With a
Sword Vol. 6: Death
Marz, Ortega, Reed, more

Red Sonja She-Devil With a
Sword Vol. 7: Born Again
Reed, Geovani

Red Sonja She-Devil With a
Sword Vol. 8: Blood Dynasty
Reed, Geovani

Red Sonja She-Devil With a
Sword Vol. 9: War Season
Trautmann, Geovani, Berkenkotter

Red Sonja She-Devil With a
Sword Omnibus Vol. 1
Oeming, Carey, Rubi, more

Red Sonja vs. Thulsa Doom
Vol. 1
David, Lieberman, Conrad

Savage Red Sonja: Queen of
the Frozen Wastes
Cho, Murray, Homs

Red Sonja: Travels
Marz, Ortega, Thomas, more

Sword of Red Sonja: Doom
of the Gods (Red Sonja vs.
Thulsa Doom 2)
Lieberman, Antonio

Red Sonja: Wrath of the Gods
Lieberman, Geovani

Red Sonja: Revenge of the
Gods
Lieberman, Sampere

Savage Tales of Red Sonja
Marz, Gage, Ortega, more

VAMPIRELLA
Vampirella Masters Series Vol 1
Grant Morrison & Mark Millar
Morrison, Millar, more

Vampirella Masters Series Vol 2
Warren Ellis
Ellis, Conner Palmiotti, more

Vampirella Masters Series Vol 3
Mark Millar
Millar, Mayhew

Vampirella Masters Series Vol 4
Visionaries
Moore, Busiek, Loeb, more

Vampirella Masters Series Vol 5
Kurt Busiek
Busiek, Sniegoski, LaChanc, more

Vampirella Archives Vol 1
Various

Vampirella Archives Vol 2
Various

Vampirella Archives Vol 3
Various

Vampirella Archives Vol 3
Various

Vampirella Vol. 1
Crown of Worms
Trautman, Reis, Geovani

MORE FROM GARTH ENNIS
Dan Dare Omnibus
Ennis, Erskine

Garth Ennis' Battlefields
Vol. 1: The Night Witches
Ennis, Braun

Garth Ennis' Battlefields
Vol. 2: Dear Billy
Ennis, Snejbjerg

Garth Ennis' Battlefields
Vol. 3: The Tankies
Ennis, Ezquerra

Garth Ennis' The Complete
Battlefields Vol. 1
Ennis, Braun, Snejbjerg, Ezquerra

Garth Ennis' Battlefields
Vol. 4: Happy Valley
Ennis, Holden

Garth Ennis' Battlefields
Vol.5: The Firefly and His
Majesty
Ennis, Ezquerra

Garth Ennis' Battlefields
Vol.6: Motherland
Ennis, Braun

Garth Ennis' The Complete
Battlefields Vol. 2
Ennis, Braun, Holden, Ezquerra

Just A Pilgrim
Ennis, Ezquerra

JIM BUTCHER'S

The DRESDEN FILES

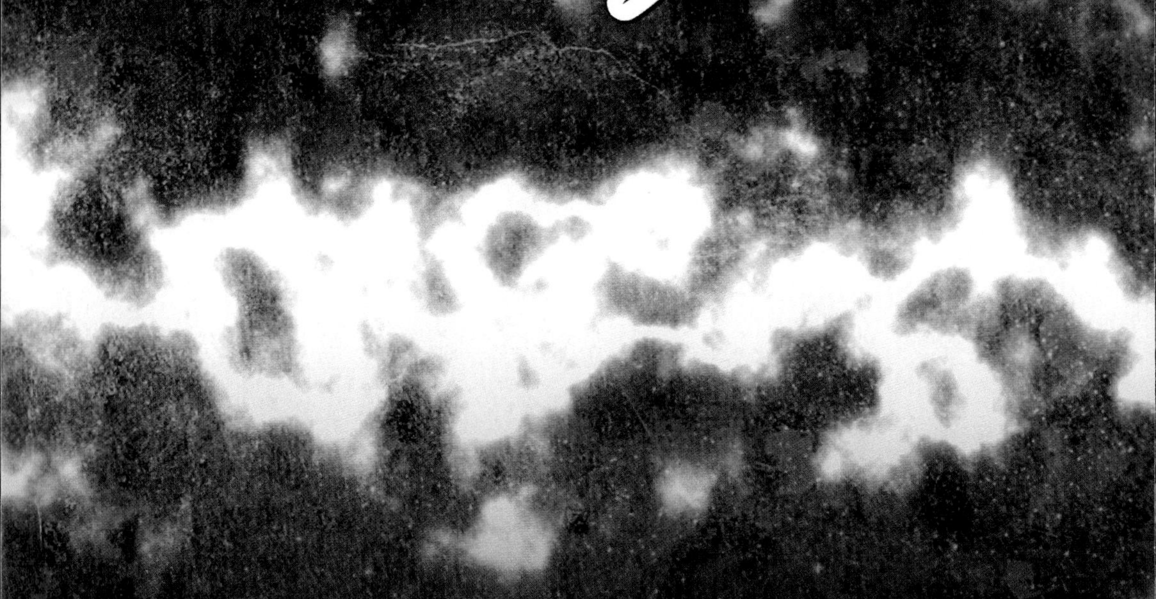

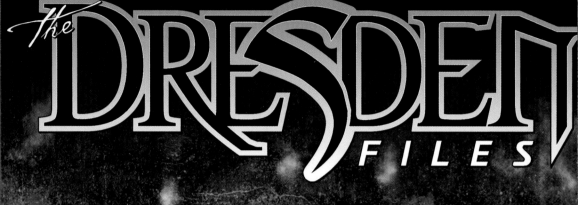

FOOL MOON

volume one